The Sacred in the Modern World

Praise for THE SACRED IN THE MODERN WORLD

"This lucidly written study of *The Sacred in the Modern World* deserves the widest possible audience. In one of the most impressive restatements of Durkheim's theory of sacred forms, Gordon Lynch helps us to make sense of contemporary social life. Whether you are intrigued by the power of public media, disturbed by the moral certainties that justify extreme acts of violence, or interested in the rhetoric of humanitarian appeals, you will profit from reading this book. Lynch's voice is without peer in this area and cannot afford to be ignored."

Christopher Partridge, Lancaster University

"Offering a clear, authoritative and thought-provoking account of the entanglement of secular and sacred phenomena today, *The Sacred in the Modern World* will be of great interest to a range of readers, and essential reading for those seeking to make sense of the normative claims to authority evident within many contemporary inter-group disputes about rights, identities and wellbeing. Illuminating how such claims often depend upon patterns of implicit sacralisation, Lynch's innovative and valuable analysis reorients the sociological imagination beyond 'religion' to focus on the mechanisms through which social life continues to be shaped by evolving constructions and enactments of the sacred."

Phil Mellor, University of Leeds

The Sacred in the Modern World

A Cultural Sociological Approach

Gordon Lynch

OXFORD
UNIVERSITY PRESS

OXFORD
UNIVERSITY PRESS

Great Clarendon Street, Oxford ox2 6DP

Oxford University Press is a department of the University of Oxford.
It furthers the University's objective of excellence in research, scholarship,
and education by publishing worldwide. Oxford is a registered trade mark of
Oxford University Press in the UK and in certain other countries

First published 2012
First publised in paperback 2014

Published in the United States of America by Oxford University Press
198 Madison Avenue, New York, NY 10016, United States of America

British Library Cataloguing in Publication Data

Data available

Library of Congress Cataloging in Publication Data

Library of Congress Control Number: 2011941286

ISBN 978–0–19–955701–1 (Hbk)
ISBN 978–0–19–870521–5 (Pbk)

In memory of Leonard Patrick (Len) Lynch
(1925–2008)
and for Hani
for all you have taught me about the sacred

Now emotion is naturally refractory to analysis, or at least it lends itself uneasily to it, because it is too complex. Above all when it has a collective origin it defies critical and rational examination. The pressure exerted by the group on each of its members does not permit individuals to judge freely the notions which society itself has elaborated and in which it has placed something of its personality. Such constructs are sacred for individuals. Thus the history of scientific classification is, in the last analysis, the history of the stages by which this element of social affectivity has progressively weakened, leaving more and more room for the reflective thought of individuals. But it is not the case that these remote influences which we have just studied here have ceased to be felt today. They have left behind them an effect which survives and which is always present; it is the very cadre of all classification, it is the ensemble of mental habits by virtue of which we conceive things and facts in the form of co-ordinated or hierarchized groups.

(Émile Durkheim and Marcel Mauss, *Primitive Classification*, 1903)

Contents

Acknowledgements

On completing this book, I am struck once again at the fiction of a single author's name appearing on its cover. Academic writing often seems to me to be a practice of collage, in which we draw on the insights and inspirations of others, and our contribution is to try to piece these together in a creative way that may generate new insights, or at least clarify old ones. This book is no different, and I am indebted to many colleagues whose ideas have inspired and shaped the argument to be developed in the coming pages. The original formulation of my argument, much changed since then, came during an invaluable conversation with Linda Woodhead in the back of a mini-van in a car park in Beijing. Johanna Sumiala has been a constant inspiration and encouragement to me, through both her writing and our periodic conversations. Mia Lovheim and Jolyon Mitchell have also been hugely helpful through their constructive criticisms of this material, and Tom Beaudoin's support and stimulation remain invaluable. My ideas about the mediatization of the sacred were helped by my involvement in events run by the Nordic Research Network for the Mediatization of Religion and Culture, which led me to engage more with the work of Stig Hjarvard. In the spring of 2010, I was able to spend time as a visiting research fellow at the Center for Cultural Sociology at Yale University, which proved invaluable for clarifying many of the arguments I came to develop in the book. My warm thanks to Jeffrey Alexander, Ron Eyerman, and Philip Smith for making that possible and for being so generous with their time and encouragement, as well as to everyone at the Center for making me so welcome, including Nadine Amalfi, Anna Lund, Vered Vinitzky-Seroussi, and Alison Gerber. Johanna Sumiala and Lynn Schofield Clark have been very generous in reading drafts of this material and offering detailed comments. Terhi Utriainen has helped my thinking about ontological theories of the sacred, and Colum Kenny also kindly shared his insights about the context of the Irish industrial school system. I have been very grateful for the opportunities given to me to present material from this book at workshops, seminars, and conferences, including at the universities of Oslo,

Uppsala, and Yale, as well as at an International Study Commission for Media, Religion, and Culture workshop in Sao Paulo, and my particular thanks to Jan-Olav Henriksen, Stewart Hoover, David Morgan, Anders Sjoborg, Phil Smith, and Ron Jacobs for either making those events possible or acting as respondents. Over the past couple of years, I have been fortunate to be able to work with a very able group of doctoral students, whose work is a constant source of stimulation to me: Steph Berns, Claire Forbes, Sarah Harvey, Pauline Muir, William Potter, Ruth Sheldon, and Anna Strhan. My thanks also go to Paul Tremlett for his input into that graduate work, and to Sasha Roseneil for her collegiality and insight. Work on this project has also been made possible by an AHRC Research Fellowship award, and I am grateful to both the AHRC and my anonymous peer reviewers for their support with this. Over the past three years, Rosie Cox has been an enduring source of sanity and support, without which my academic life would have been much the worse. The book has benefited greatly from the support and professionalism of staff at the Oxford University Press; my thanks to Tom Perridge for initiating this project, and to Elizabeth Robottom, Tessa Eaton, and Hilary Walford for supporting the book through the production process. I am grateful to all of these, as well as numerous other colleagues to whom my work is indebted. Where the act of putting the author's name on the book cover is not a fiction is the point at which the author has to take final responsibility for its content. The final shape of my argument is my responsibility alone.

I remain ever grateful for Duna's enduring patience, love, and support, and for all that she continues to bring to our life together.

Finally, this book is dedicated to two other people. During the period of writing this book, my father, Leonard Patrick Lynch, died, and my son, Hani Edward Lynch, was born. Their lives have shaped me so indelibly, and I can easily see how the content of this book bears their own mark. It is to them both, with love and gratitude, that I dedicate this book.

Gordon Lynch

Canterbury
2011

Introduction: Why do we Need a Sociology of the Sacred?

> We hold these truths to be sacred and undeniable; that all men are
> created equal...
>
> > (Thomas Jefferson, first draft of the Declaration of
> > Independence, 1776)

Much of our everyday lives is lived out through mundane activities and concerns. We rise, wash, try to organize our days, take children to school, get through the business of the day at home or at work, do the necessary chores, find time (if we are lucky) for entertainment or catching up with family and friends, and retire once more to bed. Most of our actions are unreflexive, negotiated through mundane spaces and objects, and using skills so familiar that we are barely conscious of them; brushing our teeth, making coffee, negotiating our daily journeys.[1] Sometimes our lives are interrupted by some unusual or intense experience—a holiday, a romance, a serious illness, a bereavement—in which, for a time, we become conscious of our lives, our sense of time, our bodies, in new ways. But these irruptions, welcome or unwelcome, are typically the exception to the quotidian rule of our daily lives.

Then there is another element of social life, which transfigures, and even overturns, the mundane. A few minutes' walk away from my previous office, on 7 July 2005, a bomb exploded on the upper deck of a London bus in Tavistock Square. In the midst of people's mundane daily journeys, Hasib Hussain, one of four suicide bombers who attacked London that day, intentionally or unintentionally detonated his device, ripping open the rear end of a bus and killing thirteen people. The explosion reflected the apparent arbitrariness of everyday life, as Hussain had probably not intended the bus as his initial target and may have been on it only because his bomb had a faulty battery or he had not been able to get onto the underground. Yet, despite the arbitrariness that led to Hussain's presence on the bus, the moment of violence was shot through with sacred significance.

It was a sacred commitment that led Hussain, and the other bombers, to plan, build their bombs, and then detonate them, sitting and standing next to ordinary people whom they did not know. As Mohammad Sidique Khan said in his posthumously shown martyrdom video: 'I and thousands like me are forsaking everything for what we believe. Our driving motivation doesn't come from tangible commodities that this world has to offer. Our religion is Islam, obedience to the one true God, Allah and to follow in the footsteps of the final prophet and messenger Muhammad. This is how our ethical stances are dictated.' It was this sense of obligation to a sacred form that led this former classroom assistant from Leeds to kill and injure people sitting near him on an underground train at Edgware Road because of their assumed complicity in the profanities of Western foreign policy. The explosion was also given sacred significance in the responses of those who mourned the loss of loved ones, and for those for whom the victims became a symbol of an assault on the idea of a free, tolerant, and democratic society. As metal was rent apart by the explosions, so it was forged and shaped into fifty-two columns, one for each victim of the 7/7 bombings, placed in a memorial in Hyde Park; a symbolic space for preserving the memory of the attacks, and for reasserting the sacred bonds of society against the profanity of the violence. As the subsequent public inquiry into the 7/7 bombings unfolded during 2010, daily news stories were carried that conveyed sacred moments of human contact; of commuters holding people who had been strangers to them moments before the blast, to comfort them while they died.

Although it does not always take such dramatic forms as the bloody events of 7 July, the sacred is woven through contemporary social life. Modernity has often been cast in academic and popular imagination as a secular age. This may be true of some societies. However, even if we accept that we live in more secular times than previous generations, we do not live in a de-sacralized age. Durkheim was concerned about the persistence of the sacred in modern life, wondering about the basis of social solidarity and moralization in societies where traditional sacred forms were falling away. In the century that has passed since he wrote *The Elementary Forms of the Religious Life*, however, there has been more than enough evidence of the enduring power of various forms of the sacred for both good and ill, as we shall see in the coming pages.

This book is concerned with naming and reflecting on the sacred in the modern world. As Durkheim and Mauss commented, in their conclusion to *Primitive Classification*, to think about the sacred—particularly one's own sacred commitments—is never an easy task. They recognized that our bonds to the sacred evoke, and are reinforced by, particular sentiments. Moving beyond these emotional performances requires disciplined reflection that examines the historical and social formation of specific instances of the sacred. But, even as we learn the capacity for such reflection, we never entirely shake ourselves free of emotional ties to particular sacred forms. Perhaps we should not seek such freedom, for, if we are unable to feel anything to be sacred, then we may have cut our moorings to society and the possibility of a life with moral depth. But we need insight to be able to name the forms of the sacred that move us, to understand their histories, as well as the light and shadow that they cast. Without this, our complex, pluralist societies are in danger of repeating cycles of conflict through sacred reflexes that do more harm than good. This is a small hope in the face of entrenched and new conflicts around the world. But, like a client in therapy, any understanding of our condition that makes it possible to move beyond simply acting out creates new conditions of possibility. It is for this reason that we need a sociology of the sacred, to help us to see the sacred in our lives, to understand where it animates our feelings and our institutional practices, to recognize its role in the formation of subjectivities, and to learn how it binds people together as well as profoundly separating them. With such understanding, we can ask in what ways the sacred might be a constructive force in social life, whether or not we might in fact forge better social bonds without the sacred, and how we might live together in the midst of a plurality of sacred forms. Responding to such questions means adopting a critical approach to our most assumed understandings of reality. Despite the challenges of this process, it remains a crucial intellectual project for our time.

***

In addressing these questions, this book is concerned with powerful motive forces shaping contemporary life. More narrowly, it is also the refinement of a theoretical project within my own field of the study of religion. One of the defining features of the sociology of Western religion since the 1960s has been the attempt to conceptualize the focus of this subdiscipline beyond the study of traditional, institutional forms of religion. The progressive de-Christianization of many West European societies, together with the emergence of new forms of religious identity, affiliation, and practice in North America, have led sociologists to develop a range of conceptual and empirical projects to understand significant developments beyond the boundaries of traditional religious institutions. This has generated a significant research literature on new religious movements, new age and alternative spiritualities, neo-paganism and Wicca, the emergence of a broader 'holistic milieu', and wider discourses and practices of 'spirituality', which form part of a longer tradition of religious liberalism in the West.

While this work has been valuable in analysing new religious structures and practices, it has tended to focus on groups and practices that are relatively marginal in terms of their size and influence within the wider population.[2] Although it can reasonably be argued that 'occultural' content has now become widespread through popular media and culture in the West, the numbers of people actively involved in alternative spiritual structures and practices are a small fraction of the populations of Western Europe and North America. There remains a need, then, to find ways of conceptualizing what Thomas Luckmann referred to as 'the invisible religion' of socially significant sources of meaning and value within increasingly de-Christianized societies.[3] This has been a central concern of my own research over the past ten years, which initially made use of functionalist definitions of religion to explore the ways in which forms of media and popular culture, including popular cinema, the post-rave dance scene, and lifestyle media served as sources of significant meaning, value, and community beyond institutional religion. More recently, however, I have become critical of the value of this functionalist framework, arguing that it risks imposing essentialized notions of 'religion' upon social and cultural phenomena in a way that has little genuine analytical or explanatory power. My attempt to articulate a sociology of the sacred is thus a renewed response to Luckmann's challenge in a way that seeks to avoid these shortcomings and hopefully to offer a more insightful basis for social analysis.

In developing this project, I also want to make a distinction between the sociology of religion and the sociology of the sacred. As we will see in Chapter 1, the concepts of 'religion' and the 'sacred' are often conflated in both popular and academic discourse. Equating 'religion' and the 'sacred' with each other is analytically unhelpful, however, as it blurs two related, though distinct, foci of study. One of the most significant developments in the study of religion in recent decades has been a growing reflexivity concerning the category of 'religion'. Challenging the assumption that there is some universal or cross-cultural phenomenon that can be defined as 'religion', scholars' attention has turned to the ways in which the category of 'religion' emerged out of the particular European intellectual and political context over the past three centuries. Far from being a neutral category of analysis, the concept of 'religion' has performed essential cultural work in demarcating the kinds of social institution and subjectivity appropriate to modern, liberal, and Enlightenment societies. The study of 'religion' has also been implicated in various transnational and cross-cultural projects, from the colonial governance of non-Western societies to the development of social institutions for a new global age. This reflexivity has led to calls for the study of religion to be reconfigured as the study of the operations of the discourse of 'religion' in academic thought and other arenas of social life. An alternative, and somewhat broader, approach is to treat 'religion' as a socially constructed phenomenon, and the study of religion as the study of whatever is constructed as 'religion' in a particular context. What these new approaches open up, though, is a welcome move beyond confining the study of religion to specific groups that are regarded as manifesting core traits of the essential phenomenon of religion. Instead, researchers are also becoming interested in how concepts, symbols, and practices associated with 'religion' circulate through contemporary society beyond the boundaries of traditional religious institutions, as well as the ways in which different social institutions (such as the legal or educational systems) play an active role in the construction of 'religion'. By studying groups and practices conventionally thought of as 'religious', this more reflexive approach also offers the possibility of disclosing 'secular' assumptions that structure both academic enquiry and the organization of modern society.

If we think of the sociology of religion in terms of the sociological study of that which is taken to be 'religion' in particular contexts, then this intellectual project needs to be distinguished from the sociology of the sacred. In the coming pages, the cultural sociology of the sacred will be described in terms of studying the nature and significance of what people take to be absolute, normative realities that exert claims on the conduct of social life. While there is clearly a degree of overlap between these two sociological projects, there are also important differences. Contemporary sacred forms often have a significant religious past, and sacred forms associated with particular religious traditions and communities play a part in the multiplicity of sacred forms within contemporary society. But the wider range of sacred forms that exert considerable influence over contemporary life cannot be easily encapsulated within the concept of 'religion'. Gender, human rights, the care of children, nature, and the neo-liberal marketplace all have sacralized significance in modern social life, but our understanding of the nature and operation of these sacred forms is not helped by framing these as 'religious' phenomena. Similarly, discourses and symbols of religion circulate through contemporary culture in ways that do not necessarily have normative significance or draw together a community of adherents in the way that sacred forms do. Examples of this include the circulation of religious symbols and narratives through entertainment media in which they serve as backdrops or cultural references with little normative significance for their audiences, and the construction and framing of 'religion' in legal or policy contexts. The content and structure of sacred forms range much further than the conventional conceptual boundaries of 'religion'. Religion, on the other hand, as it is constructed and circulated through contemporary society, is a far more diffuse range of phenomena than the more specific, normative structure of sacred forms. To make an analytical distinction between the sociology of religion and the sociology of the sacred is, therefore, to demarcate two important fields of study. Without such a distinction, the study of the nature and significance of religion and the sacred becomes blurred in ways that generate unwarranted assumptions about the legitimate boundaries of the study of 'authentic' religion, and blunt the conceptual frameworks that might help us to interpret the nature of the sacred in the modern world.

***

This book forms part of a renewed interest in the notion of the sacred in sociology, media studies, and the study of religion. Following Robert Bellah's work on civil religion,[4] since the 1980s there has been an ongoing refinement of cultural sociology as a theoretical and empirical project in which questions of sacred symbols and values play a central role. Similarly, the growth of interest in neo- and post-Durkheimian approaches to the study of media over the past two decades, associated with the emergence of media anthropology,[5] has generated a growing literature on media, ritual, and the sacred. Within the study of religion, recent critiques of ontological theories of the sacred (discussed in Chapter 1) have created new opportunities for rethinking the value of the concept of the sacred for social and cultural analysis.[6] This project therefore builds on this growing academic interest in the sacred, and benefits from many invaluable contributions by previous writers on this subject.

One of the challenges in writing this book is to present material to readers from different disciplines who have very different degrees of familiarity with it. Theoretical points made in the following discussion will at times seem blindingly obvious to readers well versed in cultural sociology, but may well be new to readers in the critical study of religion, and vice versa. Writing in a tradition of scholarship emerging out of the writings of Émile Durkheim is also complex, given the range of interpretations and uses to which Durkheim's work has been put. Working across disciplines and literatures always therefore runs the risk of producing simplistic or under-theorized accounts that take debates backwards rather than forwards.[7] The extent to which I have also fallen into this trap will be for others to judge. I hope, though, that this book will contribute to an awareness of an interest in the study of the sacred across different disciplines, and open up conversations between disciplines and literatures that have been developed only to a limited extent in the past.

The five chapters of this book attempt three consecutive tasks. In Chapters 1 and 2, I attempt to outline some basic theoretical principles for a cultural sociology of the sacred. The intention here is not to provide any kind of systematic theory of the sacred—the value of which is uncertain, for reasons I explore later. Rather my aim is to note some of the key theoretical principles that we can take to be characteristic of the sacred as a cultural structure, which can help us to operationalize it for research, and which can underpin attempts to use the sacred as a concept for social and cultural analysis. A major task in the opening chapter is to distinguish the cultural sociological approach advocated in this book with various ontological theories. This is partly to ensure that my use of the concept of the sacred gets a fair hearing among those who are otherwise inoculated against the use of this term through their rejection of an Elidean tradition of religious studies. But it is also mainly because differentiating between ontological and cultural sociological theories of the sacred helps to clarify some fundamentally different theoretical assumptions in these approaches and thus some of the underpinnings of the cultural sociological approach. Differentiating between ontological and cultural sociological theories of the sacred is not always easy. Even Durkheim can be read as supporting a particular kind of ontological understanding of the sacred. However, distinguishing between these approaches can encourage a theoretical clarity that is not always present when some writers draw together different theorists of the sacred across this conceptual divide. A second task in Chapter 1 is to offer a critical rereading of Durkheim's theory of the sacred, which rids it of less useful elements, such as Durkheim's tendency towards generalized binary thinking and his notion of the common social ontology underlying all individual sacred forms. By the end of this chapter, I begin to identify some key theoretical claims that I wish to make about sacred forms. These are further extended in Chapter 2, as I discuss how the work of Edward Shils, Robert Bellah, and Jeffrey Alexander addresses a range of issues that are central to the nature and significance of sacred forms in the modern world. Through Chapter 2, the influence of Alexander's 'strong programme' in cultural sociology on my argument will become clear. Indeed, the book as a whole can be read as an attempt to think critically about, and through, understandings of the sacred associated with Alexander's 'strong programme'. Having reviewed the work of Shils, Bellah, and Alexander, I set out some of the key theoretical claims underpinning a cultural sociological approach to the study of the sacred and offer some comments on the kind of knowledge offered by cultural interpretation grounded in these claims.

Some readers may find it helpful to begin with Chapters 1 and 2 if they want to understand the theoretical orientation of the book. Other readers may find it more fruitful to turn first to Chapters 3 and 4, which represent the second major stage in the book's argument, in which I use case examples to explore the utility of the sacred for analysing specific social and cultural phenomena. Chapter 3 explores why the systemic abuse and neglect of children within the Irish industrial school system was possible for much of the twentieth century, arguing that this happened partly because of a contingent relationship between the dominant sacred form of the Irish Catholic nation and the subjugated form of the sacrality of the care of children. In Chapter 4, a case is made for thinking about public and social media as the primary institutional structure for the reproduction and contestation of sacred forms in contemporary society. The tensions this creates for public broadcasters are then discussed in relation to the strong public reaction against the BBC's decision not to broadcast a humanitarian appeal on behalf of those suffering from the conflict surrounding Israel's Operation Cast Lead offensive on Gaza in 2008–9.

Chapter 5 represents a final stage of the argument, moving into normative reflection about our relationship with sacred forms. One could think of the final stage of this argument as an example of a normative project within cultural sociology (similar to the normative concerns that run through Jeffrey Alexander's *The Civil Sphere*), or as an inclusive theological project that encourages critical reflection on the sacred regardless of one's religious or secular position. To me, these are really simply two different ways of describing the same process. Noting the potentially destructive effects of sacred forms on social life, this chapter argues that the sacred is an inevitable communicative structure for human society and that life without the sacred is almost certainly impossible for us. The question then turns to how we might live with sacred forms in ways that mitigate as much as possible the shadow that they can cast on social life. In the Conclusion, I offer a summary of the theoretical definition of the sacred that has emerged from the preceding discussion, and suggest a number of questions for further study.

There is a sense in which all the work in this book is incomplete in terms of the breadth and depth of this argument. I make no claims for it beyond it being an initial attempt to formulate an intellectual project through which we might better understand and critically reflect on the sacred forms that shape our contemporary lives for better or ill. My hope is that this book will stimulate more people to take this project forwards, to develop its theoretical underpinnings, and, in particular, to refine its arguments through more detailed analyses of sacred forms in specific social and historical contexts.

1

Ontological and Durkheimian Theories of the Sacred

> In a word, society substitutes for the world revealed to us by our senses a different world that is the projection of the ideals created by society itself.
>
> (Émile Durkheim, *Sociology and Philosophy*, 1924)

It is nearly a hundred years since two of the most influential theoretical texts on the sacred were published; Émile Durkheim's *The Elementary Forms of the Religious Life* and Rudolf Otto's *The Idea of the Holy*. Despite this—or perhaps because of the criticisms that mounted up against their approaches—the term 'the sacred' is still widely used today without clear theoretical underpinnings. Indeed, in much academic and popular usage, the 'sacred' is often treated as a simple synonym for religion, with sacred texts referring to the scriptures of established religions, sacred spaces to sites of religious worship, and so on.

This book seeks to extend a body of scholarship that attempts, against such vernacular uses, to use the concept of the sacred in theoretically grounded ways as a means of social and cultural analysis. The aim of this opening chapter is to clarify fundamental differences between the two very different theories of the sacred exemplified by Otto and Durkheim, and to present arguments in favour of adopting the latter approach. By the end of this chapter, Durkheim's foundational contribution will be discussed, as will the ways in which his contribution needs to be reinterpreted to form the basis for a viable sociology of the sacred. This will clear the way, in the next chapter, for considering how contributions by later writers have helped to establish a more detailed theoretical framework for the study of the sacred on which the remainder of the book will be based.

Ontological theories of the sacred

Durkheim and Otto's theories of the sacred are not simply foundational contributions, but have formed the basis for two radically different approaches to this subject: the *ontological* and the *cultural sociological*.[1] Otto's treatment of the sacred in terms of a universal human capacity to experience sacred presence is an example of a wider range of ontological theories that conceive of the sacred in terms of fundamental structures within the person or the cosmos itself. Otto's work drew partly from William James's theory of religion as 'the feelings, acts, and experiences of individual men [*sic*] in their solitude, so far as they apprehend themselves to stand in relation to whatever they may consider the divine'.[2] While Otto agreed with James's basic observation about the primacy of religious experience, he argued that this experience of the sacred could be defined more clearly as 'mysterium tremendum', a sense of sacred awe, fascination, and dread. Furthermore, Otto contended that James's account was limited by his attention only to human feelings rather than the structures that those feelings disclosed.[3] These structures were the 'numinous', the sacred presence shrouded in mystery yet experienced as 'objective and outside the self',[4] and the structure of human consciousness, 'an original and underivable capacity of the mind',[5] through which the numinous could be experienced through the sensory and material conditions of individual experience. Otto's theory of the sacred thus pointed to a human capacity for a particular kind of religious experience, as well as the indefinable, mysterious phenomenon of the numinous that gave rise to such experiences.

Otto's theory of the sacred was far from unique, and shared common ground with other scholarship of his time on mysticism, a subject on which Otto himself also lectured. Evelyn Underhill, Baron von Hügel, and Rufus Jones were all popular writers of that period who detected in the mystical traditions of the great world religions a common spiritual experience, of 'union between God and the soul'.[6] William James similarly described mysticism in terms of a transient and transformative moment of direct experience of the ineffable.[7] Such a notion of universal mystical experience remains influential today among some religious liberals and practitioners of alternative spiritualities. Otto's phenomenological approach was also further developed by influential figures in the study of religion such as Gerardus van der Leeuw, Joachim Wach, and, most influentially, Mircea Eliade.

While Eliade's seminal book, *The Sacred and the Profane*, begins with a tribute to Otto, it also substantially extends his ideas. Eliade draws a contrast between his own work and Otto's by observing that the latter's interest in the emotional apprehension of the sacred represents a focus merely on the 'irrational' elements of religion. Eliade, by contrast, declared an interest in the 'sacred in its entirety',[8] by which he meant attention to the different dimensions of the human response to the sacred, including the phenomena of sacred space, sacred time, ritual, and myth. These various dimensions contributed to a particular way of being in the world—the *homo religiosus*—characterized by a fundamental orientation to transcendent, ontological reality. In this sense, Eliade preserves Otto's emphasis on the 'wholly other' nature of the sacred that elicits particular kinds of human response. However, Eliade moves beyond Otto's notion that this response is characterized by specific kinds of religious feeling, arguing that the religious response to sacred reality may take different forms of subjective and cultural expression (albeit through common structures such as sacred space, time, and myth).[9]

Another distinctive element of Eliade's understanding of the sacred, compared to Otto's, was his contrast between sacred and profane as two modes of being in the world.[10] Seeing the *homo religiosus* as the historically more typical human experience of being in the world, he saw the profane human experience of life in a desacralized cosmos as a modern phenomenon. By contrast with the *homo religiosus*, whose life is structured in relation to an ultimate reality, the modern, desacralized life follows the pattern described by existentialists such as Sartre and Camus in which 'modern nonreligious man [*sic*]...regards himself solely as the subject and agent of history, and refuses all appeal to transcendence'.[11] While Eliade saw the sacred mode of being as more common in pre-modern times, he was also sceptical of the ability of the modern person fully to free him or herself from this religious past. Rather than embracing fully a post-religious existence, contemporary life is run through with 'camouflaged myths and degenerated rituals', both at the level of the attempts to inject meaning into personal life and of wider social and political movements organized around collective ritual and myth.[12] The modern, desacralized way of being may, therefore, have the grandeur of 'a tragic existence', but it is at the same time based on a series of 'denials and refusals' of the historically rooted religious mode of being in the world that is the more common form of the human condition. Furthermore, Eliade concludes, modern attempts to find meaning in the face of existential crisis will always remain transient and fragmented if they fail to connect with a transcendent reality that forms a more universal and general point of reference for life. The 'unquenchable ontological thirst'[13] that drives religious life cannot therefore be adequately met by the partial meanings crafted by the lonely existential self. But, although the people today may have 'lost the capacity to live religion consciously', they still retain an unconscious memory of their religious inheritance, which keeps alive the 'possibility of reintegrating a religious vision of life'—work that might be furthered by philosophers, psychologists, and theologians.[14] Far from being a cool, analytical theory of the sacred, Eliade's ideas speak of a nostalgia for a lost religious past, as well as the hope that some form of recovery from the 'fall' of modern, post-religious life might be possible.

The line of scholarship represented by James, Otto, and Eliade defines the sacred in terms of recognizable patterns of subjective experience, whether these be particular forms of religious experience ('mysterium tremendum'), or an existential way of being in the world structured around transcendent reality.[15] Otto and Eliade go beyond James's emphasis on religious feeling, however, to emphasize the importance of the ontological reality that evokes such subjective responses. In this sense, for Otto and Eliade, the sacred is both an adjective, referring to a particular quality of human experience, and a noun, referring to a sacred that transcends understanding.[16]

Ontological theories and the poststructuralist turn

This ontological tradition proved to be highly influential on the discipline of religious studies in the twentieth century. Through emphasizing the essentially positive core at the heart of different human religious traditions, it formed a basis both for liberal approaches to inter-faith dialogue and for an emerging tradition of religious studies premised on the assumption that the study of 'healthy' religion could have positive cultural effects in a pluralist society.[17] It also, as that century drew to an end, became increasingly criticized as a theoretical approach. The critique has been particularly advanced in recent years by a new generation of scholars who have contributed to a poststructuralist turn in the study of religion, including Russell McCutcheon, Timothy Fitzgerald, Tomoko Masuzawa, Jeremy Carrette, and Richard King.

For these scholars, ontological theories of an ahistorical essence to the sacred that can be properly discerned only through the expertise of the religious scholar is an anathema. As Russell McCutcheon puts it:

one cannot argue for religion as a historical event [as Eliade does] *while at the same time* asserting that there is always a kernel left over once we separate it from the historical chaff, a kernel whose special nature dictates the use of special skills exercised by special hermeneuts. Ironically, many of us might have jobs in autonomous religion departments precisely because few have yet to recognise the contradiction.[18]

To suggest that there is some kind of universal, essential experience underlying the *sui generis* phenomenon of religion or the sacred is problematic precisely because the categories of 'religion' and the 'sacred' are themselves contingent, historically situated, and non-universal concepts. From this poststructuralist perspective, essentialist claims about the universal basis and structure of religious experience should be regarded not as attempts to uncover the objective nature of the world, but as discursive practices formed in specific historical contexts with socio-political consequences. From a poststructuralist perspective, the ontological approach of Eliade and others exemplifies the ways in which scholars deny the social and political conditions of both their objects of study and the ways in which they think about them—an observation given particular poignance in the light of Eliade's own early involvement with fascism in Romania.[19]

This poststructuralist critique has not, however, led to the demise of ontological theories of the sacred, which continue to flourish in contemporary scholarship on religion. This is partly because it has been absorbed into newer ontological theories of the sacred. Thomas Csordas, for example, has recently argued that 'the origin of religion, the sacred, the holy' lies in the inherent ambiguity of the human experience of embodiment, characterized by the lack of a stable, embodied centre for the self, which gives rise to a fundamental experience of alterity that finds expression through the metaphors and practices of religion. For Csordas, then, the *concept* of religion may indeed have specific historical and cultural roots, but this does not mean that one cannot say anything about universal ontological phenomena to which this culturally specific term points. Similar arguments have been made in relation to cognitive theories of religion, in which their advocates claim to be able to identify common cognitive structures and processes, which have subsequently come to be thought of as 'religious'.[20] Such neo-ontological theories, often mindful of the poststructuralist critique of religion, nevertheless represent a direct rejection of Russell McCutcheon's claim. From this perspective, the concept of 'religion' can indeed be cast off as historically specific chaff, without losing the kernel of the ontological structure and experience that the concept of 'religion' attempts to grasp.

There is another way in which ontological understandings of the sacred have been seen as compatible with poststructuralist thought.[21] A recurring concern in the work of major poststructuralist theorists such as Jacques Lacan, Jacques Derrida, Luce Irigaray, and Hélène Cixous has focused on the limitations of language and representation. Ignoring Wittgenstein's famous dictum, 'That whereof we cannot speak, let us be silent', this trajectory of poststructuralist scholarship has sought to find ways of acknowledging the significance of that aspect of existence that exceeds and escapes our capacities of representation. As Jacques Derrida commented, for example, 'there are only contexts... nothing exists outside context, as I have said, but also that the limit of the frame or the border of the context always entails a clause of non-closure. The outside penetrates and thus determines the inside.'[22] To attempt to capture this in language is always an impossible task: 'the trace is always, in being discussed, effaced by the very language which makes it known.'[23] Despite the impossibility of capturing that which always eludes systems of representation, poststructuralist writers have nevertheless sought to point toward it through evocative or non-rational styles of writing, reflecting the approach to the sacred taken by Bataille.[24] It has also been alluded to through concepts such as jouissance, alterity, the mystical, the aesthetic, the material or sensual ground of reading and writing, the sublime or the unconscious, the erotic, the transgressive, the subversive or disruptive; the otherness or lack that is desired but that can never be captured or possessed. This otherness that exceeds the limitations of language is also described in sacred terms using analogies from apophatic theology that recognize the transcendence that eludes any concepts of the divine (the 'Godhead beyond God', as Meister Eckhart put it).

The poststructuralist interest in the sacred that transcends representation has been taken up in more sociological terms by Bernhard Giesen.[25] Giesen is critical of the failure of social theory to take account of that which goes beyond discursive classification, arguing that the capacity of classificatory systems to create a sense of stability in categorizing the world depends on their allusion to an unspoken, 'Archimedian point'[26] that lies beyond classification. Giesen links this poststructuralist emphasis on that which transcends representation with a central part of Durkheim's theory of the sacred in *The Elementary Forms of the Religious Life*. Here Durkheim had argued that the aura of transcendence that surrounded sacred forms derived from the fundamental human sense of participating in a greater whole, which is in fact the greater whole of society. Sacred forms thus become the means by which people represent their consciousness of being part of society back to themselves. Giesen argues, though, that such an operation of being both subject (encountering the sacred form) and object (represented by the sacred form) is extraordinarily complex, and that the simultaneous awareness of being both subject and object cannot easily be held within human consciousness. As a consequence, the sacred form is encountered as something other than a mere representation of the collective life of the group, and experienced as something other, as radical alterity. Echoing the concepts of Rudolf Otto, Giesen argues that such an encounter 'breaks down the structure of ordinary life', leaving us 'taken over by a state of suspense, vertigo and awe'.[27] Like Eliade, Giesen also argues that such experiences of the sacred attach themselves to particular times, spaces, practices, and places as moments and sites of epiphany, in which the sacred takes concrete form in social life.

A cultural sociological critique of ontological theories of the sacred

The approach to the study of the sacred to be developed in this book is radically different in its focus and assumptions from these various ontological theories of the sacred. What distinguishes this cultural sociology of the sacred from ontological theories is that the former does not identify the sacred as a universal ontological structure within the human person or the cosmos. Instead it attends primarily to the sacred in terms of identifiable processes and qualities of social life, understanding sacred forms as culturally constructed within historically contingent contexts. Rather than thinking about the sacred as an ontological phenomenon that transcends signification, the cultural sociological approach understands sacrality as a particular form of cultural signification in which symbols, objects, sentiments, and practices are experienced as expressions of a normative, absolute reality. The crucial distinction here is between the claim that there is an actual ontological referent for sacred forms, and the idea that sacred forms constitute *what people take to be* absolute realities that have claims over their lives. The ontological assumption of a common experience underlying sacred forms is not only unnecessary; it also obscures the nuances of the very different kinds of subjectivity that emerge in relation to the different content and structures of specific sacred forms. An ontological approach asks what sacred forms emerge out of a fundamental experience of the sacred.[28] A cultural approach asks what specific kinds of experience (embodied ways of feeling, thinking, and acting) are bound up with historically contingent and socially constructed forms of the sacred. This is not to deny the existence or importance of what mystics, Romantics, or poststructuralists have referred to as the ground of being, the sublime, or alterity. But it is to deny that such experiences underlie the construction of sacred forms in the direct way suggested by ontological theories of Otto, Eliade, Csordas, and Giesen.

If ontological theories of the sacred have been so influential for the study of religion, and continue to find expression in new phenomenological, cognitive, and evolutionary guises, why should they be regarded as problematic for the intellectual project I am presenting here? A fundamental objection is that they blunt and limit the study of sacred forms more than they illuminate it, for three main reasons. First, *ontological theories typically provide reductive accounts of the sacred as a social phenomenon*. By positing a single, originating ontological root for the human experience of the sacred, ontological theories always reduce their analysis of expressions of the sacred to the terms of that originating experience. Contemporary fascination with Harry Potter can therefore be explained in the basic human cognitive capacity to make connections between unconnected phenomena, or the physical experience of being 'slain in the Spirit' in a Charismatic healing service can be explained simply in terms of an underlying structure of embodiment. But such reductive accounts tell us little or nothing about the historically contingent ways in which particular sacred forms vividly acquire the status of absolute, normative realities or the social processes through which they are reproduced or contested. Similarly, where such theories claim an interest in alterity (as, for example, Csordas or Giesen do), they reduce an account of otherness to a single, understandable ontological cause, rendering alterity somewhat less than radically 'other'. A basic contention of the argument to be developed in this book is that thinking of the sacred in cultural sociological terms allows us much more scope to develop nuanced accounts of the nature and operation of sacred forms under particular, contingent conditions. As we shall discuss further towards the end of the next chapter, this allows us not only to be able to diagnose specific social contexts with greater insight, but also to refine a more general theory of the sacred as a cultural structure.

Second, as will have become clear in the preceding pages, *ontological theories of the sacred typically conflate the 'sacred' and 'religion'*. While Otto and Eliade wrote about the fundamental place of the sacred within human existence, the 'sacred' was inseparable from its expressions through cultural forms of religion. Thomas Csordas, similarly, claims to see the importance of recognizing that the relations between terms such as 'religion', 'transcendent', the 'sacred', and the 'supernatural' are 'endlessly nuanced, and [that] we must be mindful of the dangers in attempting to construct a universalist definition of religion'.[29] Yet, within a few pages, he talks about the ontological roots of religion and the sacred in a way that makes no distinction between the terms. The sacred, for these writers, sooner or later becomes a synonym for religion. One of the problems with this is the assumption that religion is necessarily connected with the underlying ontological structures of the sacred. Again this trait of ontological theories of the sacred places unnecessary limits on our capacity for social analysis both of religion and of sacred forms. Within the approach to the sociology of religion that I described in the Introduction to this book, it is clear that the concept of 'religion' has far wider significance and uses beyond its reference to a posited ontological root. The category of 'religion' is variously used in contemporary society to allocate resources, to establish and limit rights and equalities, and to imagine different forms of social malaise and redemption. None of these uses relates to a common ontological experience; rather they reflect the ways in which the category of 'religion' has evolved and now circulates through contemporary society. Furthermore, the conflation of religion and the sacred has led some writers to make unnecessarily negative evaluations of sacred forms that have a cultural life beyond religious traditions and institutions (Eliade's 'camouflaged myths and degenerated rituals'), or indeed to think that the 'secular sacred' is in some sense a distinct entity from religious traditions and structures. It is precisely through the temporary suspension of the terms 'religion' and 'secular' that a sociology of the sacred is able to detect the religious roots of apparently secular sacred forms, or the common influence of particular sacred forms across what we think of as 'religious' or 'secular' domains of society. By conflating 'sacred experience' with 'religious expression', ontological theories of the sacred therefore needlessly limit our sociological imagination about what 'religion' is and does in contemporary society, as well as our understanding of the roots, nature, and significance of sacred forms. Again, a fundamental assumption of my argument is that we make considerable conceptual gains by making an analytic distinction between 'religion' and the 'sacred', and that, by making this distinction, we may actually come to see religious institutions, symbols, and practices in more sociologically insightful ways.

Finally, by limiting an understanding of the sacred to a single ontological source, *ontological theories of the sacred provide a poor basis for understanding the multiplicity of contemporary sacred forms, and the complex interplay between different sacred forms*. One of the defining features of the history of Western modernity has been the shattering of Christian cosmology that was previously taken for granted by the majority of the population. As Benedict Anderson observed in the context of the rise of nationalism,[30] it was precisely the fragmentation of this sacred canopy that created conditions for new sacred forms to arise. The past three centuries have witnessed the emergence and extension of sacred forms such as the nation state, the self, nature, human rights, and the sacrality of the care of children, alongside multiple sacred forms carried through the increasing religious diversity of the West. Late modernity is therefore defined by the simultaneous presence of multiple sacred forms, which exist in complex patterns of complementarity and con-flict, dominance and subjugation. To think of the experience of the sacred as a single phenomenon is to neglect the myriad ways that sacred forms are experienced, reproduced, and shaped through individual sub-jectivities in modern society. As noted above, a cultural sociology of the sacred focuses on the thoughts, feelings, and actions associated with contingent sacred forms in particular social and historical contexts; thinking of the sacred in terms of a single kind of ontological experience or structure can only hamper this.

The intellectual tradition of the cultural sociology of the sacred

Given this critical perspective on ontological theories of the sacred, my aim in the remainder of this chapter and the next is to outline key concepts underpinning a cultural sociological approach to the study of the sacred. Through these chapters, I will focus particularly on the work of four writers who have made crucial contributions to this task: Émile Durkheim, Edward Shils, Robert Bellah, and Jeffrey Alexander.[31] The four writers selected here are important as representatives of different theoretical and moral projects in the cultural sociological study of the sacred. In addition, their work is part of a particular intellectual lineage beginning with Durkheim at the start of the twentieth century, running through the work of Shils and Bellah from the 1950s onwards, up to the work currently being undertaken by Jeffrey Alexander. The absent figure who provides a vital link for this Anglo-American tradition is Talcott Parsons. Parsons's reception of Durkheim's theory of religion, reworked in the context of an abstract, systems theory of social structure and action, was formative both for Edward Shils (who co-authored large parts of *Toward a General Theory of Action* with Parsons), and Bellah (who studied under Parsons at Harvard). While Parsons's work was shaped by a range of European sources, the Durkheimian influence on his work was most evident in his emphasis on the integrative role of values for the maintenance of social order. But Shils and Bellah both later reacted against Parsonian systems theory in different ways,[32] and it was Bellah's intellectual project that provided a framework for

Alexander (one of Bellah's students at Berkeley) to articulate a fuller account of a cultural sociology in which attention to the sacred plays a central role. In fact, Parsons's use of Durkheim to develop an integrative model of society, and the subsequent widespread rejection of Parsonian theory by the 1970s,[33] contributed to a more general rejection of Durkheim's ideas of the sacred among many sociologists in subsequent decades.[34]

Durkheim's own understanding of the sacred is sufficiently complex to allow different, and sometimes competing, readings. His work can, therefore, be reasonably read as supporting a form of (social) ontological theory of the sacred, exemplified by Bernhard Giesen, as well as the cultural sociological approach that will be discussed in more detail in the remainder of this chapter.[35] In this sense, Durkheim has many intellectual children, and the cultural sociological approach presented here, while fundamentally inspired by his work, is not the only possible theoretical development from his ideas.

Shils, Bellah, and Alexander each extended and revised Durkheim's theory of the sacred. These writers have been more concerned with the 'pure' sacred, sacred symbols around which social collectivities form and that shape thought, feeling, and action. Their work is, therefore, distinct from that of Georges Bataille, Roger Caillois, and other members of the Collège de Sociologie who were fascinated by the concept of the 'impure' sacred that threatens to subvert the conservatism of profane social orders through the pursuit of transgression of taboo or the exceeding of constraint. Indeed, this division of interest along the lines of the pure and impure sacred has often followed geographical lines, with the impure sacred continuing to be an important influence in the work of later continental thinkers such as Michel Foucault, Jean Baudrillard, and Julia Kristeva, and the pure sacred attracting the interest of an Anglo-American seam of scholarship to which Shils, Bellah, and Alexander have been leading contributors.[36]

There is a significant difference between these two traditions of understanding the sacred. The focus on the 'pure' sacred addresses sacred forms *as* cultural structures, exploring not only the content of specific sacred forms but also the circulation, reproduction, and contestation of these structures through social life. By contrast, the focus on the 'impure' sacred conceives of the sacred in terms of experiences and states that arise precisely through the *suspension or transgression* of cultural structures. In this sense, the work of Bataille and Caillois is similar to Victor Turner's interest in the sacred significance of moments of 'anti-structure' in which conventional structures are suspended or challenged in a deeper spirit of *communitas*. In using the sacred as a concept for social and cultural analysis, we are, therefore, faced with a fork in the road between these traditions of the pure/structural and impure/anti-structural sacred. In choosing between the two approaches, it may be helpful to note that they attend to two fundamentally different phenomena. The study of the 'pure' sacred focuses our attention on processes by which particular sacred forms operate as normative constructions of absolute reality that tend to maintain their power over long periods of time, even though intense identification with them may come only in transient forms. The study of the 'impure' sacred, by contrast, focuses on fleeting moments of ecstasy, transgression, creativity, and *communitas*, which give life by temporarily releasing people from cultural structures that would otherwise become oppressive and arid. While the accounts of this latter phenomenon by Caillois and Turner may indeed offer perceptive insights into the finitude and decay of human existence (Caillois) or the importance of a fundamental sense of common humanity (Turner), there is still no convincing basis for assuming that the phenomena that they refer to stand behind the specific sacred forms that animate contemporary social life. By contrast, attention to sacred forms as normative, cultural structures provides a more promising way for thinking about how these structures emerge and operate in particular contexts. The approach set out in this book therefore follows the path of the 'pure' sacred, previously tracked by Shils, Bellah, and Alexander, although the limitations and alternatives to this approach deserve ongoing discussion.

By tracing a trajectory of the reception of Durkheim's work through Shils, Bellah, and Alexander in the next chapter, I hope to give a clearer outline of a cultural sociological approach to the sacred that is theoretically defensible and empirically useful. Before I do this, it is necessary to consider Durkheim's contribution in more detail.

Émile Durkheim: The collective construction of the sacred

Durkheim's interest in the sacred became a defining feature of the work of the last twenty years of his life. Although this interest is most associated with his major study, *The Elementary Forms of the Religious Life*, his first substantial articulation of his notion of the sacred was published nine years earlier in 1903 in his major essay, co-authored with his nephew Marcel Mauss, on *Primitive Classification*. Three preliminary comments should be made before presenting a brief account of Durkheim's theory of the sacred. First, Durkheim believed that his theory of the sacred as a social phenomenon was universally applicable, and that his studies in religion could disclose 'an essential and permanent aspect of humanity'.[37] Durkheim therefore believed that central processes and functions associated with religion could potentially be found even in modern, secular societies. While this claim to universality has been contested,[38] it raises the fundamental question of whether or not forms of the sacred can be identified in all societies. By the end of the book, we will return to this question of whether the sacred is a necessary, or indeed desirable, aspect of social life. Secondly, Durkheim's theory of religion and the sacred was developed in the context of an evolutionary framework in which he argued that the most accurate way of understanding religion was both to analyse it in the context of the simplest possible societies and to study archaic forms of religion that were not derived from previous religious forms. By creating an account of this 'original' form of religion, derived from ethnographic literature on Aboriginal and native American cultures, Durkheim argued it would be possible to understand the core of religion that ran through later, and more complex, societies and that had been built on these primitive roots. There are significant difficulties with this evolutionary approach, however. The assumption either that these early societies were homogeneous or that they bore any straightforward evolutionary relationship to modern societies has been challenged.[39] Even if Durkheim's basic assumptions about this were correct, there has also been criticism of his selective use of atypical ethnographic material and a strong case has been made that Aboriginal culture does not actually demonstrate some of the key processes and structures that Durkheim attributed to it.[40] An equally problematic aspect of this evolutionary approach was Durkheim's assertion that religious symbols should be understood as a primitive method of representing social structures and processes, and that the discipline of sociology would, therefore, remove the need for such religious symbols by providing a more direct and scientific account of the social realities to which they pointed. This assumption places the sociological study of religion in an immediately antagonistic relationship with its object of study, privileging the researcher as the one who *really* knows what is going on in a religious context rather than the religious dupes who persist in using their primitive and, to some degree, mystifying language. Durkheimian sociology of religion, in this sense, is a fundamentally secularizing project, seeking to cast away the imperfect and obsolete use of religious symbolism in the light of an authoritative, rational, and scientific gaze. While contemporary sociologists would still sympathize with Durkheim's assertion that sociological concepts and methods offer important insights into the significance of religious structures and processes beyond those attributed to them by their adherents, fewer would be comfortable with his claim that sociology can uncover *the* ultimate truth (that is, social reality) underlying religious life in a way that renders any further use of religious language obsolete.

While Durkheim's evolutionary assumptions about religion are problematic, they do not present insurmountable barriers to the use of his work. His concepts of religion and the sacred can be detached from the evolutionary framework in which they were developed. In *The Elementary Forms*, Durkheim initially presents his theory of religion and the sacred without any reference to the ethnographic data that he later uses in the book to support it. This has been identified as a weakness by some critics, who have argued that Durkheim's analysis of archaic cultures merely serves to illustrate a predetermined theoretical framework. Given that Durkheim's use of that ethnographic material has been widely criticized, it is potentially helpful to be able to extract some of the important concepts that Durkheim developed from the evolutionary assumptions and ethnographic errors that otherwise drag them down. We might similarly wish to distance ourselves from the project of defining religion that underpins *The Elementary Forms*. As noted above, the poststructuralist turn in the study of religion has raised fundamental questions about whether religion is an essence or stable phenomenon amenable to definition. Durkheim's approach to defining religion, perhaps like any attempt at such definition, also rests on a circular argument in which the various examples of religious life that Durkheim gives to support his definition are identified as being 'religious' on the basis of that definition. *The Elementary Forms* is, therefore, better approached as a theoretically stimulating resource for thinking about the sacred, rather than as the rigorous historical study or programmatic definition of religion that Durkheim intended it to be.

Finally, one of the most serious sociological objections to Durkheim's theory of the sacred is that it fails as a general theory of social life. As Jeffrey Alexander has observed, Durkheim's theory presents an undifferentiated view of social life, in which the only significant values in society are those formed through intense social interaction. This privileges an integrative view of society over the more complex realities of social pluralism and conflict, and regards only those social institutions associated with the sacred as having an important social role.[41] Furthermore, simplistic accounts of the integrative effects of the celebration of the sacred across whole societies fail to deal with the complexities and pluralism of late modernity.[42] Such a theory ignores too many of the structures, processes, and motive forces of contemporary social life to claim to be a comprehensive theory of society. At the same time, however, Alexander argues that Durkheim's work may still have considerable value if we regard it as a 'special theory referring to specified kinds of empirical process'.[43] In other words, Durkheim's theory of the sacred does not exhaust everything that needs to be said about the nature and constitution of society, but it may help us to think about specific kinds of structure and process that can have an important bearing on social life. It is in this spirit, of using a broadly Durkheimian framework as an analytical tool to help us think about specific aspects of contemporary social life, that this discussion proceeds.

Durkheim's theory of the sacred combines cognitive-symbolic, affective, and ritual elements. While some subsequent interpreters of his work have given particular emphasis to one of these individual elements,[44] it is more accurate to see these elements as inseparable and interlocking in Durkheim's thought. In cognitive terms, Durkheim saw the sacred as a focal element within cultural systems of symbolic classification. In *Primitive Classification*, Durkheim had argued that the structure of early classificatory systems derived from primary experiences of social solidarity and difference, that these systems were infused with moral sentiment rather than being organized on purely rational grounds, and that they were constructed in relation to what was taken to be sacred in a given social context.[45] The sacred thus constituted a radically distinctive element within such systems in relation to which other symbols drew their meaning. In principle, any object or category could be attributed sacred status—as a thing 'set apart'—but what defined the sacred was its radical otherness compared to all other, profane, categories. The separation of the sacred and profane was, in Durkheim's view, absolute, and far more radical than the separation between good and evil (which both represent positions on the scale of values). The sacred, by contrast, has nothing in common with the profane, existing as a *sui generis* category removed from all other forms of life. While the symbolic representation of the sacred was treated as a grounding source of power, healing, and meaning,[46] in reality the social significance of the sacred derived from its role as a symbolic representation of the moral community of its adherents. It is in this sense that Durkheim therefore saw sacred symbols as primitive attempts to conceptualize the nature and power of society.

The social significance of the sacred derived, however, not simply from its distinctive symbolic status, but from its role as the focus for intense, effervescent emotion generated through particular kinds of group activity.[47] Such emotion, stimulated by the experience of being caught up in the power of the social group, found itself channelled through sacred symbols in the same way that a lightning rod conducts a lightning strike. This meeting of the cognitive symbol and the power of group emotion enlivened the sacred, reinforcing the symbolic distinctiveness of the sacred with an experience of encountering a power greater than the individual self. Such emotion was not simply the effervescence of social interaction, but particular kinds of emotion generated in relation to the specific sacred symbol, which might include fear, respect, love, and enjoyment, as well as creative imagination.[48]

The third element, ritual, provided the structure for this process. Ritual both set the social space and conditions in which collective effervescence could be generated ('positive rites'), and provided ways of acting in relation to the sacred, which maintained its distinctive status and set down prohibitions that protected the sacred from pollution by the profane ('negative rites'). Such experiences of intense, collective engagement with the sacred, made possible through ritual, had the effect, not only of legitimating (and sometimes changing) the classificatory system of which the sacred was a part, but also giving individuals a profound sense of being members of a shared moral community. As Shilling and Mellor have argued, the fundamental structure in which these processes of thought, feeling, and action are grounded is the body.[49] Sacred thought, feeling, and practice cannot, therefore, be understood as abstract entities, but as always are performed through contingent bodies and learned through specific processes of 'body pedagogics'. Attending to the body as the ground of sacred thought, feeling, and action also makes it possible to understand the varying degrees to which thought, feeling, and practice are significant in the contingent sacred identifications formed by individuals and groups. Indeed, it raises the possibility that such sacred identifications may be grounded primarily in bodily practices associated with particular emotions, and not necessarily expressed through clearly conceptualized beliefs or ideologies.[50]

Within this theoretical framework, it is important to recognize Durkheim's fundamental emphasis on the heterogeneity of the sacred. A possible misreading of Durkheim's definition of the sacred is to think of it in terms of that which is seen as being of greatest power, value, and meaning in a given cultural system.[51] In other words, in a cultural hierarchy of what is deemed most valuable in life, the sacred stands at the top of the pile. In some ways, such a definition could be useful in terms of helping to focus on that which is most valued in a particular cultural context. But, in fact, Durkheim explicitly distances himself from such a view. In the *Elementary Forms*, he writes:

One might be tempted to define sacred things first by the place they are assigned in the hierarchy of beings. They are regarded as superior in dignity and power to profane things, and particularly to man [*sic*] when he is merely a man and does not participate in the sacred. He is represented, in fact, as occupying a lower and dependent place in relation to sacred things . . . But nothing about this representation is truly characteristic of the sacred. It is not enough to make one thing subordinate to make the other sacred in relation to it . . . Now, if we sometimes say that a person's religion consists of beings or things which he considers eminently valuable and in some way superior to himself, it is clear that in all such cases the word is meant metaphorically, and there is nothing in these relations that is properly religious in the strict sense of the term.[52]

Instead, Durkheim argued, what defines the sacred is its radical otherness in comparison to the profane. He, again, makes this point in the *Elementary Forms*, when discussing how the analytical work of a sociology of the sacred might proceed:

If one believes that sacred beings are distinguished merely by the greater intensity of their powers, the question of how men [*sic*] could entertain this idea is a rather simple one: merely identify those forces whose exceptional energy could strike the human mind vividly enough to inspire religious feelings. But if, as we have tried to establish, sacred things differ in nature from profane things, if they have a different essence, the problem is quite complex.[53]

Sacred things are, for Durkheim, radically different in nature from the profane, emerging from the human sense of the other beyond themselves that in fact derives from their experience of social life. It is the experience of living as a social being, in structures beyond the self, that constitutes the ground for this sacred 'other', regardless of the particular representational forms through which that 'other' is given concrete expression. It is the fundamental otherness of the sacred that reconstitutes the reality of social life, establishing profane forces that threaten to pollute or overwhelm the sacred, and draws together an affective, moral community that recognize its reality and claim on their lives. As we shall now see, it is Durkheim's emphasis on the heterogeneous and reality-constituting nature of the sacred that forms a vital basis for a cultural sociology of the sacred, but this project can proceed only with a significant rereading of Durkheim's position.

Rereading Durkheim

Any cultural sociological understanding of the sacred will to some degree be indebted to Durkheim's foundational work in this area, in the same way that any contemporary theorist working seriously with the concept of the unconscious would need to recognize the foundational work of Freud. At the same time, neo-Durkheimian schol-arship does not represent an uncritical reception of Durkheim's work. Indeed, this trajectory is better understood as a complex process of making use of Durkheim's work in different subsequent contexts of reception in ways that both critique his ideas and use them as a stimulus for new theoretical approaches.[54]

The critical rereading of Durkheim proposed here rests on two basic criticisms of his understanding of the sacred and the profane. First, the radical separation of the sacred and the profane reflects a tendency towards binary oppositions in Durkheim's thought that do not always adequately reflect empirical data or provide sufficiently nuanced theo-retical tools.[55] As Steven Lukes has observed,[56] in the case of the binary of the sacred and the profane, the profane becomes a residual category that includes a number of different elements (for example, the everyday, the impure sacred, and potential pollutants of the sacred) that would be better considered separately. This creates scope for further clarification about the sacred and its relation to other categories. Indeed, it is helpful to distinguish between the reality-constituting *sacred* as the intersection of symbol, emotion, normative claims, ritual practice, and social collec-tive; the *profane* as the evil that threatens this sacred form and pollutes whatever it comes into contact with;[57] and the *mundane*, as the logics, practices, and spaces of everyday life.

Secondly, Durkheim's theory of the sacred, as presented in the *Elemen-tary Forms*, can itself be read as a form of an ontological theory of the sacred.[58] Durkheim's understanding of the social source of sacred forms assumes that the power and significance of sacred forms derives from a universal trait of human experience—the experience of participating in the self-transcending reality of the social group.[59] A very similar assump-tion is also present in Victor Turner's understanding of *communitas*, in which the sacred significance of *communitas* derives from the potent awareness and recognition of 'an essential and generic human bond, without which there could be *no* society'.[60] This ontological grounding of the sacred is different from the ontological views of Eliade, or indeed of poststructuralist mystics. Durkheim's view is grounded on a social ontology, the notion of a common aspect of human experience that derives from participation in society, rather than assuming struc-tures that exist in the ontology of the pre-social person or of the cosmos itself. But it nevertheless assumes that there is some kind of universal human experience that underlies specific instances of sacred forms. As with any ontological theory of the sacred, such assumptions are unnecessary, though, and typically lack empirical verification. Durk-heim has been criticized for assuming that a particular kind of experience of society, which may, at best, be limited to simple and homogeneous societies, can be generalized across all forms of human society.[61] Mary Douglas has also noted the flaws in Durkheim's assumption that participation in ritual is closely bound up with fluid and creative experiences of collective effervescence, given that rituals are often carefully controlled, stage-managed, and experienced by their participants as long and dull.[62] As we noted earlier, the nature of particular sacred forms (and the subjectivities formed in relation to them) are historically contingent. Rather than assuming a common existential or (social) ontological core underlying all sacred forms, it is more useful analytically to ask what particular kinds of experience are associated with particular kinds of sacred forms in specific historical contexts. While Durkheim's understanding of the intersection of symbol, moral sentiment, practice, and collective experience and identity is essential for a cultural sociological theory of the sacred, his assumption that all sacred forms derive from a universal social ontology is unhelpful for nuanced analysis, and should be dispensed with. Closely associated with Durkheim's belief in the social ontological roots of sacred forms was his claim that sacred forms are symbolic representations of society itself: 'if the totem is both the symbol of god and of society are these not one and the same?'[63] Again this assumption is unnecessary for a cultural sociological understanding of the sacred.[64] If we think about sacred forms simply as symbols that stand for society, this becomes reductive, stifles historical curiosity about the contingent origins of specific sacred forms, and blunts an appreciation of the ways that the content and structure of different sacred forms shape social life in distinctive ways.

Accepting these two criticisms—of Durkheim's tendency towards unnecessarily simplistic binary thinking and his idea of the common social ontology underlying all sacred forms—does not necessarily require a wholesale abandonment of his theory. Rather, new possibilities are created for critically reinterpreting it.

The enduring analytical value of Durkheim's emphasis on the heterogeneity of the sacred is that it establishes that the radical otherness of sacred forms is experienced by their adherents as *non-contingent*—an absolute reality that stands over and above the mundane, contingent nature of everyday life. It is not necessary to assume that this radical otherness is the product of an underlying, common social ontology—the experience of being in society. Indeed, without this ontological claim, it becomes easier to think about how the specific content, structures, and identificatory power of sacred forms have emerged through particular historical processes. Moving beyond Durkheim's claim that sacred forms emerge from the experience of being in society, we can focus instead on the ways in which the assumed non-contingent status of particular sacred forms constitutes reality for their adherents.

As the opening quotation for this chapter suggests, Durkheim saw the sacred primarily in terms of its role in structuring cultural frameworks through which reality is interpreted. This point was central to Durkheim's earlier work with Mauss, in *Primitive Classification*, in which they argued that cultural systems of classification are organized, not on the basis of some form of objective rationality, but on a terrain of moral sentiment in which fundamental, sacred concepts define symbolic relationships within the system as a whole. The otherness of the sacred can therefore be understood in terms of an absolute reality on which the meanings of social life are constituted.

Sacred forms are not absolute realities in the sense of laws of nature, such as the universal boiling point of water or the laws of gravity. Rather, they are absolute realities that establish normative claims over social life. The profane/evil, as Jeffrey Alexander has argued, vividly brings its relative sacred form into focus.[65] As absolute, normative realities, sacred forms are so obvious as to become an often assumed part of people's social worlds. They operate as more fundamental assumptions than what we might explicitly describe as 'good'. Children simply are precious. It is always honourable to die for one's nation. God really does move though our lives as the breath within our breath. It is precisely through its threatened pollution—whether by child abuse, treason, or blasphemy—that such assumed realities come to figure in the foreground of consciousness as vulnerable to the harmful and polluting effects of the profane/evil. By giving more specific definition to the concept of the profane than Durkheim, the categories of the sacred and profane can also be used more effectively as tools for social and cultural analysis. The delineation of the *profane* as the evil that threatens the sacred, and the *mundane* as the logics, practices, and spaces of everyday life, enables us to think about the ways in which the mundane can be lived according to its own habits and norms, which may be interrupted only by the more fundamental claims of the sacred and the profane at particular moments. This point will be discussed further in the next chapter in relation to the work of Edward Shils.

By rereading Durkheim's theory of the heterogeneity of sacred forms as referring to absolute realities that establish normative claims on social life, it is possible to connect it with the affective, moral, and collective aspects of sacred forms that were also central to his thought. As Durkheim argued, sacred forms draw to themselves social groups that form deep emotional identifications with them, which find expression in particular moral sentiments and are recursively reproduced through practices oriented to the absolute reality of that sacred form.

Through this critical rereading of Durkheim, then, it is possible to articulate the basic claim that will underpin the cultural sociological approach to the sacred pursued in the coming chapters:

> *The sacred is defined by what people collectively experience as absolute, non-contingent realities which present normative claims over the meanings and conduct of social life. Sacred forms are specific, historically contingent, instances of the sacred. Sacred forms are constituted by constellations of specific symbols, thought/discourse, emotions and actions grounded in the body. These constellations of embodied thought, feeling and action recursively reproduce the sacrality of the sacred form and constitute groups who share these discourses, sentiments and practices. The normative reality represented by a sacred form simultaneously constructs the evil which might profane it, and the pollution of this sacred reality is experienced by its adherents as a painful wound for which some form of restitution is necessary.*

The following chapter will examine how this position might be developed to provide a fuller theoretical outline for a cultural sociology of the sacred.

2

After Durkheim: The Development of a Cultural Sociology of the Sacred

> The task of a cultural sociology . . . is to bring the unconscious cultural structures that regulate society into the light of the mind. Understanding may change but not dissipate them, for without such structures society cannot survive. We need myths if we are to transcend the banal reality of material life. We need narratives if we are to make progress and experience tragedy. We need to divide the sacred from profane if we are to pursue the good and protect ourselves from evil.
>
> (Jeffrey Alexander, *The Meanings of Social Life*, 2003)

In the previous chapter a number of objections were discussed in relation to Durkheim's theory of the sacred. Despite these, it was argued that a critical rereading of Durkheim could form a viable basis for the sociological study of the sacred. Another limitation of Durkheim's work in *Primitive Classification* and *The Elementary Forms of The Religious Life* was the relative lack of attention that he gave to the ways in which the concepts of the sacred and the profane might be deployed to study modern societies. Although Durkheim was clear that the principles he had identified remained highly relevant to modern life, this relevance was noted mainly in these two major works through occasional comments and asides. How Durkheim might have used these ideas to offer a more detailed analysis of modern life, had he not died in 1917 and lost many of his leading students in the preceding years of the First World War, is largely lost to us.[1]

Since his death, however, other writers have sought to explore the significance of the sacred and profane in the modern world. By discussing the work of three leading contributors to this task—Edward Shils, Robert Bellah, and Jeffrey Alexander—it will be possible to extend the theoretical understanding of sacred forms set out at the end of the

previous chapter, thus providing a more developed framework for analysing the nature and significance of the sacred in the modern world.

Edward Shils: The ambiguities of the sacred centre

Although the work of Edward Shils was shaped by a wide range of
theorists other than Durkheim, including Tonnies and Weber, it nevertheless represents a significant extension of Durkheim's understanding
of the sacred. In *Center and Periphery*, a collection of essays on macro-
sociology, Shils examines the relationship between the sacred, authority
and social institutions structured around the concept of the sacred
centre of society. Shils had previously collaborated with Talcott Parsons,
with whom he co-edited and largely co-authored *Toward a General
Theory of Action*. But, although Shils retained Parsons's interest in the
significance of values for the maintenance of social order, his later work
bore little resemblance to Parsons's account of social systems, which he
saw as part of a wider drift towards 'scientific' sociological theories,
which proved to be 'very abstract, very difficult to understand, and
even more difficult to use in the understanding of the world as we know
it from our experience'.[2] Shils retained a strong interest in theorizing the
role of the sacred in the maintenance of society, but came to recognize
that the 'growth of [sociological] knowledge is a disorderly movement'
shaped by an emerging interplay of contexts, challenges, and insights.[3]
As a consequence, *Center and Periphery* presents theoretical insights developed across individual essays rather than a highly systematized theory,
which were forged in the context of a range of experiences and intellectual challenges during and after the Second World War. These included
debriefing German prisoners of war, studying social relations in the
Russian army, researching far-right organizations in the United States,
examining family relations in the East End of London, reviewing Lazars-
feld's major study of voting in the 1948 presidential election, and reflecting on the social and cultural significance of the coronation of Queen
Elizabeth II in 1953.[4] Each of these deepened his interest in questions of
social integration and of the ongoing significance of sacred values for
different kinds of national and subnational organization.

A starting point for Shils's theory of centre and periphery is his claim
that people need some kind of sacred order at the centre of their lives,
because this addresses the basic human need 'for incorporation into
something which transcends and transfigures [a person's] concrete individual existence'.[5] While this sacred order, expressed through core values, played an important role in social integration and the possibility of

renewal and critique of social institutions, it was not the only integrating force in social life. Shils recognized a much wider range of social motivations that bound people together in mundane, everyday interactions: 'personal attachments, moral obligations in concrete contexts, professional and creative pride, individual ambition, primordial affinities, and a civil sense.'[6] These mundane dynamics played an integral role in the maintenance of everyday social order, and the systematic articulation and intense identification with a sacred order of values were a less common but nevertheless potentially powerful phenomenon. Indeed, those who sought to structure social life on the basis of explicit and consistent sacred values might be regarded by some people as charismatic and prophetic figures and, at the same time, by others as unpalatable zealots, ideologues, and fundamentalists.[7] The sacred was not then, in Shils's view, the only possible basis of social integration, nor one whose power was uniformly felt throughout society, but it remained a potent force, for good or for ill, both for social integration and for the challenging of habituated practices of everyday life.

Shils saw sacred order as not purely symbolic, but as woven through particular forms of social structure. At the heart of Shils's understanding of the sacred is an interplay between the sacred 'symbols, values and beliefs which govern a society' and the major social institutions that mediate this 'central value system' (which include political, economic, religious, educational, and media institutions).[8] In particular social contexts and historical moments, one specific figure or institution might come to represent this sacred centre above all others—as in the case of the British monarchy at the time of Queen Elizabeth's coronation.[9] The central sacred order could generate legitimacy and aura for its mediating institutions, which derived both from those institutions' association with those sacred values and from the 'sentiments of sacredness' experienced by some people in the face of institutional power.[10] But the institutional mediation of the sacred also inevitably involves some attenuation, as the norms of institutional life become routinized and it becomes impossible for all participants in an institution to experience intense identification with the sacred over an extended period of time.

The sacred centre of a society is, therefore, closely bound to the elites and institutions that express and reproduce that central value system. The association of the sacred centre with institutional elites means that the central value system implicitly or explicitly legitimates the traits, qualities, or rewards normally associated with those who hold elite office. This means that certain kinds of people may be seen as particularly suitable mediators of the sacred (for example, in terms of their abilities, cultural backgrounds, gender, ethnicity, and so on). The association between institutional authority and the sacred centre can also mean that institutions exert a particular allure for some people as important social structures and spaces that promise 'the capacity to do vital things [and] a connection with events which are intrinsically important'.[11] At the same time, however, the central value system is not simply the sum of the interests of key social institutions at any given point in time. The sacred centre typically has idealistic values—'a utopian potentiality'[12] which can be drawn on by charismatic individuals and movements to critique the specific failings of elites or institutions. Indeed, tensions are naturally likely to arise between the institutional tendency to normalize social life on the basis of 'recently and currently acknowledged criteria of legitimacy' and the capacity of the charismatic articulation of the sacred to disrupt such institutional conventions by challenging them in the light of core values.[13]

The sacred centre can also inspire deeply ambivalent emotional responses in those over whom it exerts any influence, including an unconscious resentment at authority expressed through desires to breach the sacred order. A primary function of public celebrations of the sacred, suggested Shils, was, therefore, precisely to provide a defensive strategy, a reaction formation, through which these unconscious desires could be converted into a reassuring reconnection with the sacred.[14] People living at the periphery of key institutions' symbolic or territorial influence may also be likely to feel less regard for their authority or the sacred order that they mediate. Similarly, those sections of society that do not enjoy the qualities and traits normally associated with institutional elites are unlikely to feel much identification with the sacred order expressed by those institutions.[15] Shils's account of the sacred centre of society is, therefore, attentive to its ambiguities; of the ambivalent relationship between the sacred order and its institutional mediation; of the uneven popular assent to the sacred order; and of the ambivalent emotional reaction to the sacred within the individual. Furthermore, the sacred functions as just one kind of social force alongside the mundane dynamics of everyday life, which can both attenuate the power of the sacred as well as be subject to the sacred's radical critique. Such analysis adds much needed complexity to more simplistic accounts of the socially integrative role of sacred values that are sometimes attributed to neo-Durkheimian approaches.

Shils's nuanced account of the sacred is complemented by an awareness of the importance of historical context. His analysis of the symbolic significance of the 1953 coronation as a powerful moment of collective identification with sacred values at the heart of British society is predicated on an awareness of the historical conditions that made such a moment of identification possible. As Shils comments, republican sentiment had run high in British society in the previous century. But the coming-together of a sense of a common social order made possible through experiences of two major wars, the creation of the welfare state, the decision of the Royal Family to stay in London during the Blitz, and a sense of a shared social project across class boundaries made it possible in the early post-war period for the monarchy to function as a powerful symbol of those collective values.[16] Alongside this recognition of the role of specific historical conditions in shaping the nature of sacred forms, Shils also developed a more general theory of the transformation of the social conditions for encountering the sacred from premodern to modern times. Shils argued that premodern societies typically left large sections of their populations on the periphery of key social institutions, and that these excluded groups oriented their lives more around alternative sacred orders constituted around the context of their everyday lives. By contrast, however, 'when in modern societies, a more unified economic system, political democracy, urbanization and education have brought the different sections of the population into more frequent contact with each other and created even greater mutual awareness, the central value system has found a wider acceptance than in other periods of the history of society'.[17] In other words, the impulse of liberal, democratic, and capitalist societies towards the greater inclusion of all members of society as citizen/consumers has led to more people engaging with key social institutions and thus becoming associated with the sacred centre that they mediate. Paradoxically, this greater degree of exposure to the sacred centre of society does generate more opposition to this centre, but also generally makes this opposition less effective. For, although greater interaction with the institutionally mediated sacred centre may inspire more expressions of resistance against it, the greater degree of popular identification with that sacred centre prevents such resistance from generating any genuinely revolutionary change. As Shils puts it, 'in the modern societies of the West, the central value system has gone much more deeply into the heart of their members than it has ever succeeded in doing in any earlier society'.[18] Social integration around the central, sacred value system is not then an inevitable function of any social system, but is encouraged by the operations of particular kinds of modern institution.

There is much to be valued in Shils's work. His discussion of the sacred in terms of institutional life demonstrated how Durkheimian ideas of the sacred could be used in the context of modern social structures.[19] His understanding of the ambiguities of the sacred gave a far more nuanced account of the limits of the socially integrative power of the sacred than Durkheim's *Elementary Forms*, or indeed than superficial summaries of his essay with Michael Young on the 1953 coronation. His account of the nature of, and interaction between, sacred and mundane social ties also opens up important insights into the ways in which the sacred can be both present and absent in everyday life. Furthermore, his awareness of the effects of social and historical context on the mediation of the sacred open up possibilities for thinking about the historical contingency of sacred forms. There are also limitations, however. His notion of the institutional mediation of the central values system was not expressed in ways that help us to think about the different forms of the sacred that may be simultaneously present within a particular social or institutional space. As we shall note shortly, Robert Bellah's work is more attentive to the ways in which competing and powerful moral orders may be embedded within a society's core institutions. There is still a potentially helpful ambiguity in Shils's work, even at this point, however. Shils's notion of the sacred refers both to the central values system around which a particular society is formed, and also to the values held sacred by specific revolutionary, ideological, and religious groups. This allows for the possibility of a plurality of forms of the sacred, expressed through different kinds of social structure—for example, the nation state, the diasporic community, the transnational organization or movement, or other kinds of subcultural structure. This is, at best, a reading through Shils's work rather than a set of issues that he adequately addressed himself. Shils's treatment of the role of the sacred in legitimating core social institutions is less critical than that of Marxist-influenced scholars, who understand the sacred legitimation of institutional authority with greater suspicion as an ideological operation.[20] But then Shils intended his work to be a form of resistance against the reductive interpretation of all forms of human thought and values in terms of political ideology,[21] just as he was critical of the failure of liberal and radical scholars to recognize the enduringly 'religious' dimensions of social and cultural life.[22] While some might regard Shils as having an overly benign view of institutional power (his enthusiasm for the positive effects of patriotism being a case in point), his work nevertheless opens up important possibilities for using the sacred as a concept for contemporary social and cultural analysis.

Robert Bellah: Civil religion in America

A third important contribution to the cultural sociological study of the sacred has been Robert Bellah's work on civil religion. Whereas Shils was primarily interested in theorizing the sacred in relation to social structures, Bellah's work on civil religion sought less to extend a theory of the sacred than to examine how the sacred might be used as a tool for analysing a particular historical and social context—the American republic. Indeed, after his seminal original article on American civil religion, first published in 1967, Bellah's interests increasingly turned to the specifics of this case, as he sought to clarify the content, structure, and implications of this form of the sacred. This led him to write about the complex relationship of American civil religion to other moral traditions and structures in American society,[23] the threat posed to the moral core of civil religion by the rising tide of individualism,[24] and the development and vulnerability of the project of civil religion through American political history.[25] In this body of work, Bellah is clearly not a disinterested commentator on the concept of the sacred and its relevance to American public life. At one point in his 1967 article, he writes that 'the civil religion at its best is a genuine apprehension of universal and transcendent religious reality as seen in or, one could almost say, as revealed through the experience of the American people'.[26] This reflects Bellah's moral idealism—his belief that moral traditions articulated and celebrated through specific social and historical processes have the ability to point to essential, universal values.[27] His commitment to the moral vision that he sees enshrined in the best of American civil religion lends an edge of social and political critique to his work. In his original article on civil religion in 1967, his argument is thus closely tied to opposition to the Vietnam War and support for the civil-rights movement, and his later work increasingly laments the failure of American society to live up to the moral vision of civil religion.[28] Bellah's work therefore exemplifies how a theory of the sacred may enable not only sociological description but also a moral critique that blurs into political philosophy and theology.

A useful starting point for summarizing Bellah's concept of American civil religion is his argument that traditional notions of religion are unhelpful for understanding operative forms of the sacred in the modern world. In a footnote to his 1967 article, Bellah suggested that part of the reason why scholars had previously paid insufficient attention to the notion of civil religion was 'certainly due to the peculiarly Western concept of "religion" as denoting a single type of collectivity of which an individual can be a member of one and only one at a time'.[29] As we noted earlier, the recognition that modern life is lived out in the presence of multiple forms of the sacred is essential for any adequate understanding of the contemporary sacred, and gives greater emphasis to the pluralist nature of society than Durkheim's simpler, integrative model of the sacred appears to allow.[30]

American civil religion therefore operates as a sacred system that is connected to, though also distinct from, American Christianity.[31] It is, in Bellah's Durkheimian phrase, 'a collection of beliefs, symbols and rituals with respect to sacred things and institutionalized in a collectivity'.[32] This civil religion is constituted around the sacred values of universal human rights and freedom, enshrined in the principles of democratic society, in which freedom is viewed in positive moral terms as the freedom to pursue a just and civically responsible life.[33] This system of sacred values finds expression in particular sacred texts[34] such as the Declaration of Independence, the Constitution,[35] seminal speeches such as the inaugural presidential addresses of George Washington and J. F. Kennedy, and rituals such as the celebration of Thanksgiving and Memorial Day, as well as through material forms such as the American flag and national cemeteries. Through participation in the symbolic and ritual world offered by this civil religion, Americans are able to experience themselves as part of a national collective, oriented towards sacred values of freedom, democracy, and justice.

Integral to Bellah's account of civil religion, though, was the idea that this sacred system was legitimated not simply by the moral or political authority of the American nation, but by the higher authority of God. The discourse of American civil religion therefore situates its sacred values in a transcendent framework. As J. F. Kennedy put it in his inaugural speech, 'the same revolutionary beliefs for which our forebears fought are still at issue around the globe—the belief that the rights of man come not from the generosity of the state but from the hand of God'.[36] Bellah recognizes that the centrality of the concept of God for authorizing these sacred values risks excluding those who find themselves unable in good conscience to use such theological language,[37] even though the 'God' of civil religion is not that of any one single religious tradition. But, in the same way that Shils recognized the utopian potential of the sacred to critique the shortcomings of the social institutions that laid claim to it, so Bellah argued that this transcendent source of the sacred was a necessary basis of social critique. As he put it, 'without an awareness that our nation stands under higher judgment, the tradition of civil religion would be dangerous indeed'.[38] Its vision of the collective of the American nation has been used not only to bind people to a common moral vision, but also to exclude and oppress minorities from native Americans onwards. Its notion of the American republic as bearing a specific historical mission to spread the sacred values of freedom and democracy has been used to legitimate a wide range of imperialist military adventures, including, in our own recent past, the war in Iraq. It also creates possibilities for others to make use of the language of American civil religion to associate themselves with this sacred project for their own political interests, as, for example, in the case of governments that have recently attached themselves to the moral discourse of the War on Terror in order to legitimate security and military action against their own political opponents. Without the capacity to refer to a higher moral source than the state, Bellah therefore argues that civil religion degenerates into the symbolic legitimation of the immediate interests of the state, with all the expediency, injustice, and violence associated with this. Bellah appears to locate such failings not as an inherent part of any sacred system, because he keeps the faith that sacred systems can, at their heart, maintain some kind of transcendent moral vision. Rather he sees these failings as part of the vulnerability of any sacred system to be subjected to 'demonic distortions',[39] or, in the case of American civil religion, the almost inevitable failure of American society to sustain a commitment to such an exacting moral vision.[40] Whether Bellah is right to maintain this faith in the essential purity of vision of sacred systems—or whether sacred forms by their very nature cast moral shadow as well as light—is a question we will return to in Chapter 5.

Bellah's account of American civil religion represents the most widely discussed attempt to use Durkheimian theory to analyse a sacred system in a specific social and historical context. Although it does not seek to add directly to a theoretical understanding of the sacred, its sociological and historical analysis nevertheless provides important insights. First, the case of American civil religion points to the historically contingent nature of social forms of the sacred. By this, I do not mean simply that the content of American civil religion was contingent upon the memory of religious persecution in Europe of the founders of the Republic, concepts of the individual, freedom and rights emerging out of the Protestant Reformation, or longer traditions of republican thought in the classical Greek tradition with whom some of the founding fathers were familiar. Rather, the social structure of the sacred system of American civil religion is also historically contingent in terms of identifying a sacred system with symbols and structures of the nation state. As comparative work on civil religions has demonstrated, the emergence of sacred systems associated with the nation is not a universal phenomenon, but is linked to historical processes of radical formation or transformation of specific nation states.[41] Just as American civil religion was forged at the birth of a new nation, so, around the same time, a new sacred system of symbols, values, and rituals was being created in revolutionary France to mark its radical shift away from the influence of the monarchy and the Church.[42] Social forms of the sacred are historically contingent, then, not only in terms of their symbolic and material content, but also in their structures. Civil religion at the level of the nation state is not a universal phenomenon, common to all nations. Caution must, therefore, be taken in asserting universal models of the sacred, applicable to all human societies. While some basic principles of the sacred may be more widely applicable, careful attention needs to be given to the particular historical and social contexts within which sacred forms develop.

A second significant point deriving from Bellah's work is that the relationship between the sacred and core social institutions is not necessarily straightforward. As we noted above, Shils's theory of the sacred centre closely associates sacred value systems with core social institutions. These institutions play an essential role in expressing and developing the sacred centre, and also draw their legitimacy from their relationship with it. Bellah's account of American civil religion, however, suggests that this relationship may be more complex. In his later article on 'Religion and the Legitimation of the American Republic', Bellah revises his assessment of the close relationship between American civil religion and key institutional elements of American political life. He suggests that American public life has always been constituted not only on the republican moral vision encapsulated in civil religion, but by a liberal political tradition that envisages the role of the state in terms of maintaining public order, not impinging on the freedom of individuals, and creating the basis for the effective operation of the free market.[43] These two traditions, of republican civil religion and liberalism, are fundamentally antagonistic, argues Bellah, and the liberal political order is kept from descent into anomie and the collapse of meaningful democracy by the capacity of civil religion to inculcate healthy civic values. At the same time, however, Bellah also argues that there are aspects of American political institutions in which the liberal tradition is more dominant than civil religion, in particular the Constitution of the United States, which makes no mention of God and does not use the discourse of civil religion.[44] As a result, American civil religion has no legal grounds, and the legal system is not charged with maintaining its sacred values. Indeed, Bellah concludes, religious institutions may have played a more important role in maintaining American civil religion than political ones.

This social and historical analysis suggests a far more complex relationship between the sacred order and core social institutions than is suggested in parts of Shils's work. Indeed, Shils's notion of the sacred centre is called into question by Bellah's case example. Does political liberalism represent the central values system of American public life, or civil religion? Bellah's analysis suggests that the answer is neither, and demonstrates that societies may be constituted around competing sacred visions rather than integrated around a single sacred centre. This also raises the possibilities that core social institutions may again not be oriented around a single sacred values system, that sacred forms may have varying degrees of purchase on different social institutions, and that the relationship between sacred forms and specific institutions is, again, historically contingent. This suggests that, for all of the value of Shils's work in drawing attention to the implications of the institutional expression of the sacred, a more nuanced understanding of this may be needed that pays greater attention to plural forms of the sacred in social life and the historically specific relations between particular social institutions and particular forms of the sacred.

Jeffrey C. Alexander: The sacred and the strong programme in cultural sociology

Since the early 1980s, Jeffrey Alexander has led the development of a theoretical framework for cultural sociology and has explored this framework through a series of case studies, including computer technology, the Watergate scandal, the emergence of the Holocaust as a symbol of universal moral evil, and, more recently, responses to the events of 9/11 and the role of cultural meaning in the 2008 US presidential election.[45] His theoretical treatment of the cultural sociological study of the sacred is more extensive than that of either Shils or Bellah, and his work represents an essential reference point for any contemporary understanding of the sacred as a social phenomenon.

Although Alexander traces his interests in part back to Weber's work on the significance of religious concepts of salvation in structuring social life,[46] his approach to cultural sociology clearly reflects the project of a 'religious sociology' that he identifies in Durkheim's later work.[47] However, Alexander's use of the term 'cultural sociology' to describe his intellectual approach, rather than 'religious sociology', reflects the fact that his work is a substantial reworking of Durkheim's project that draws on a wider range of cultural theories, including semiotics, hermeneutics, pragmatism, and theories of performance. As such, his work is both a major intervention in the recovery of culture as a focus for sociological theory and empirical investigation, and the most fully articulated socio-logical account of the sacred to be developed by any contemporary thinker.

The intellectual project of cultural sociology can be understood in terms of different levels of theoretical intent. Across the body of Alexander's work, there is an ambivalence about the possibility of devel-oping universal social theory, with some of his work aspiring to such generalizability,[48] and other parts eschewing this as an achievable aim.[49] Even if his most recent work does not aim to present a 'general model of culture', there are still important theoretical aims in sight. First, Alexander seeks to clarify the significance of culture within social theory. He rejects the notion that culture is simply the expression of underlying social structures, and instead argues for the 'relative autonomy' of culture (discussed later in this chapter) in which culture is taken seri-ously on its own terms as a dynamic force in social life. Culture is not simply the product of 'real' (that is, material) social structures, or used instrumentally in the operation of those structures, as in the case of Bourdieu's theory of taste.[50] Nor is culture to be defined as a specific area of society (as in the 'culture industries' or 'popular culture') that may be studied using sociological concepts and methods already honed from the study of other aspects of social life. Rather, culture is properly understood as 'not a thing but a dimension, not an object to be studied as a dependent variable but a thread that runs through ... every conceivable social form'.[51] It is in this sense that Alexander has referred to his approach as the 'strong programme' in cultural sociology, which emphasizes the capacity of cul-tural meanings to shape social life. His emphasis on the importance of cultural structures does not deny the importance of material structures, for example, in terms of the social significance of class and inequality. But it does provide an account of society in which attention to the sacred, as a central element of cultural structures of meaning, plays an important role in explaining social phenomena.

Second, Alexander's approach to cultural sociology addresses theoret-ical issues that are central to the discipline of sociology, such as the perennial debate about the relationship between structure and agency in social life. Alexander argues that cultural meanings play a pivotal role in the relationship between structure and agency. Cultural struc-tures, as codes of meaning, provide the medium through which social structures are interpreted and derive much of their social power. Cul-tural structures also provide a framework in relation to which subjectivity is formed and particular forms of agency are experienced and practised.[52] Cultural structures therefore play a bridging role between the 'inner' and 'outer' forms of social life, as both are formed and enacted in relation to socially shared systems of meaning. As Alexander puts it, 'socially-constructed subjectivity forms the will of collectivities; shapes the rules of organizations; defines the moral substance of law; and provides the meaning and motivation for technologies, economies and military machines'.[53] This account therefore privileges neither agency nor structure, but sees both as occupying a symbiotic relationship through the shared medium of codes of meaning. Such cultural structures are not some kind of *deus ex machina*, operating beyond any form of social influence, but are themselves produced through particular historical processes. Nor do they compel social actors to behave in particular ways. Rather they provide a horizon of meaning in which social actors engage their social and material worlds, and that renders possible and meaningful particular kinds of emotional performance— desire for material objects; hope for salvation by technology; fear and disgust at symbolic constructs of evil.[54] This theoretical account attempts to demonstrate both the relative power and the limits of agency and structure. Rather than the intentional action of an autonomous social actor, Alexander presents agency as the performance of subjectivity in the context of, at best partially understood, morally and emotionally charged systems of meaning. Social structures do not, therefore, simply determine thought or action, but are subject to the meanings that are projected onto them, which set important parameters for their influence on social life.

Third, attempts to address such issues of sociological meta-theory provide the intellectual context for Alexander's more concrete theoretical aim of developing a rigorous hermeneutical approach to making sense of specific social and cultural situations. It is here that Alexander's neo-Durkheimian understanding of the sacred performs important conceptual work. In his analysis of particular forms of social life, Alexander thinks of cultural structures in semiotic terms as codes of meanings that are structured around morally and emotionally laden constructions of the sacred and the profane/evil.[55] He reads Durkheim's understanding of the role of the sacred in classificatory systems through Saussure's contemporaneous structuralist theory of language, using Saussure's observation about the arbitrary relationship between the sign and the external world to make a related point about the arbitrary construction of the sacred in systems of meaning.[56] Sacred forms are, therefore, cultural expressions not determined by some form of universal ontology, but socially and culturally constructed through particular historical trajectories. They are 'shifting cultural constructions' subject to means of symbolic production, which are 'fatefully affected by the power and identity of the agents in charge, by the competition for symbolic control, and the structures of power and distribution of resources'.[57] Like Bellah's civil religion, even cherished forms of the sacred—which in Alexander's case include the capacity for a universal moral sympathy constructed around notions of human rights, the valuing of democracy, and the practice of a particular kind of critical rationality—can be understood, not as timeless truths, but as the products of particular cultural histories whose preservation and extension demand ongoing cultural labour.

Alexander makes this point about the historical contingency of sacred forms most extensively in a widely read essay on the Holocaust, in which he argues that the Holocaust came to be perceived as a unique, profane evil only through a gradual historical process.[58] In the immediate aftermath of the Second World War, discoveries of the nature and extent of the concentration camps and mass exterminations were initially interpreted primarily as expressions of the more general evil of German nationalism, and survivors of the camps were not accorded any significant moral status. Over time, though, the weakening grip of anti-Semitism in Western societies, and the effect of powerful identificatory narratives with Jewish suffering (notably, for example, through the publication and dramatization of Anne Frank's diaries) led to a shifting perception, with greater emphasis placed on the profundity of the evil of the Holocaust. As a consequence, far from being simply a symptom of the evils of German nationalism, the Holocaust came to represent the greatest profanation on which Nazism could be judged to be evil. As Alexander has argued, then, the sacred meaning of the Holocaust is not static, but dynamic and historically contingent, with its meanings and uses continuing to evolve in contemporary society.

While Alexander's work has emphasized a semiotic understanding of cultural structures as systems of meaning constructed in relation to the sacred and the profane, he has also sought to expand this primarily 'textual' emphasis to give more weight to lived performance.[59] Drawing particularly on recent work on the theory of performance, Alexander has advanced a theory of cultural pragmatics that conceives of public expressions of the sacred in dramaturgical terms and that enables him to revisit the role of 'ritual' in relation to the symbolic representation of the sacred. From this perspective, sacred symbols are enacted in society by being used in publically performed 'scripts', in which meanings are evoked as part of specific, historically contingent projects. The social potency of the sacred symbol remains latent while it is simply a symbol within a wider classificatory system of meaning, and its power is activated only when it is utilized in the public performance of a cultural script. The performance of such emotionally laden scripts charts dynamic relations between the sacred, evil, and the mundane, and invites audiences to form sympathetic identifications with the sacred and against that which profanes it. The dramatic conceptual frame is further developed with reference to 'directors' (those social agents who seek to initiate and shape such scripts), 'actors' (those implicated in the acting-out of the script), and *mise en scène* (the social, cultural, and physical space that provides a meaningful frame for the sacred performance). The capacity to conduct such social performances of the sacred with any success is also related to control of the means of symbolic production and distribution, in the form of particular media, spaces, or social networks.[60]

Such an understanding of the social performance of the sacred also entails a critique of more traditional ways of conceiving the significance of ritual in relation to the recursive reproduction of the sacred. Alexander rejects the notion—evident, for example, in Bellah's 'Civil Religion in America'—that ritual practices in pre-modern societies provide an adequate model for understanding the social reproduction of the sacred in contemporary society. Such uses of 'primitive ritual' to interpret contemporary social practices are flawed because they ignore two defining features of late or postmodernity: social actors' greater degree of reflexivity in relation to the cultural practices in which they engage, and the effects of social differentiation that make it increasingly difficult for any single ritual practice, focused around a particular sacred symbol, to compel sympathetic participation across a wide population. Challenging Shils's assertion of the growing public consent to the central values system through modernity, Alexander argues that such reflexivity and plurality make it more likely that public performances of the sacred will evoke scepticism from sections of their audience who regard them as inauthentic, instrumental, or based on an inadequate form of the sacred.[61] Ritual leaders are no longer the 'unproblematic, authoritative disseminators of meaning that they were in the past'.[62] Participation in a given ritual thus loses its taken-for-grantedness in social contexts in which many different sacred rituals are present, and forms of the sacred are plural and contested. In such a context, 'participation in, and acceptance of, ritual messages are more a matter of choice than obligation'.[63] Although such reflexivity is never complete, and people are still bound emotionally and unreflexively to forms of the sacred, the moral and cultural plurality of modern society makes simple models of ritual increasingly irrelevant for contemporary social analysis and instead demands concepts that allow for plurality, contestation, and failure in social performances of the sacred.

Alexander has used this theory of social performances of the sacred to analyse events surrounding 11 September 2001. From the perspective of sacred drama, the attacks of 9/11 can be understood in terms of the performance of a script, directed by the leadership of Al-Qaeda, intended to elicit a sympathetic response from a Muslim audience that would identify with the martyrs giving up their lives to destroy profane symbols of American economic, political, and military power. While these attacks were indeed celebrated, or viewed sympathetically, among some Muslim audiences, American reactions to the attacks demonstrated that audience responses to sacred dramas cannot be easily predicted or controlled. While the part ascribed to the American public in the drama plotted by Al-Qaeda was that of a shocked, humiliated, and symbolically crushed society, American responses took a different form, as the symbolic violence done to America was absorbed by the sacralization of the sites of the assault (particularly the city of New York and 'Ground Zero'), as well as of those individuals and organizations that suffered in the assaults. While the physical space of American territory had been profaned by such dramatic violence, this was increasingly seen as an assault on material structures, which left the immaterial, sacred core of the soul of American society untouched. Indeed, the public grieving and memorialization of the events of 9/11 themselves became a counter-performance of a sacred drama that evoked sympathetic national and international identification with the victims of the assault as sacred symbols of freedom and democracy. This sacred drama, swiftly developed by neo-conservative political actors into the War on Terror, became another iteration of a performance framed in terms of the protection of the sacred from evil. In turn, this counter-performance provided further evidence for some Muslim audiences of the profane nature of American militarism. And so the performance of an Islamist sacred drama on 9/11 was not simply followed by a counter-performance of American defiance and patriotism, but formed part of a cyclical pattern of performance and counter-performance in which different audiences found their perceptions of the evil of their opponents merely confirmed and reconfirmed. The events of 9/11, therefore, not only demonstrate how, in pluralist societies, sacred performances do not elicit only one intended response from their audience, but show how patterns of performance and counter-performance of the sacred can be implicated in entrenched patterns of violent conflict.

Cultural sociology, as developed by Alexander, is not simply a theoretical project, but also a therapeutic one, with Alexander likening cultural sociology to a kind of cultural psychoanalysis. In the same way that Sigmund Freud famously described the task of psychoanalysis as increasing conscious understanding of unconscious processes ('where id was, let ego be'), so Alexander sees the task of cultural sociology as enabling greater awareness of cultural structures that continue to evoke powerful responses in contemporary social life. As he puts it:

The secret to the compulsive power of social structures is that they have an inside. They are not only external to actors but internal to them. They are meaningful. These meanings are structured and socially produced, even if they are invisible. We must learn how to make them visible...To reveal to men and women the myths that think them so that they can make up new myths in turn.[64]

The ultimate aim of such analysis is thus not simply an intellectual understanding of the significance of the sacred in modern life.[65] Nor is it to reach a kind of social life freed from the cultural structures of meaning and the sacred—for no such social life is possible; 'without such structures society cannot survive'. Cultural sociology does not then simply engage with questions of social theory and explanation, but moral questions about the kinds of symbols, practices, and traditions that are needed to sustain just, tolerant, and democratic societies. In this sense, it preserves Durkheim's concern both for sociological explanation and for reflection on the moral orientation of society. Alexander has grown sceptical about the value of theoretical universalism—and instead describes his work as a dialectics of culture that moves between theory and concrete social analysis in order to illuminate both. Yet his work remains open to the possibility of a moral universalism for social life, albeit one forged through a range of sacred symbols and recollections of cultural trauma that resonate in different social contexts.[66]

Theoretical foundations for a cultural sociology of the sacred

In providing a brief summary of the work of each of these writers, my intention is not systematically to integrate their individual contributions. Such an attempt would both fail to do justice to the distinctiveness of their intellectual projects and imply that some form of 'authoritative', integrated sociological theory of the sacred is possible or desirable. Like Alexander, my approach is post-foundational, in that it regards theory, not as an objective account of social reality, but as a framework within which particular ways of thinking and acting in relation to society become possible.[67] This understanding of theory has been articulated clearly in Thomas Tweed's recent influential contribution to the theory of religion, *Crossing and Dwelling*. Tweed draws an analogy between theory and the perspective of a traveller journeying through a landscape that changes, not only with the traveller's own progress, but with the ever-evolving environmental conditions that shape what the traveller is able to see.[68] Sociological theory is not, then, a pure insight into the heart of social reality, but perspectival, produced in a specific time and space, and forged for particular concerns and purposes. The value of theory lies in its usefulness in helping us to see and act in ways that do justice to social complexity, that make meaningful connections between different aspects of the social, and that encourage critical, reflexive approaches to social structures and actions. The perspectival nature of theory does not mean that it cannot be challenged or disconfirmed. Theoretical accounts of a social landscape can be as lacking in insight as a poorly executed piece of landscape painting, and theoretical claims about the significance of particular processes and structures can be challenged by other, better-substantiated claims. In providing ways of seeing, thinking about, and acting in the social, theory therefore provides the grounds for the kinds of interpretative, moral, and therapeutic projects exemplified by Durkheim, Shils, Bellah, and Alexander. My intention, then, is not to integrate the work of these writers, but to situate my work under their intellectual lineage, because their work stimulates useful theoretical insights for our contemporary condition.

At the end of the previous chapter, an initial definition of the sacred was given in the light of a critical rereading of Durkheim:

> *The sacred is defined by what people collectively experience as absolute, non-contingent realities which present normative claims over the meanings and conduct of social life. Sacred forms are specific, historically contingent, instances of the sacred. Sacred forms are constituted by constellations of particular sacred symbols, thought/discourse, emotions and actions which recursively reproduce the sacrality of that sacred form and draw together groups who share these discourses, sentiments and practices. The normative reality constituted by a sacred form simultaneously constructs the evil which might profane it, and the pollution of this sacred reality is experienced by its adherents as a painful wound for which some form of restitution is necessary.*

The work of Shils, Bellah, and Alexander can significantly develop this definition in relation to modern societies, and their work adds four important elements to it.

First, *as a social phenomenon, the sacred is morally ambiguous*. While Durkheim's interest in the 'pure' sacred in the *Elementary Forms* focused on the socially and morally integrative effects of the sacred, subsequent treatment of the sacred has been more complex. Although Shils, Bellah, and Alexander each argue that specific forms of the sacred can symbolize and energize important normative values, they also recognize that the concrete instantiations of the sacred can be morally flawed. Shils saw that the sacred had the potential not only to bind societies together around a common set of values, but also, in times of charismatic upheaval, to destroy viable ecologies of everyday life. Bellah's high view of the moral vision of American civil religion is, at the same time, tempered by a recognition of the ways such a sacralized view of the American project can be used to legitimate military and cultural imperialism. Alexander's description of the 9/11 attacks in terms of the staging of a particular form of Islamist sacred drama demonstrates that the term 'sacred' should not be taken, in sociological terms, as a mark of normative goodness, but as bound up with the construction of 'good' and 'evil', in which the pursuit of the 'good' can be the cause of much violence and suffering. While people take the sacred forms with which they identify to be profound representations of the good, in reality such sacred commitments can be the source of much harm—a point to which we shall return in Chapter 5.

Second, the work of Shils, Bellah, and Alexander draws attention to *the historical contingency of sacred forms*. Durkheim's *Elementary Forms* was written against the backdrop of his concern about what forms of the sacred could evolve in modernity as well as his growing conviction that the emerging 'cult of the individual' might be viable as a focus for cultural and moral integration. However, while Durkheim's evolutionary approach assumed that forms of the sacred would change, and become more diverse and complex with greater social and cultural differentiation, the historical contingency of sacred forms was not directly addressed in any detail in his work. As noted earlier, Shils and Bellah opened up these questions of historical context more directly. Alexander has further demonstrated—for example, in relation to the Holocaust—how forms of the sacred and profane emerge through historical action negotiated through systems of power, social institutions, and specific forms of symbolic production and mediation. An awareness of the historical contingency of the sacred therefore involves, not simply the synchronic analysis of what objects are deemed sacred within a given cultural context, but a diachronic analysis of how the social power of particular sacred forms rises and falls. As we have seen, there are also specific questions about how the social and cultural conditions of late modernity affect the nature and performance of sacred forms. This includes the different positions held by Shils and Alexander on whether modernity deepens identification with sacred forms with the extension of key social institutions or whether performances of the sacred in contemporary society are necessarily more fragile, contested, and prone to failure.

Third, Shils, Bellah, and Alexander have begun to explore the ways in which *modern society is characterized by the emergence of multiple sacred forms* in the wake of the fragmentation of more inclusive sacred canopies, which offered overarching sources of meaning and identification. Shils's language of the 'central value system' is not particularly helpful in this regard, but his work began to show an appreciation that multiple sacred forms could operate at a national and subnational level. Bellah's discussion of the tension between American civil religion and liberalism did more to open up discussion of how multiple sacred forms may be mediated through the same, key social institutions. Alexander's discussion of sacred forms, ranging from computer technology to the Holocaust, has helped to demonstrate further the range of sacred forms in modern society. Understanding the implications of the simultaneous presence of multiple sacred forms is, however, an area requiring more work than that undertaken by these writers. One of the limitations of Alexander's semiotic approach is that it tends to focus on how specific systems of meaning construct the sacred and profane, rather than considering the interplay between different sacred forms and the effects of multiple sacred forms on individual and social life. In the same way that societies are no longer primarily oriented around a common sacred form, so individuals tend not to orient their lives around single sacred forms unless they live in a religious or cultural context that encourages and supports this very difficult task.[69] At a social level, the simultaneous presence of these multiple sacred forms means that sacred forms exist in contingent patterns of complementarity, conflict, dominance, and subjugation. The following chapter explores one such pattern, between dominant and subjugated sacred forms.

Fourth, *the presence of the sacred in social life needs to be contextualized in relation to the mundane logics, practices, emotions, and aesthetics of everyday life.* Shils's work has been particularly important in clarifying this point, through his discussion of the ways in which mundane social interactions have their own logics, which do not necessarily derive from sacred forms. Social life, at the level of the everyday, may be more commonly practised with reference to the logics of particular mundane contexts, and with little or no conscious reference to sacred forms. Such an understanding of the mundane clarifies how intense identification with sacred forms may be transient and associated with specific contexts, and can transfigure, critique, or disrupt ecologies of mundane life.

These ideas are the basis for a cultural sociology of sacred forms. The analysis of sacred forms in particular contexts is essential for refining these concepts as a framework for social and cultural analysis. In the final part of this chapter we shall turn our attention to the kind of cultural explanation that such an understanding of the sacred makes possible, and how the analysis of the sacred in specific social and historical contexts can refine our theoretical understanding of it.

The nature of cultural explanation as knowledge and practice

The nature of sociological explanation with reference to cultural structures has been a central preoccupation of those working within the 'strong programme' of cultural sociology. As noted earlier, this approach is clearly defined against attempts to analyse culture purely on the basis of other social structures (for example, economic or class relations, or material conditions or interests). Jeffrey Alexander has also been critical of forms of cultural study that are wholly descriptive, identifying a mistaken view of Geertz's 'thick description' in terms of a kind of academic journalism that simply describes what meanings are present in a given context. By contrast, Alexander argues for an approach to cultural explanation that both identifies the codes of meaning that are present in a given context, but also accounts for the ways in which these relate to other kinds of social structure and institutional dynamics, as well as 'paying attention to institutions and actors as causal intermediaries'.[70] This approach to cultural explanation can be understood in terms of the 'strong programme's' view of the 'relative autonomy' of culture, in which culture is recognized as having the potential to shape social life, while cultural structures are at the same time always bound up with particular social institutions, structures, practices, and spaces. Cultural explanation always needs to work within this conceptual framework, in which there is a recognition of both the social significance of cultural meaning and the ways in which cultural meanings relate to social structures and processes.

Anne Kane has described this attention to the relationship between cultural and social structures in terms of distinguishing between studying the 'analytic autonomy' and 'concrete autonomy' of culture. The former refers to abstracted cultural systems identified by the researcher, and the latter to the ways in which those systems function in particular historical contexts. At the level of 'analytic autonomy', then, cultural explanation is concerned with 'the elements and internal logic of a cultural structure, establishing how [these] symbolic processes work' and explaining 'the development of culture—that is, how it reproduces and/or transforms itself'.[71] This involves both a theoretical understanding of how cultural systems operate, and an abstracted account of the meanings of a particular cultural system. Alongside this, explanations of the 'concrete autonomy' of culture involve explaining how this abstracted (and therefore, in certain respects, 'fictionalized'[72]) cultural system interacts with the basic elements of historical and social events: 'conditions, actors, contingent events, and arenas of action'.[73] Such contextually grounded accounts become the means through which the social significance of cultural structures is demonstrated. Studying the 'analytic autonomy' of culture is necessary for establishing the structural properties of culture and the content of a given cultural system. Studying the 'concrete autonomy' of culture in specific historical settings is necessary for establishing how such cultural structures shape, and are shaped by, concrete instances of social life. Cultural explanation thus proceeds on the basis of a dialectical analysis of the analytic and concrete autonomy of particular cultural structures, in which close readings of concrete situations refine abstracted accounts of cultural systems, which are then used to reread concrete situations, which in turn revise understandings of how those cultural systems operate, and so on.

If we think of cultural explanation as an articulation of the relationship between cultural meaning and social structure in a given context, what are the implications for how we might think of such explanations as a form of knowledge? First, cultural explanation is a form of hermeneutics; indeed, the dialectical process described above can be conceived of as a hermeneutical circle. Alexander and Smith refer to this approach as structural hermeneutics, in the sense that it combines both a structuralist interest in defining the content of meaning systems with a hermeneutical interest in making sense of how meanings operate in terms of the 'texture and temper of social life'.[74] But, even if we do not tie an understanding of cultural meaning, or sacred forms, quite so strongly to a structuralist approach, understanding the significance of cultural meaning in relation to social life remains a fundamentally interpretative practice that identifies meaningful patterns between culture and social life. Furthermore, if the cultural explanation being undertaken seeks to track the unfolding relations of cultural meanings and social structures through time, this explanation will typically take a narrative form. This narrative is not necessarily historical, in a full disciplinary sense of the term, but represents an attempt through narrative to make sense of patterns developing through time (as in the case of

Alexander's historical narrative of the changing sacred significance of the Holocaust).

Second, recognizing the hermeneutical nature of cultural explanation has particular implications for the status, rigour, and value of such knowledge. As a sense-making activity, such hermeneutical work itself represents a particular form of cultural practice. This also has implications for the status of knowledge produced through such explanatory work. The cultural structures that the researcher identifies through his or her explanatory account do not represent objective knowledge, but, as Geertz put it, 'analysis penetrates into the very body of the object' and 'we begin with our interpretations . . . and then systematize those'.[75] The 'facts' uncovered by such study are thus meaningful on the basis of the theoretical framework that the researcher brings to his or her study, a framework that should be open to revision and expansion on the basis of the encounter with those 'facts'. This also means recognizing the researcher's own subjectivity as an essential part of this interpretative process. Indeed, a researcher's analysis of sacred forms is likely to have a particular sensitivity when he or she is able to combine critical reflection with a subjective awareness of the meanings and feelings elicited by a particular sacred form (which itself raises interesting questions about a researcher's ability to make sense of sacred forms that he or she regards as highly problematic or with which he or she feels no strong cultural identification). But such recognition of the interpretative nature of such explanatory work does not mean that it is 'merely' subjective, in the derogatory sense of this knowledge being less valid than objective, scientific knowledge. Rather, it involves the recognition that cultural explanation is an interplay of the repertoires of meaning that the researcher brings to his or her study (including his or her theoretical understanding of culture and of the sacred), and the repertoires of meaning that the researcher is able to detect in his or her field of study.[76] This interplay produces knowledge that is not objective, but that is, at its best, open to the ways in which social realities challenge the researcher's theoretical presuppositions, insightful in making connections between cultural meaning and social process, and extensive in accounting for a wide range of meanings, structures, and processes that have relevance for the particular explanatory narrative being developed.

As interpretations of particular social and cultural contexts and processes, cultural explanations do not fulfil traditional, positivist criteria for generalizability. Indeed, the purpose of such cultural explanation is to serve as not 'a predictive science of laws, but a generalized science that can establish models'.[77] Cultural explanations primarily account for what is happening in a particular context, but, when offered on the basis of rigorous theorizing and reflection, have the potential to illuminate other contexts, both by serving as a catalyst for stimulating ideas of what explanations may or may not work in other contexts, and in terms of helping to clarify more general theoretical issues about the operation of cultural meaning or sacred forms. Cultural explanations can, therefore, contribute to a broader theory of contemporary social life, but do so slowly, through building up a gradual picture of different contexts and by taking account of the significance of widespread features of late modernity such as mass migration, pluralism, the expansion of neoliberalism and market economies, individualization, and the expansion of digital media.

Following Alexander's account of cultural sociology as a form of cultural psychoanalysis, cultural explanation can also have therapeutic value. In the context of individual psychotherapy, Donald Spence commented that the therapeutic process was one of finding a 'narrative home' for the patient's experience.[78] The same holds true for the therapeutic possibilities of cultural explanation. It is by finding a 'narrative home' that makes sense of the ways in which cultural meanings are bound up with social structures and processes that people have the potential to reflect on social life (including those parts that seem intractably conflictual or unpromising for measured reflection) and, in doing so, identify ways of being and acting that may prove more constructive. Rather than 'acting out' the emotions and conflicts of particular sacred forms, cultural explanation holds the potential to 'defuse' the often deeply felt bond between cultural meanings and social practices,[79] creating a space in which cultural explanation, at its best, can help people to think about the shadow side of their sacred commitments. This is the project that this book will explore.

3

Dominant and Subjugated Sacred Forms: Interpreting the Systemic Abuse and Neglect of Children in the Irish Industrial School System

> Many witnesses who complained of abuse nevertheless expressed some positive memories: small gestures of kindness were vividly recalled...Often the act of kindness recalled in such a positive light arose from the simple fact that the staff member had not given a beating when one was expected.
>
> > (Conclusions from the *Report of Ryan Commission to Inquire into Child Abuse*, 2009)
>
> The thing that I missed most was love. No love. I don't think the nuns knew the meaning of it...How could they comprehend it in their minds that you loved Jesus, but you can't love little children. Jesus said suffer the little children, he didn't say beat the fecking hell out of them.
>
> (Mary Norris, former resident of St Joseph's Industrial School, Killarney, from M. Raftery and E. O'Sullivan, *Suffer the Little Children*, 1999)

Modern social life is characterized by the presence of multiple sacred forms, and these sacred forms are historically contingent and under continual reproduction and contestation. Understanding the significance of these sacred forms thus involves making sense of the ways in which sacred forms intersect with each other, as well as historical processes through which their power as foci of collective and moral identification grows or weakens. Making sense of the different relations and patterns of interaction around sacred forms in modern society will be a long project, and the ideas presented in this book provide an initial framework that will need to be supplemented and clarified with further research.

This chapter will focus on the significance of sacred forms in relation to the systemic abuse and neglect of children within the residential child-care system in Ireland during the twentieth century. Through its narrative of the operations of power and the suffering of vulnerable children, this case demonstrates the power of sacred forms both to legitimate and to challenge institutional structures and practices that stifle human life. But, as we shall see, this case also demonstrates a particular pattern of relationship that is possible between two simultaneously present sacred forms—a hierarchical relationship of dominance and subjugation—as well as how such hierarchical relations are maintained or change under particular historical, social, and cultural conditions.

The nature and context of child abuse and neglect in industrial schools

In 1954, an Irish member of parliament raised a question in the house about a complaint he had received from one of his constituents, a woman whose son was resident at the Artane industrial school run by the religious order, the Christian Brothers. Her son had been hospitalized with injuries including a broken arm after one of the Christian Brothers in the school had given him an extensive beating with a sweeping brush.[1] The order had subsequently refused the mother permission to visit her son in hospital. Responding to this question, Sean Moylan, the Minister for Education, whose department was responsible for the funding, regulation, and inspection of the industrial schools, said:

I cannot conceive any deliberate ill treatment of boys by a community motivated by the ideals of its founder. I cannot conceive any sadism emanating from men who were trained to have devotion to a very high purpose. The point is that accidents happen in the best-regulated families and in this family there are about 800 boys. These boys are difficult to control. At times maybe it is essential that children should be punished. This is an isolated incident; it can only happen again as an accident...I would point out to parents that any guarantee I give them of full protection of their children is no licence to any of the children to do what they like.[2]

This was not the first time that such instances of violence against children within the industrial school system had received government attention in Ireland. Eight years earlier, a local councillor had been in correspondence with the Department of Education about the case of Gerard Fogarty, a 14-year-old boy who, having run away from the industrial school in Glin, County Limerick, was flogged naked with a leather cat-o'-nine-tails by one of the religious order running the school and then forced to swim in the salty waters of the Shannon estuary.[3] In this instance, Fogarty was given early release from the school, but, as in 1954, this case did not lead to any major review of the industrial school system or of the conditions in which its young residents were forced to live.[4]

With the publication of the Ryan Commission to Inquire into Child Abuse in 2009, a formal acknowledgement was made that such instances of violence against children in residential care in Ireland were neither accidents, nor isolated incidents, as Sean Moylan had claimed.[5] The Commission had been established in 2000 in the wake of a major television exposé of children's experiences of the residential care system, *States of Fear*, produced by Mary Raftery. This series followed a growing number of testimonies from survivors of the system through biographies, newspapers, and websites published during the 1990s, as well as an earlier television programme, *Dear Daughter*, broadcast in 1996 on experiences of abuse in the Goldenridge industrial school.[6] The degree of public and media attention given to *States of Fear*, however, meant that it provided a focal moment in crystallizing a sense of public scandal at children's experiences of emotional, physical, and sexual abuse in a childcare system run by religious organizations and regulated by the state.[7] The power of the television series in focusing this sense of outrage is demonstrated by the decision of the then Irish prime minister, Bertie Ahern, to make a public apology for this abuse at 5 p.m. on 11 May 1999, just a few hours before the final episode of *States of Fear* was due to be broadcast. The fact that the Department of Education had supported the making of *States of Fear* through providing access to its archives and other information similarly reflected a political decision to work with the grain of this growing sense of outrage, while politicians were, at the same time, trying to assess how the threat of litigation against them by survivors of the system might be most effectively assessed and minimized.[8]

Part of the expression of public outrage focused on the ways in which cases of sexual abuse had been dealt with, reflecting the wider sense of scandal over cases of sexual abuse by Catholic priests, brothers, and nuns. While the Ryan Commission's report detailed numerous accounts of sexual abuse within the Irish residential care system, another significant source of scandal within the report was its detailed review of the systemic neglect and cruelty to which children in industrial and reformatory schools were subjected. To understand children's experiences of this system, some historical context should be given.

For much of the twentieth century, Ireland's residential school system followed a structure that had developed in the latter half of the nineteenth century. By the mid-nineteenth century, the numbers of poor and vulnerable children in Britain and Ireland were at a level where the existing system of workhouses and other charitably run residential schools and orphanages could not meet demand. Interest turned to the model of the 'industrial school', which, by that time, had become well established in Germany, Scandinavia, and Switzerland, and which was designed to provide a residential environment in which children would learn skills for future employment in industry or agriculture. By 1868, a legislative framework was in place in Britain and Ireland to certify both reformatory schools (for children found guilty of criminal offences) and industrial schools (for children who were destitute, neglected, at risk of turning to crime or of moral corruption, or guilty of misdemeanors). Industrial schools soon became far more numerous in Ireland than reformatory schools.[9] Legislation for industrial and reformatory schools was subsequently consolidated in the 1908 Children's Act, which, although soon subject to further revision in Britain, remained the primary legislative framework for childcare in the independent Irish State until 1991. The 1908 Act emphasized the duty of the state, through the court system, to intervene to remove children aged under 14 from family environments in which their physical or moral well-being was at risk. The perceived risk of moral contamination from unsuitable families—and perceived importance of the industrial schools for children's moral and spiritual formation—meant that children committed to these schools through the courts were sentenced to attend them for the maximum period possible (usually until their fifteenth or sixteenth birthday). They were also often sent to schools in remote locations or far from their family homes, and parental visiting rights were closely controlled.[10] Many children committed to industrial schools had already lived for many years in their family environment, but some children appeared as 'defendants' in those committal proceedings aged 3 or 4, with little understanding of the process they were experiencing and with no formal advocate acting on their behalf.[11] The poor economic conditions that continued to prevail in Ireland after independence, together with the sharp rise in births outside marriage,[12] meant that there was a substantial group of primarily poor, working-class children[13] who were considered by the courts to be socially or morally vulnerable. Between 1936 and 1970, 170,000 children were resident at around 50 industrial schools in Ireland (around 1.2 per cent of the age cohort), with the total numbers in these schools remaining above 6,000 in every year between 1936 and 1952.[14] The numbers of children began to fall in these schools in the 1950s, and then more rapidly in the 1960s, partly as a reflection of the improving economic context, and partly as a result of courts' increasing reluctance to send children to these schools.[15] The number of schools also began to shrink accordingly, with twenty-six industrial schools closing between 1960 and 1983, before the remaining schools came under the jurisdiction of the Department of Health.[16] By 1970, there were only 1,740 children in industrial schools in Ireland, and, by 1984, the Department of Health's policy was to seek to maintain children in their own family environments for as long as possible, and to work towards keeping the numbers of children in residential care at less than 1,000.[17]

The industrial and reformatory school system in Ireland involved the state, the legal system, the Church, and other child welfare agencies. By 1913, in Britain, a review of reformatory and industrial schools had raised concerns about the large degree of autonomy that voluntary organizations had in running government-funded educational institutions, and these were brought under closer state management, until industrial schools in Britain were closed in the 1930s. In Ireland, however, the Catholic Church was far more successful in maintaining control over the management of these schools. Prior to partition, Catholic industrial schools had outnumbered Protestant industrial schools in Ireland by nearly ten to one, and after 1921[18] the Catholic Church became virtually the exclusive provider of residential childcare in the new Irish State.[19] Robert Orsi has commented on the importance of the spiritual formation of children within religious groups, which extends beyond a commonsensical transmission of religious tradition to a new generation to the way in which 'children's bodies, rationalities, imaginations, and desires have all been privileged media for giving substance to religious meaning... not only *for* children, but *through* them too, for adults in relation to them'.[20] The formation of children thus becomes a practice through which the sacred takes material form. In the context of British colonial rule, such processes had a particular political edge. Catholicism had a unique significance in Irish culture in providing a symbolic and material resistance against British rule, leading the British government to recognize the necessity of working with the Catholic Church in Ireland if it was to be able to maintain governance. The Christian Brothers, who were to run some of the largest industrial schools, were formed primarily as an educational order in the early nineteenth century in the context of anxiety over the proselytization of Catholic children in Protestant schools and orphanages, and the Brothers sought to combat the British, Protestant threat with a patriotic ethos of 'Faith and Fatherland'.[21]

Catholic religious orders therefore ran industrial and reformatory schools in Ireland, but, in line with the 1908 Act, these schools operated in a wider institutional framework. As noted above, admission to the schools was through the court system, and both religious and non-religious child welfare agencies were involved in presenting children for committal.[22] More significant than the voluntary agencies, however, was the role of the state. Although owned and run by religious orders, the industrial schools were legally certified, inspected by, and funded by the state, through the Department of Education. Avoiding the potential problems of making direct payments to religious orders, the funding system established by the British government, and largely unchanged after Irish independence, was for schools to be paid a per capita grant based on the number of pupils they had in residence. The nature and level of this grant remained controversial for much of the twentieth century. The religious orders consistently argued that it was insufficient. The Department of Education veered between agreeing periodic increases in the capitation grant and arguing that the lack of transparent and consistent accounting across the school system meant that it was difficult to make a strong case for this. By funding the schools on a per capita basis, however, an economic incentive was built into the system to have children committed to the schools. The Ryan Commission concluded that this led to demands by school managers for children to be committed to industrial schools 'for reasons of economic viability of the institutions'.[23] The capitation grant also meant that conditions in the schools began to worsen further, as numbers of residents declined from the 1950s onwards.[24]

In addition to being reliant on state funding, the industrial schools were also subject to regulations that provided the basis for the certification of individual schools by the government. The content of these rules remained largely unchanged from the time that industrial school certification began in 1868 until the review of the system in the Kennedy report of 1970. The rules were established to provide a framework for a safe and secure training environment that would prepare children for adult life. In practice, children more commonly experienced the schools as places of abuse and neglect.

These rules stated that children were to be given 'neat comfortable clothing in good repair, suitable for the season of the year'.[25] It was common practice in the industrial schools, however, for children's clothing to be laundered and distributed on a collective basis, so that no child had his or her own specific clothing. The collective distribution was sometimes made with little attention to whether clothing fitted the child or not, and the circulation of clothing also encouraged the spread of lice and scabies. In his 1962 private report on conditions at the Artane industrial school, Henry Moore complained to the Archbishop of

Dublin that children's clothing at the school was dirty, unhygienic, uncomfortable, and of generally poor quality, given that the material for the clothing was largely manufactured at the school by the boys themselves. The laundry rotation at Artane was such that the boys at the school would have their shirts and trousers changed every week, and their underwear only every fortnight. Of particular concern to Moore was the fact that children had overcoats only if they had been able to pay for these out of their own money, and that it was common to see hundreds of the children at the school walking to Mass on a Sunday morning in winter wearing only thin jackets and trousers. Children working outdoors at industrial schools were also left for long periods in wet and soiled clothing.[26]

A similar gap between the aspiration of official regulations and actual practice in the schools was evident in relation to issues of diet and health. In 1912, the rules stated that children were to be given 'plain, wholesome food, according to a scale of Dietary to be drawn up by the Medical Officer of the school and approved by the Inspector'.[27] In 1933, this rule was further developed with the statement that 'such food shall be suitable in every respect for growing children actively employed and supplemented in the case of delicate and physically under-developed children with such special food as individual needs require'.[28] The reality was very different from this. In its conclusions, the Ryan Commission stated that children in residential care were frequently hungry, and that the food they did receive was 'inadequate, inedible and badly prepared',[29] noting the evidence of witnesses that they had been reduced to scavenging from waste bins and eating animal feed. The lack of supervision of mealtimes at many boys' schools also meant that older boys would steal food from younger or weaker boys, who were unable to defend themselves. At one point at Artane, a group of boys managed to steal wafers from the Sacristy to eat. All the boys at the school were then searched for evidence of wafer fragments, and, if they found any on them, were given an immediate flogging.[30] Health care was also largely inadequate.[31] The Cussen Commission of Inquiry into the industrial and reformatory school system concluded, in 1936, that there was no effective system of medical inspection in the schools. Little changed in the wake of the Cussen report, however. At Artane, in 1962, Henry Moore commented that he failed to understand 'the indifference of Departmental Inspectors to the seriously inadequate medical facilities in the school. Apart from the twice-weekly visit of the Doctor there is no matron or nurse in attendance. A brother without qualifications and who was transferred from the care of the poultry farm is now in charge of all medical requirements.'[32] The general lack of access to medical care in the residential schools meant that children went without treatment for chronic conditions that were to have significant consequences for their health in adult life. Enuresis among the children was not seen as something requiring medical or psychological treatment, but led to beatings or public humiliation when a child was found to have wet his or her bed (as many did, given the traumatic environment of the school). Although the rationale for the schools was to provide an appropriate education and training for the children to prepare them for adult life, in practice most schools provided very limited education and tended to use the children as an unpaid workforce, forcing them either to undertake manual tasks to maintain the running of the school itself or to produce goods that could be sold.[33] The level of work could be particularly arduous for the younger children in the schools, who were set tasks that were physically exhausting and to standards that they struggled to meet. While the financial viability of individual schools varied across the system,[34] and independently audited accounts were in short supply,[35] when such accounts were forthcoming it was evident that many schools providing poor living conditions for children were at the same time being run at a profit.[36]

Arguably, though, the most traumatic breach of the rules governing conduct in these schools related to the punishment of children. These rules stated that punishment of children should consist of '(a) forfeiture of ranks and privileges, or degradation from rank, previously attained by good conduct; (b) moderate childish punishment with the hand; (c) chastisement with the cane, strap or birch'.[37] Although a culture of corporal punishment persisted for much of the twentieth century, the rules regulating the conduct of residential schools also made it clear that the use of corporal punishment was to be administered in an accountable and controlled way. As the list of punishments above suggests, the harsher forms of corporal punishment were framed as a last resort, following milder forms of physical punishment or other sanctions. Furthermore, where children were considered to be guilty of serious misconduct requiring more severe punishment, these incidents were to be recorded in a punishment book that would be made available during periodic inspections of the school by the Department of Education. Such an understanding of the use of corporal punishment bore little relation to the culture of systemic violence experienced by children in these schools. Children in the schools were beaten frequently, often without warning, and for reasons such as looking at the clock during lessons, failing to give a correct answer during catechism, or being the last child to reach the dormitory from the washrooms. Beatings were also administered without any clear rationale at all. Individual children could be beaten several times a day, over periods of days and weeks. The methods of punishment used against children far exceeded those in the official rules. Children were kicked, burned, or held under water, and were beaten with fists, the backs of washing brushes, hurling sticks, and (in the case of one brother) by a section cut from the rim of a solid rubber tyre.[38] Beatings were given spontaneously, with staff apparently having free licence to administer beatings without any managerial oversight. These physical punishments were never properly recorded, as required by the official regulations, and were used, again in breach of the regulations, as the first resort of punishment for any perceived misdemeanour. So normalized was this culture of violence that the Ryan Commission report commented that it was 'notable that witnesses described daily, casual and random physical abuse as normal and wished only to report the times when the frequency and severity of the abuse was such that they were injured or in fear for their lives'.[39] Within this culture, the decision by a member of staff to withhold a beating in a situation where it had become normal practice could be interpreted by the children as an act of kindness.[40] It was not unknown for children to require medical treatment as a consequence of this violence,[41] and medical staff would have clearly seen evidence of physical injury against children. The Ryan Commission concluded that the extent and degree of violence used against children in the residential schools exceeded sporadic acts of individual members of staff and reflected a systemic and widespread culture of violence across all the residential schools that it studied.[42] Part of the underlying intention of this systemic violence appears to have been to create a climate of fear in which it was believed children would be more manageable and subject to moral formation. Not only, therefore, was violence used to terrorize individual children receiving beatings, but, by beating children publicly (or within earshot of other children), all children in the school were made to feel under constant threat of violence. Those who attempted to abscond from school were particularly subjected to public punishment—for example, by having their heads shaved as well as being publicly beaten. At some schools, when children absconded, a collective punishment was given to all the children, so that those absconding would then be subject to further mistreatment by their peers. As one brother put it, complimenting the work of a nominated disciplinarian: 'He didn't tolerate disobedience in word or act. Returned runaways had to "walk the line" for longish periods until they were broken.'[43] Members of staff were similarly bound up in this system of abuse. In one incident at Artane, a 17-year-old teacher of a class of young children was beaten by an older brother for failing to beat the younger children often enough. The Ryan

Commission further concluded that the extent and degree of the violence used against children was such that the Department of Education must have known that 'violence and beatings were endemic in the system itself',[44] yet no action was taken to prevent this. Within all this, the role of the children was to be subject to the authorities and the conditions within which they were raised. As one former resident of the Letterfrack industrial school recalled: 'the most terrible law in Letterfrack was we must not complain. In the words of Brother Kelly, "it is sinful in the eyes of God to complain".'

Such systemic violence, neglect, and humiliation inevitably scarred those who experienced their childhood in these residential schools. Some former residents bore the physical effects of injuries received, or of medical conditions that did not receive proper treatment. The Ryan Commission report commented that those witnesses who went on to have their own families struggled to manage their own parental roles. While some former residents did manage to go on to have successful careers, the Commission noted that 70 per cent of the 1,090 witnesses who testified to it did not receive any secondary-level education, with most spending the rest of their lives in manual or unskilled occupations. Thirty per cent of former residents who testified to the Commission also reported significant mental health problems, including suicidal behaviour, depression, alcohol and substance abuse, and self-harm.[45] More spoke, more generally, about the ways in which their lives had subsequently been marked by poverty, social isolation, and a struggle to form stable and secure adult relationships. The wounds experienced by most former residents of these schools ran deep, leaving an indelible mark on the rest of the course of their lives.

Hierarchies of sacred forms and the persistence of abuse

Since the early 1990s, the growing sense of public scandal over the disclosures of the treatment of children within the industrial and reformatory schools has raised the question about how such systemic abuse and neglect were possible in a system regulated and funded by the state and run by mainstream religious institutions.[46] One explanation, suggested by Raftery and O'Sullivan in their book accompanying the *States of Fear* television series, was that the system was run largely on the basis of financial expediency by the state and the Church. Attempts to reform the system (for example, through encouraging foster care rather than residential care) were, they argue, resisted by Catholic institutions, which wished to preserve their power and status within Irish society.[47]

While economic and political self-interest were doubtless enmeshed in the reasons behind the persistence of this system, to explain it simply in terms of the desire to save money and to make profit, or to maintain the exercise of power, is insufficient. As Viviana Zelizer's series of studies of values and markets has shown, economic practices are never purely rational calculations but are always framed in the context of broader values and meanings.[48] To give children in residential care a bare subsistence diet, or to provide them with inadequate clothing or health care, is not simply a 'rational' economic calculation—as is evident by the moral outrage that would be caused if such 'rationality' were to be deployed by a childcare agency today. Rather, it reflects a particular meaning and status given to children within that residential school system, embedded in a wider understanding of the sacred, which made such practices of 'care' seem reasonable and legitimate.

Another way of addressing the sense of public scandal over children's treatment, used by many of the religious orders that ran the schools, is to construct various forms of episodic narrative.[49] Here the moral contamination of children's abuse and neglect is contained in the past in an attempt to keep its polluting effects from the present. Versions of this narrative include the claim that abuse was practised by only a few staff, whose actions were largely unknown in an otherwise functioning system, that poor standards of care in the industrial and reformatory schools reflected poor standards of care of children more generally in Ireland prior to the 1960s, and that contemporary notions of 'abuse' and 'children's rights' had little cultural influence until relatively recently. Another related distancing strategy was to situate claims of abuse in the 'narratives' or 'claims' of former residents. As a senior figure in one religious order put it, in evidence to the Ryan Commission, 'when we have met ex-residents and talking to them and listening to how it was for them and how they experienced it, you know, it has really saddened us a lot and we, like, we would always say, well, look, we are really sorry that these are your memories'.[50]

While performing symbolic work in attempting to keep at bay the moral contamination of former residents' accounts of abuse and neglect from the present-day operations of the religious orders, these narratives are historically inadequate. As the Ryan Commission concluded, the reported evidence of abuse and neglect was so widespread across institutions that this had to be understood as a broader, systemic issue rather than a series of isolated cases.[51] Conditions of neglect occurred because of structural decisions—for example, not to give children a regular supply of eggs or milk at a school attached to a large working farm—rather than the isolated acts of a few malevolent individuals. To claim that instances of abuse were not known about or properly understood fails to recognize evidence of complaints made to the police and the Department of Education about individual cases.[52] The suggestion that those running the schools were unaware that there was anything inappropriate about the conditions under which the children were living is challenged by evidence that religious orders were complicit with the Department of Education in presenting unrealistically positive images of conditions in the schools during their periodic inspections. Similarly the claim that child abuse was not a concept understood until recently, while correct to some degree in terms of awareness of the extent and psychological consequences of abuse, obscures the fact that the sexual and physical abuse of children was already subject to criminal law and that modern discourses of child welfare were increasingly widespread in Atlantic societies by the start of the twentieth century. The figure of the child played an important role in the political rhetoric of Irish Republicanism. Furthermore, as a member of the League of Nations from 1923, the Irish Free State was part of a transnational organization that had already begun to adopt a discourse of the rights of children through its endorsement of a World Child Welfare Charter (later to become the UN Declaration of the Rights of the Child), which included the stipulations that 'the child must be given the needs requisite for its normal development . . . the child that is hungry must be fed, the child that is sick must be nursed . . . and the orphan and the waif must be nurtured and succored'. Keeping the moral contamination of the abuse and neglect of children quarantined in the past through a clear, episodic distinction between contemporary understandings of the sacrality of the care of children and earlier practices of raising children fails to do justice to a more complex historical picture.

Instead of these episodic narratives, a more satisfactory understanding may be gained through thinking about this case in terms of hierarchies of sacred forms. By this I mean that, when multiple sacred forms are present in a given social context, one possible form of relationship between them is one in which a particular sacred form dominates another, making it difficult through various operations of power for that subordinated sacred form to become an intense focus of public thought, feeling, and action. Thus, while the subordinate sacred form may continue to be circulated through cultural texts and practices, the cognitive, emotional, and practical investment in the dominant sacred form is such that the power of moral identification with the subordinate form is weakened. Such hierarchical relations between sacred forms are not static or immutable, however. As we have noted before, Jeffrey Alexander has commented that sacred forms are 'shifting cultural constructions' subject to means of symbolic production that are 'fatefully affected by the power and identity of the agents in charge, by the competition for symbolic control, and the structures of power and distribution of resources'.[53] This is very much evident in the case of the industrial and reformatory school system in Ireland through the twentieth century in which the hierarchical relationship between two sacred forms was under continual negotiation, and was eventually reversed by the time that century had drawn to a close.

'The destiny which God has in mind for the children of the Gael': The sacrality of the Irish Catholic nation

The first of these sacred forms, dominant in Irish society for much of the twentieth century, was the sacrality of the Irish Catholic nation. This sacred form fused the hoped-for, and then newly formed, independent Irish State with a sense of national identity grounded in Catholic symbolism and piety. This fusion of Catholicism and nationalism took a myriad of forms—from claims of Ireland as a Christian civilization in political and religious rhetoric,[54] to the use of Catholic symbolism to celebrate the martyrdom of those struggling for Irish freedom,[55] to the early twentieth-century fashion for Irish landscape painting and the idealization of the West coast of Ireland as the last repository of authentic Irish culture. It bound together the longing for an Ireland free from colonial rule, in which an authentic Irish cultural life would become possible again, with the sense that such a cultural life was impossible if not fed by the deep wells of Christian piety that were woven through the history of true Irish civilization. As the early twentiety-century Irish literary critic Daniel Corkery put it, the authentic Irish racial mind was informed by religion, nationalism, and a sense of the land, and any Irish art not absorbed by any of these three things was not authentically Irish.[56] The pervasiveness of this sacred form in the opening decades of the twentieth century was such that, at the moment of greatest division within the new Irish State—the post-treaty civil war of 1921–2—the two opposing sides largely sought to draw on it to legitimate either their support for, or their rebellion against, the Irish Free State. Supporters of the Free State claimed it as an authentic, albeit pragmatic, realization of the hope for a free Irish Catholic nation.[57] Those opposing the treaty claimed that violent resistance against the Free State was legitimate, as one anonymous Republican put it, 'when the majority [supporting the treaty] are bent on compromising issues of transcendent importance',[58] and the treaty had constituted the breach of 'sacred national principles'.[59] As another Republican priest put it, 'the Irish Republic is not only the symbol of our independence. It is a Christian and holy thing. It is the shrine wherein rise the sacred incense of Ireland's devotion and Ireland's holy aspirations...the road to that destiny which God has in mind for the children of the Gael.'[60] The symbolic struggle over which side had the right to deploy the symbolism of the Irish Catholic nation in this context was further evident in the decision by the Catholic Church in Ireland to excommunicate anyone who violently resisted the Irish Free State after 1922.[61]

The appeal of this sacred form in the context of the Irish struggle against colonial rule is not difficult to perceive.[62] As Ireland fought towards greater independence from Great Britain, so the task of defining an Irish identity distinct from the Protestant culture of the Anglo-Irish power elites acquired particular significance.[63] The trauma of the Great Famine of 1845–52 had profoundly disrupted Irish rural life, with the death of more than a million people and the associated migration of another two million largely breaking the transmission of Irish folk traditions.[64] While there were movements to maintain or reinvent[65] such folk traditions in the early twentieth century, and an attempt to encourage the widespread use of the Irish language in the early years of independence, these failed to effect widespread cultural change.[66] By contrast, Catholicism was deeply woven into Irish cultural life. Historically, Catholic practices and institutional structures had played an active role in resisting the authority of the British occupation, from ecclesiastical involvement in the struggle for Catholic emancipation to the Church's role in opposing conscription in Ireland to the British army in 1918.[67] Alongside this association of Catholicism with cultural and political resistance, the closing decades of the nineteenth century had also seen widespread, popular adoption of new Catholic devotional practices in Ireland from continental Europe—including perpetual adoration, novenas, devotion to the Sacred Heart, pilgrimages, processions, and retreats.[68] These practices, together with the visual and material artefacts that focused piety in the home, and the expansion of Catholic institutions including churches, convents, schools, orphanages, and hospitals, gave renewed cultural life to Catholic symbols and sensibilities.[69] This found expression, not only in high levels of regular Catholic observance within the wider population, but also in periodic spectacular demonstrations of public piety, such as a Mass for 500,000 people held in Phoenix Park, Dublin, in 1929 to celebrate the centenary of Catholic emancipation, and the attendance of a million people at a Mass at the same site three years later as part of an international Eucharistic Congress.[70] As an institutional structure, the Catholic Church also played a central role in Irish society, providing both key social services as well as one of very few opportunities for career advancement for the many unable to secure advancement through inheritance of land. By the time of the formation of the Irish Free State, Catholic institutions had already become dominant across Irish civil society.[71] Given the exceptional levels of migration from Ireland from the 1840s onwards,[72] the Catholic Church also provided both a physical and an imagined structure that connected the global Irish diaspora—constructed symbolically as an alternative, spiritual, transnational structure to the dominant order of the British Empire.[73]

Within the sacred form of the Irish Catholic nation, sexuality became a touchstone of the moral purity of the nation.[74] One of the striking characteristics of Irish society in the late nineteenth and early twentieth centuries was the comparatively high proportion of the population who remained either unmarried or who married late. In part, this was a consequence of the discouragement of early marriage, given the problems this posed for families having to make further subdivisions of agricultural smallholdings.[75] Alongside these economic realities, the aspiration of abstinence from sex outside marriage remained a widespread cultural norm, although actual sexual practices often diverged from this. Catholic moral teaching on sexual relations shaped not only personal sensibilities but public policy as well. These included stringent legal restrictions on divorce and the censorship of printed material from 1929 being applied to any written work advocating, or giving information about, birth control.[76]

The strength and cohesion of the Irish nation rested on its moral purity, and this purity was inseparable from Catholic piety and sexual mores. Anxiety over the moral decline of Irish society fed both political and ecclesiastical concerns about a perceived decline in sexual morality that set the context for the Carrigan Report on Sexual Offences in 1931, whose findings were never publicly published, following advice from leading clergy that they might raise wider doubts about the moral integrity of the Irish nation.[77] The spread of cinemas, mass print media, and dance halls across Ireland posed both a real and an imagined challenge to this moral order. However, even as such processes of cultural modernization began to challenge the conservative Catholic hegemony, these popular cultural threats were used to mobilize renewed commitment to the sacred order they threatened to undermine.[78] As a joint pastoral letter issued in 1927 by leaders of the Catholic Church in Ireland put it:

These latter days have witnessed, amongst many other unpleasant sights, a loosening of the bonds of parental authority, a disregard for the discipline of the home, and a general impatience under restraint that drives youth to neglect the sacred claims of authority and follow its own capricious ways ... The evil one is ever setting his snares for unwary feet. At the moment, his traps for the innocent are chiefly the dance hall, the bad book, the indecent paper, the motion picture, the immodest fashion in female dress—all of which tend to destroy the virtues characteristic of our race.[79]

This sacred form of the Irish Catholic nation, which shaped both imagined visions of Irish collective life as well as the sexual subjectivities of individuals, provided a central source of symbolic legitimation for the industrial and reformatory school system. The concern for the moral purity of the pious nation can be seen in the grounds on which some children were committed to the schools, where, for example, they were perceived as being at risk from exposure to sexual immorality when their mothers were engaged in extramarital sexual relations. Similarly, children's subjection to sexual abuse in family or institutional settings was commonly thought about, in terms not of psychological harm to the child, but of moral taint,[80] and sexually abused children might find themselves further punished for their (albeit unwilling) involvement in polluting behavior.[81] In this context, children exposed to 'immoral' family settings could be perceived as 'moral dirt',[82] fundamentally stained and at risk of extending moral pollution if not subjected to firm moral correction. Violence against children, in this symbolic world, was not simply the random act of individual sociopaths, but a 'sensational form', a means in which a particular sacred form was physically mediated. Through beatings, children were meant to understand their place in the moral structure of this particular religio-national sacred form.[83]

The idea of the reformatory and industrial schools as sites of moral and spiritual formation—reflected in Sean Moylan's comments about Artane—similarly legitimated the exercise of power by religious orders through those institutions, making it harder to concede that this power might be deployed in abusive ways. In its conclusions, the Ryan Commission criticized 'the deferential and submissive attitude of the Department of Education' towards the religious orders that ran the schools,[84] and argued throughout the report that the Department of Education would have been aware of the poor conditions to which children in the schools were being subjected. Such deference could be thought about in terms of political pragmatism. The popular influence of the Catholic Church was such that no professional politician would seriously entertain alienating the Church, and the twentieth century provided numerous examples of the ways in which the Church influenced successive Irish governments' policy on issues of child welfare and personal morality. But to see such deference to the Church in terms of political expediency would be to miss the importance of the symbolic framework of the Irish Catholic nation, which was largely shared by the clergy and political classes, or indeed of the importance of deference to moral, political, and religious authority within this sacred form.[85] In this context, the refusal of politicians like Sean Moylan publicly to countenance the harm being done through the industrial school system reflected a desire, however strategic or reflexive, to protect the sacred form of the Irish Catholic nation from the taint of moral scandal. The meanings of this sacred form were therefore woven through the processes through which children were committed to industrial schools, legitimated the institutional structures of power through which children were neglected and abused, and created a cultural climate in which an overt challenge of the schools' practices through the statutory inspection system or wider public debate was experienced as a threat to social order. The sacred form of the Irish Catholic nation did not simply determine the structures and practices of the industrial school system. As we noted at the end of the previous chapter, cultural structures do not determine social life in such simple or direct ways, but interact with economic, social, and historical processes to generate particular kinds of social life. But this sacred form did shape a cultural environment in which an industrial school system based on mid-nineteenth-century concepts and practices was able to remain an integral part of the Irish childcare system well into the twentieth century, and long after these had been discredited in most other Western societies.[86]

The sacrality of care for children

Alongside the sacred form of the Irish Catholic nation, another sacred form was also present in twentieth-century Irish culture that had relevance to conditions in the industrial schools: the sacrality of the care of children. The cultural meanings of 'childhood' are neither immutable, nor (as we can be tempted to imagine in the light of contemporary sacred commitments) have they followed a neat historical trajectory from relative ignorance or indifference to greater knowledge and compassion. When Phillippe Aries wrote that 'in medieval society the idea of childhood did not exist',[87] he meant neither that the childhood lacked particular cultural significance in any pre-modern society,[88] nor that children in medieval families failed to receive love or devotion. Rather

Aries's seminal history of meanings of childhood in the West demonstrates how the 'short childhood' of the medieval period, in which the main transition was between a dependent infant phase and entry into the social world of adulthood, became gradually displaced by the concept of a 'long childhood' as a transitional phase between infancy and adult life.[89] The idea of a 'long childhood' became more culturally widespread from the late sixteenth century through the intertwining discourse of the need for social and moral formation of children (in opposition to a perceived sentimentalized coddling of children) and the gradual emergence of educational institutions that aspired to promote this formation.[90] The development of educational institutions at the same time delineated the meaning of the family in new ways, constructing the family as a structure for the moral and spiritual formation of the child in conjunction with the formative work of the school environment.[91] For centuries, the social reach of this new understanding of childhood was uneven, and refracted through class and gender. Those who became 'children' through the new educational institutions were primarily middle class, as the upper classes were still often able to make swift transitions from infancy to places of social status, and the lower classes were largely beyond the ambition of the new schools and colleges. Similarly, the age at which children entered and left school remained relatively unregulated, and girls were seen as not suitable subjects for such educational formation.[92] Through the nineteenth century, however, the reach of institutions focusing on the education and containment of children (refuges, orphanages, schools, and reformatories) started to become more systematic in response to the social changes of industrializing societies in which children were more vulnerable to being displaced from family structures.[93] As a consequence, the idea of a 'long childhood' as a period of formation distinct from adulthood started to become embedded more consistently across society. During the same period, the study of child development became increasingly established, in both popular and scientific forms, which generated fuller accounts of what it meant to be a normal and healthy child.[94] The idea of a long period of formation for the development of the healthy child still took considerable time to find practical realization through improving economic and welfare conditions. For most working-class children, economic and demographic realities meant that they could not remain outside the labour market for long, as their families were often reliant on their income,[95] and it was generally only in the post-war period that the cultural concept of a long childhood began to match the lived experience of the majority of children in the West.[96]

The emergence and pace of industrialization in Ireland were much later and slower compared to Great Britain and the United States. Nevertheless, these processes of economic and social change were bound to prevalent discourses framing the care of children. These included the sentimentalization of adult relations with children, the notion of the child as vulnerable to poor social conditions and corrupting moral forces, the emphasis on giving children appropriate moral and technical formation to join the new forms of labour market, and anxiety about displaced children as a source of social and moral disorder. The economic importance of the child as wage-earner meant that, into the early twentieth century, adult–child relations particularly in the working classes were often framed in terms of the 'useful child', in which the child's role was to repay their parents' investment, even though the notion of the inherent value and rights of children were becoming more common among educated elites through best-selling books such as Ellen Key's *The Century of the Child*.[97] But, as Vivianna Zelizer has shown, by the 1930s there had been a significant shift away from the notion of the economically 'useful child' to that of the 'economically "worthless" but emotionally "priceless" child'.[98] Associated with the legal and moral proscription of child labour[99]—beyond very limited instances—this consolidated the notion of the long childhood as a protected period in which children should receive appropriate material, emotional, intellectual, and moral nurturing. A later, but concomitant, development of this protected, long childhood was the emergence of the concept of the 'teenager' as someone in the latter stages of this long childhood, simultaneously protected from, and trying to access and negotiate, adult social realities.

It was through this consolidation of the notion of a long childhood that the care of children began to acquire the status of an autonomous sacred form.[100] Concern about the moral and material well-being of children had commonly been framed before the twentieth century in the context of particular religious or political systems of meaning. But, as the twentieth century progressed, the sacrality of the care of children increasingly acquired an autonomous significance (bound to the similarly autonomous sacred form of human rights) that transcended religious and cultural particularities and in which social agents and institutions were expected to submit to common principles of child nurturance and protection.[101] This found expression in the formation of new child protection legislation, new forms of professionalization (social work, youth work, child psychology and psychotherapy), new ways of framing children's malformation as 'abuse' grounded in the notion of children's rights and autonomy as social agents, the extension of discourses of universal rights and needs of children through transnational institutions,[102] and mediated scandals of child neglect and abuse (including the *States of Fear* documentaries), which provided a focus and structure for public commitment to this sacred form.

Maintaining hierarchies of sacred forms: Brother René and the failure of Edward Flanagan's challenge to the system

To return to our earlier discussion, one interpretation of the public scandal over the industrial school system is to place these two sacred forms—of the Irish Catholic nation and the care of children—in an episodic relationship. In this episodic narrative, contemporary disgust at the conditions of the industrial school system can be seen as a projection of a more recent sacred commitment to the care of children on to earlier historical conditions. It is certainly the case that the extent and political efficacy of the public scandal generated by *States of Fear* became possible in a cultural context in which the care of children had become firmly established as a sacred form, and the programme's revelations could therefore be experienced as a profound breach of the sacred. But the relationship between the sacrality of the Irish Catholic nation and the autonomous sacred form of the care of children was more complex in Irish society than a simple episodic separation. Instead, both ran through twentieth-century Ireland in a shifting, hierarchical relationship.

Two examples demonstrate the co-presence of these sacred forms. The first illustrates the ways in which sensitivity to both sacred forms could create powerful tensions within the individual subject. In a remarkable part of the Ryan Commission's report on conditions at the Carriglea Park industrial school, a detailed account is given of the correspondence of one of the brothers with management responsibility, Brother René,[103] who had asked to be released from his order several times. A running theme in Brother René's correspondence with others in his order is his acute awareness of his failure to maintain a suitably nurturing environment for the children in his care. In 1952, he wrote to his superiors:

Lacking every qualification for the work in Carriglea I had recourse to harshness and severity. As a result many of the past pupils have lost the faith and some are active, capable and influential communists. When these become sufficiently vocal it may be some help to the Brothers if they can say concerning me and in defence of the Congregation he is not in the Order now. I recall the relief it was to the Brothers to be able to say this about another... years ago when a Dáil deputy spoke bitterly of the punishment he received in school from the man concerned.

My utter failure in Carriglea caused me great remorse. Having no fitness for the work it was only to be expected that my efforts would result in failure and harm.[104]

Six years earlier, in a previous plea for dispensation from his order, he expressed similar sentiments, writing that 'despite the opinions of at least some kindly people I know myself to have been a hopeless failure and one who should never have been placed over such unfortunate boys for whom only the best is good enough'.[105] At the heart of the chronic depression expressed through Brother René's letters was not only a sense of his own professional unsuitability for the work he had been given, but the painful pull of two unreconciled sacred commitments. Underlying his repeated requests for dispensation was an awareness that devotion to his allotted place within the sacred order of the Irish Catholic nation meant that he had profoundly failed another sacred commitment to the 'boys for whom only the best is good enough'. It is indicative of the operations of power in this context that, despite his ongoing sense of guilt and failure in his role, he lacked the institutional autonomy to be able to extricate himself from that position, and his repeated requests for dispensation were never granted.

A second, longer example illustrates both the simultaneous co-presence of the sacred forms of the Irish Catholic nation and the care of children in Irish society in the middle decades of the twentieth century, as well as how a hierarchical relationship between them was maintained. On June 1946, Fr Edward Flanagan arrived in Ireland for a tour of the country that included speaking on the radio and at live events in major cities, visiting childcare institutions, and meeting politicians (including the Irish President). By this time, Flanagan was already a celebrity in the United States and Ireland. He had established his first residential children's home in Omaha in 1917, moving this in 1921 to a farm, which then became known as 'Boys Town'. Boys Town adopted a relatively progressive ethos, admitted children with no restrictions in relation to their religion or ethnicity, and gave residents a degree of self-government. Flanagan's work received much greater public attention with the release of the Hollywood film *Boys Town* in 1938, for which Spencer Tracy won an Oscar as lead actor for his portrayal of Flanagan. Flanagan's raised public profile led to him being consulted as an expert on childcare across America, and developing a broader international role in planning for institutional childcare in the wake of the disruption caused by the Second World War.

On arriving in Ireland, Flanagan admitted that he knew relatively little about institutional childcare in the country, but commented optimistically to the *Irish Times* that young people in Ireland 'should be the most ideal in all the world. I am hoping they are, and have reason to believe they are.'[106] While his public engagements and lectures continued to be reported during his month-long trip, the positive tone of his comments about the Irish context soon changed. Speaking to journalists in Dublin on 19 June, Flanagan made clear both the ecumenical nature of Boys Town and his opposition to the use of physical punishment on children, as those using it generally had too little understanding of its psychological effects on children.[107] Four days later, at a public lecture in Dublin, Flanagan said that staff he had met on a recent visit to a children's training institution in Belfast had shown 'little common-sense...trying to get inside the mind of the child'.[108] By the time Flanagan gave a public lecture in Cork on 7 July, his comments were becoming even more forthright: 'From what I have seen since coming to this country your institutions are not all noble, particularly your borstals [reformatory children's institutions], which are a disgrace.'[109] Flanagan also went on to comment that, while a politician in Dublin had told him that Irish prisons were well run, they were in his view 'a disgrace to a Christian Catholic people'.[110] While Flanagan's public criticisms of the residential school system were highly embarrassing to the Irish establishment, it was not until he had returned to America and continued to make these criticisms to the American press that a political response was made. Responding to a question in the Dáil about Fr Flanagan's comments, the Minister for Justice, Gerry Boland, expressed surprise that a priest of Flanagan's standing 'should have thought it proper to describe in such offensive and intemperate language conditions about which he has no first-hand knowledge' and said that Flanagan's claims about the extent of physical punishment in residential schools were so exaggerated that he was sure that no one in Ireland would believe them.[111] This political attack was later reiterated by another member of the Dáil, who objected to the 'series of falsehoods and slanders' that Flanagan had published about the Irish residential childcare system on his return to America, which had led, amongst other coverage, to a newspaper cartoon of a muscular warder whipping a boy with a cat-o'-nine-tails.[112] Flanagan should, he claimed, have the 'moral courage to...correct the grave injustice he has done not only to the legislators of this country, but to the decent, respectable, honest men who are members of the Irish Christian Brothers'.[113]

The public row between Flanagan and the Irish Establishment triggered further debate in the letters pages of the *Irish Times*. Although one letter was published immediately after Boland's response to Flanagan—accusing Boland of trying to coerce Flanagan's bishop into silencing him[114]—the main correspondence through the letters page took place between the end of August and mid-October. A roughly even number of the letters published supported or criticized Flanagan, although all framed their contributions in terms of the punishment and reform of offenders, even though most of the children committed to industrial schools had committed no serious legal offence. Some correspondents praised Flanagan for opening up a much-needed debate about conditions in residential schools and prisons, although his supporters tended to focus more on his comments on prison conditions than on the residential schools.[115] Others saw him as a weak liberal whose attempts to 'molly-coddle' wrongdoers were further contributing to the moral decline of Irish society. One correspondent, signing himself 'An Old Teacher', declared that 'in a life-time of teaching I always found that *fear is the only effective deterrent* for young or old' (emphasis in original). He went on to recall being warmly applauded by an audience at a lecture by the progressive judge Henry MacCarthy[116] when he denounced MacCarthy by saying that 'in my years of teaching I found only one *ology* effective with the young; that was *stickology*, NOT *psychology*' (emphasis in original).[117] Another correspondent, P. O'Reilly, commented that 'through original sin children are naturally vicious little savages, and it needs a rigorous discipline with fear as a wholesome deterrent to mould them into decent citizens'.[118] When another correspondent replied to O'Reilly's letter, saying that it demonstrated Ireland's 'singular capacity for the production of a particularly disgusting type of prig',[119] O'Reilly gave a robust response: '*We in Eire are the salt of the earth*, the last bulwark of Christianity, and if we are severe enough on law-breakers, young and old, it is because we still retain a clear perception of right and wrong, of black and white'.[120] The correspondence on this issue stopped in mid-October, around the time another leading Irish newspaper published an editorial, using similar language to that used in the Dáil, accusing Flanagan of making comments that were 'reckless and so far removed from the truth that nobody in this country is likely to pay much attention to them'.[121] One of the last letters published in the *Irish Times* on this subject, on 19 October, was sent by Flanagan himself, in which he wrote:

The integrity of the individual is sacred. Christian charity requires this integrity be respected, even in the penal institution. Desire for revenge expressed in cruel and thoughtless physical punishment is blind to the demands of Christian charity and justice.

Flogging and other forms of physical punishment wound that sense of dignity which attaches to the self. The result of such negative treatment is that the boy comes to look upon society as his enemy. His urge is to fight back, not to reform.

The child is not born bad. It is not born to be bad. The boy who makes mistakes is a spiritually sick boy. He is the victim of bad environment, bad training, bad example. In short, he is a product of neglect.[122]

Despite the media coverage given to Flanagan's criticism of residential childcare in Ireland, these criticisms had no effect on conditions within the residential schools and failed to create a significant public demand for reform. In a public statement in October 1946, Flanagan said that 'the good people of Ireland can be trusted to do what Christian charity demands if they know the facts. The problem is to get the facts before them.'[123] A few months later, though, Flanagan lamented that 'I don't seem to be able to understand the psychology of the Irish mind', and wrote privately to friends about the culture of fear in which people in Ireland held back from saying things critical of the government.[124] He nevertheless intended to continue his campaign, planning to visit a wide range of penal institutions in Ireland in the summer of 1948, but died of a heart attack in May 1948 while on a trip to Berlin as part of planning for post-reconstruction childcare.

By articulating a notion of the sacrality of the care of children, embedded in his own institutional practices at Boys Town, Edward Flanagan sought and failed to bring change to childcare practices embedded in the sacrality of the Irish Catholic nation. Those opposing Flanagan in the Irish political classes did not do so by explicitly rejecting his vision of the sacrality of the care of children, but acted in ways that sought to minimize the likelihood that emotional and moral identification with that sacred form would challenge existing structures and practices, thus maintaining the dominant sacred form of the Irish Catholic nation.

This case illustrates four dimensions of social and cultural life that make hierarchical relations between a dominant sacred form and a subjugated sacred form possible. First, such hierarchies are reproduced or changed through the historically contingent events of individual and group biographies. The fact that Flanagan died before making a return visit to Ireland meant, for example, that the possibility of building a stronger movement in support of his views never materialized, and criticisms of the industrial school lacked a focal, public figure to articulate them.

Second, hierarchies become possible or unstable in relation to the social spaces and structures through which public meaning construction and decision-making take place. The ability of social agents to maintain or challenge such hierarchies depends both on the nature of those spaces and structures, and the kind of access that different social agents have to them. In Flanagan's case, while he had access to media coverage as a public figure, he was essentially an outsider to the social and political system of Irish society. He was able to control the public spaces offered by his radio broadcasts and public lectures, but had no influence within the key social institutions of the state or the Church, which had the power to bring change in the residential care system. No media institution was prepared to act as a clear advocate for his views either. No newspaper editorials were written in support of him, and no daily newspaper was prepared to report details of the case of Gerard Fogarty,[125] of which Flanagan was fully aware. As a consequence, Flanagan had no access to an institutional structure or public space in Ireland that would enable him to maintain a sustained critique of the residential schools. By contrast, his detractors had control of key social institutions, which meant that they could both seek to discredit his criticisms, and maintain the symbolic status quo of the Irish Catholic nation.

Third, hierarchies of sacred forms are related to who holds power in a given context, as well as to the nature of that power. Flanagan's celebrity status gave him a form of power as a public figure able to articulate a particular critical narrative about Irish society. But this power was a symbolic power—the power to put meanings and narratives into the public realm. By contrast, Flanagan's critics in the government and the Church had not only the symbolic power of being able to produce narratives for public consumption, but allocative and regulative power to make decisions about the use of resources and the regulatory framework of social practices. Without access to allocative and regulative power, or social spaces and structures that enable effective challenges to be made against such power, it is difficult for advocates of subjugated sacred forms to produce social change.

Finally, hierarchies of sacred forms are also made possible by the cultural logics of sacred forms as these operate in particular contexts. These logics include *the cultural mechanisms by which a dominant sacred form is reproduced*: for example, Catholic piety remained widespread in 1940s Ireland, which meant that the notion of the Irish Catholic nation remained embedded in everyday spaces and practices. They also include *the social and cultural role that particular sacred forms perform in a given context*. The project of Irish nation-building was still in its early stages in the 1940s, which meant that the sacred form of the Irish Catholic nation was still performing important work as a source of collective identification and morality. Another element of these logics is *the ways in which the reception of cultural meanings is shaped by the content of dominant sacred meanings*. The sacred form of the Irish Catholic nation was so closely bound to the legitimation of the practices of both the state and the religious orders that to present a strong moral challenge against those practices was to impute the sanctity of the nation itself. Flanagan addressed this directly by making clear his view that the conditions in penal institutions in Ireland should indeed be regarded as a shame and disgrace to a 'Christian Catholic people'. But to challenge practices and institutions associated with a dominant sacred form through inviting people to experience collective shame is always difficult. Given the human propensity to avoid experiences of shame, this move is rarely possible unless people's identification with a dominant sacred form is already weakening, people are able to identify others who can be blamed as the source of shame, or people become drawn to another sacred form that begins to displace the dominant one and become an alternative source of remoralization. The context of Flanagan's intervention was such that, while some of his audience were clearly ready to experience conditions in the residential schools as shameful, this was not sufficiently widespread to produce a sustained protest movement. Instead, commitment to the sacrality of the Irish Catholic nation meant that it was possible either to reject Flanagan's views as a failure to see the true nature of children under original sin as 'vicious little savages', or simply to say that Flanagan's comments implied such profound moral failings in institutions at the heart of the Catholic nation that they could not possibly be true.

In summary, a hierarchy of sacred forms is made more likely when there is no clear social structure or space through which widespread identification with a subjugated sacred form is possible; when power is held and deployed in ways that maintain a dominant sacred form; and when the logics of cultural meanings are such that a dominant form is widely reproduced and performs important work and challenges to that dominant form are experienced as too threatening to social and moral order to be given credence. As Jeffrey Alexander has argued, for an effective challenge to be made to the content or use of a dominant sacred form, it is usually necessary to mobilize a social movement to effect that change. Where such social movements struggle because of a lack of institutional resources or power, or because of difficulties in finding a sympathetic audience for their narrative, the prospects of bringing change in relation to dominant sacred forms are poor.

This does not mean that the subjugated sacred form is necessarily obliterated or removed from the repertoire of available cultural meanings in a given social context. Sentimentalized images of happy, healthy children circulated throughout Irish society, from NSPCC reports to the rhetoric of leading politicians like Eamon de Valera. But it does mean that the subjugated form lacks the capacity or moral and emotional force to dislodge commitments, practices, and ways of seeing, organized around the dominant sacred form. However, the subjugated form—if not cast as a profane source of pollution—can also remain a latent presence and potentially be animated as a strong focus for moral and emotional identification at a later point in time. Such proved to be the case for the sacrality of the care of children in Irish society.

Shifting hierarchies of the sacred: Cultural change in Ireland from the 1960s

So how was it, then, that the hierarchical relationship changed between the dominant sacred form of the Irish Catholic nation and the subjugated form of the sacrality of the care of children? It was only through the 1990s that a significant shift in public opinion took place in which the moral authority of the Irish Catholic nation, and its institutional elites, came under serious challenge, as concern grew about the abuse of children. In the late 1980s, one Irish publisher considered Paddy Doyle's biographical account of his childhood experiences of life in the industrial school system 'brilliant but too risky to be published'. Similarly when, in 1990, a local newspaper began to publish allegations of sexual abuse against a priest in the Ferns diocese, a public protest was mounted against the paper for daring to make such allegations, and copies of the paper were burnt by protestors in the street.[126]

Although the decisive shift took place in the 1990s, the groundwork for this had been laid in preceding decades. The growing unease of some of those in the judicial system to commit children to industrial schools from the 1950s onwards reflected a sense, voiced by others in Irish society, that the residential system was not in the best interests of the child. The very notion that the child could have interests separate from its symbolic positioning within the Irish Catholic nation hinted at a shift in a horizon of meaning in which the care of the child could be seen as raising its own moral demands. A number of other institutional and cultural changes took place in the 1960s that both weakened people's uncritical identification with the Irish Catholic nation and created the potential for more powerful identification with the care of children as a sacred form.

One of the significant cultural shifts to begin in the 1960s was the public discussion of sex. Notions of the 1960s as a decisive sexual revolution tend to neglect the fact that changes starting in the 1960s (for example, in relation to the use of the contraceptive pill) became more widespread only in later decades.[127] Nevertheless, the greater willingness to talk openly about sexual desire and experiences in Britain and America also began to find its counterpart in Ireland. This stimulated renewed attempts to reinforce traditional Catholic teaching, albeit through new media forms such as Ireland's leading agony aunt column, which advocated abstinence before marriage, or books and pamphlets written to convey Catholic sexual teaching in language that young people would understand.[128] At the same time, however, discussions of sex found their way into the public domain without being filtered through this Catholic hegemony (partly as a result of revisions made to the Censorship of Publications Act in 1967[129]). Lee Dunne's autobiographical account of his life as a Dublin teenager, published in 1965, spoke openly about his emerging sexual experiences in ways that challenged notions of Ireland as a morally pure society:

Apart from the scruff from the slums, our girls are all virgins until they go to their wedding beds. They believe in the Commandments of God and they listen to their priests. Maybe they do, but in the privacy of the cinema with only a thousand people in it they forget exactly what it was the priest has said and they remember only that they want to touch and be touched and to get as much out of it as they can.[130]

Although the film version of Dunne's book was banned in Ireland in 1970 (and only subsequently released in 2006), the book itself and a successful stage play based on it marked a new public willingness to talk openly about the realities of sex. At the same time, while advertisements for contraceptives were still banned (and even an advert for a device to facilitate the rhythm method was controversial within the Church[131]), growing numbers of women began to use the contraceptive pill under prescription, and the medical profession made it clear that its role was to treat its patients according to the patients' consciences with regard to birth control and not to be guardians of Catholic sexual ethics.[132] By the time that traditional Catholic teaching on sexuality and birth control was reiterated in the papal encyclical *Humanae Vitae* in 1968, a growing number of adults in Ireland recognized that this was out of touch with the realities of their lives.[133] The first family planning clinic in Ireland subsequently opened in Dublin in February 1969. The gap between orthodoxy and reality was demonstrated more starkly in the 1990s, as media exposés began to reveal details of high-profile Catholic clergy who had themselves had long-standing sexual relations and fathered children.[134]

Three other related developments should be noted here. First, more open discussion of sex and other social taboos was becoming possible in a changing media landscape. An important development in this regard was the creation of Ireland's first television channel. RTE had been broadcasting radio programmes in Ireland since 1926 and made its first television transmission on 31 December 1961.[135] The 1960 Broadcasting Act, which established the regulatory framework for this new venture, stated that, when a broadcast was made that provided 'any information, news or feature which relates to matters of public controversy or is the subject of current public debate, the information, news or feature is to be presented objectively and impartially'.[136] In practice, this gave RTE producers freedom to produce content contrary to the views of both the government and the Church. Although both senior clergy and government ministers subsequently expressed their disapproval with some of the content of RTE television, formal government influence over its editorial policy was limited to the extreme measure of dissolving the entire Broadcasting Authority if it seriously breached its remit (something that only ever happened once, in 1972, in relation to RTE coverage of paramilitary groups in Ulster[137]). In addition to this relative editorial freedom, the costs of programme production meant that RTE television had to rely largely on American imports for its drama and entertainment, with home-produced programmes focusing on current affairs. Over time, this current-affairs output engaged with more controversial issues, not least as a way of holding audience attention in the face of greater competition from television channels in Britain and Northern Ireland.[138] Most of RTE's television producers in the 1960s had established their professional experience outside Ireland, and tended to have socially liberal views and lifestyles.[139] The new channel also provided opportunities for an emerging generation of producers and presenters who were more willing to challenge older certainties of the Irish Catholic nation. Notable among these was Gay Byrne, the presenter of the chat show *The Late Late Show*, a programme whose live format and controversial treatment of issues such as sex and politics attracted a growing public audience.[140] While the content of RTE broadcasts may not have mocked the establishment as systematically as the new breed of satire being produced in British television, they did create a new atmosphere of debate.[141] The development of media spaces and practices that allowed critique of institutional power continued in subsequent decades, with investigative journalism demonstrating its power to effect political change, and the growing phenomenon of newspaper opinion pieces allowing direct criticism of institutional authority. The later emergence of the Internet allowed greater circulation of views and information, exemplified in the growing number of blogs written by survivors of the residential care system.[142]

Secondly, this more critical cultural environment was also nurtured by the significant expansion of Irish education from the 1960s onwards. It was only in the 1960s that secondary-level education was made freely available to all children in Ireland. This was followed, in 1967, by the introduction of a state grant system to enable people to attend university. Through the expansion of education, more children and young people were trained into practices of critical and autonomous thinking, which subverted more traditional practices of deference to the structures of the Irish Catholic nation. Thirdly, as in Britain, the changes of the 1960s led to the emergence of the women's movement in Ireland during the 1970s, which developed public campaigns on issues including domestic violence and rape. The first women's refuge was opened in 1974, and the Dublin Rape Crisis Centre in 1979. These new structures created space for the disclosure of experiences that were not openly discussed at the time, and the Rape Crisis Centre in particular received growing numbers of accounts of sexual abuse of men and women in Catholic institutions.[143]

While these changes in Irish society reflected similar developments in Britain, another significant shift in identification with the sacred form of the Irish Catholic nation happened as a result of the wider economic and political context of the Irish State. Recognizing the economic benefits of membership, Ireland formally applied to join the European Economic Community in 1962. As part of the process of assessing this application, Ireland was required to undergo an audit of its democratic structures, including its public education system, by the OECD. The OECD report on the Irish education system was published in 1965, with a series of 'confrontation meetings' held between the review team and senior civil servants over the following year. The review process made clear that the industrial school system was not suitable for a modern, European nation in which there should be educational opportunity for all and in which children should be educated to engage with the wider community of Europe (for example, through the teaching of continental languages). Moreover, the defensiveness, and at times dishonesty, of evidence from staff at the Department of Education reflected their awareness that the industrial school system, as it ran in practice, was not something of which they could be proud.[144] Less than three months after the final confrontation meeting with the OECD team, the Department of Education announced the setting-up of the Kennedy Commission into Industrial Schools and Reformatories. The Commission's subsequent report failed to disclose the extent of neglect, or physical or sexual abuse, in the residential schools, but did state that the ethos, quality of staffing, and physical environment of the schools were unsuitable for a satisfactory educational environment. It recommended that residential care for children be used only as a last resort and that residential schools should be abolished and replaced by smaller group homes that could provide an environment closer to that of a family.[145]

Significant changes were brought about, not only by the new forms of scrutiny of Irish society required by involvement in European structures, but by a new sense of the Irish nation that such involvement encouraged. Since its membership of the EEC was finally approved in 1973, Ireland has received more than 17 billion euros in structural and social cohesion funding, with a succession of funding initiatives since 1989 seeking to raise the standards of Irish infrastructure and standards of living to EU standards.[146] Together with neo-liberal economic policies, this led to rapid economic growth in Ireland from the mid-1990s, which came to an abrupt end in 2008. One of the consequences of this period of growth was that a well-educated cohort of young Irish adults who had emigrated in the poor economic conditions of the 1980s returned to work in Ireland in the 1990s, having had experience of a range of different societies. This fed, more generally, into an emerging sense of Irish cosmopolitanism, of Ireland as a modern, culturally and economically vibrant country, no longer defined in relation to the history of British colonialism. While this sense of cosmopolitanism may have been particularly concentrated in the major urban areas and the younger age groups, it nevertheless brought about a fundamental shift in the way in which the Irish nation was conceived by a growing proportion of its population.[147]

If we bear in mind the significance of structure, power, and the logics of cultural meanings for maintaining hierarchies of sacred forms, it is possible to see how these changes in post-1960s Ireland created conditions in which the hierarchy of the Irish Catholic nation over the sacrality of the care of children was weakened and ultimately overturned. In this period, a new range of structures emerged that created spaces and resources for challenging the dominant Catholic hegemony, including new media outlets and practices, the expanding education system, and the women's movement. In addition to this, engagement with transnational structures (such as the OECD and the EU) encouraged both greater self-scrutiny of Irish society, as well as new ways of conceptualizing the Irish nation. The locus of power also shifted through these processes. The expansion of media meant that media professionals acquired greater symbolic power in putting narratives and cultural meanings into the public realm and were more prepared to use this power to critique institutional authority. The rise of the

Internet also created a context in which people could put views and narratives into the public domain without needing the support of formal media organizations. Alongside this, while politicians and religious leaders retained allocative and regulative power, this power was increasingly subject to the scrutiny of relatively autonomous media institutions, which could place considerable public pressure on those whose behaviour could be cast as hypocritical, scandalous, or in breach of sacred commitments. The autonomous power of the Irish political classes was also curtailed with the new obligations associated with the economically lucrative membership of the European Union. Furthermore, these social and political changes were also bound up with changes in the logics of how the sacred form of the Irish Catholic nation operated. The extension of practices of debate and critical thinking through the media and educational system meant that deferential adherence to the demands of the Irish Catholic nation became increasingly alien to many people. With the emergence of a new, European, and cosmopolitan vision of the Irish nation, the cultural role of the vision of the Irish Catholic nation defined in opposition to British colonialism significantly diminished. And, as the vision of the Irish Catholic nation became less culturally useful, so it became less threatening to imagine that challenging that sacred form would constitute a fundamental risk to social and moral order.

As the emotionally conflicted letters of Brother René demonstrate, there was always potential for identification with the sacrality of the care of children in the earlier decades of twentieth-century Ireland. But, as the case of Edward Flanagan also shows, this identification never became powerful enough to challenge the residential school system because its advocates lacked structural resources and power, and it could exist in a subjugated and sentimentalized form only under dominance of the sacred form of the Irish Catholic nation. It was only with the social and cultural conditions associated with the end of the 'long nineteenth century' in Irish society from the 1960s onwards that identification with the Irish Catholic nation could begin to weaken significantly, and only in the further radical changes of the 1990s that its hegemony became seriously under threat. In the cultural space left by the weakening of the sacred form of the Irish Catholic nation, the growing public testimonies of survivors of the residential school system could begin to form a new focus for moral and emotional identification, and the sacrality of the care of children could be emphasized such that no Irish institution could again be exempted from its demands. Sean Moylan's reassurances about the soundness of the residential school system could not contrast more clearly with the concluding comments of the Murphy report on sexual abuse in the Catholic Archdiocese of Dublin, published shortly after the Ryan Commission report in 2009:

> The Commission has no doubt that the clerical sexual abuse scandal was covered up by the Archdiocese of Dublin and other Church authorities over much of the period covered by the Commission's remit. The structures and rules of the Catholic Church facilitated that cover-up...The welfare of children, which should have been the first priority, was not even a factor to be considered in the early stages. Instead the focus was on the avoidance of scandal and the preservation of the good name, status and assets of the institution and of what the institution regarded as its most important members—the priests. In the mid 1990s, a light began to be shone on the scandal and the cover up. Gradually, the story has unfolded. It is the responsibility of the State to ensure that no similar institutional immunity is ever allowed to occur again.[148]

There are, of course, no straightforwardly happy endings, and the public scandal of the residential school system in Ireland has become entangled in controversy over the process of redress, and allegations of profiteering by organizations keen to get a commission from survivors' compensation packages. But this case demonstrates not only that sacred forms have the potential both to legitimate and to challenge practices that blight human lives, but that the relative power of sacred forms is also subject to the choices of human agents, and the ever-changing social, cultural, and political contexts in which they live.

4

The Mediatization of the Sacred: The BBC, Gaza, and the DEC Appeal

> I have never been more appalled by the human race than I am at BBC's decision. Gutlessness reaches new lows. Mark Thompson, make all the mealy mouthed platitudes you like, but the whole world knows you for what you are... You were so quick to condemn Jonathan Ross for a rude comment, but when hundreds are dead, injured and maimed by phosphorus bombs, then you sit on the fence. You hero! Shame on you, shame on you, shame on you! You gutless gutless man.
>
> (Post on the BBC Editors' blog in response to Mark Thompson's explanation for why the BBC would not be broadcasting an humanitarian appeal for Gaza, 24 January 2009)

All sacred forms are mediated. The interaction of symbol, thought, feeling, and action that characterizes sacred forms is possible only through media that give sacred forms material expression. Media enable communication about, and interaction with, those forms. Such media include images, sounds and material objects, spaces, institutional practices, and even the bodies of those who are taken, in some way, to embody or exemplify the sacred.[1] Sacred meanings are not, therefore, free-floating signifiers but materially mediated. Identification with sacred forms is not simply an intellectual assent to the content of that form, but an embodied, affective, and aesthetic engagement with its mediation.

There is considerable scope for developing our understanding of the material mediation of sacred forms in general.[2] However, in this chapter, attention will focus on the significance of 'media' in the narrow sense of public media. By public media, I mean regional, national, and transnational communication across a range of platforms (that is, print media, radio, television, the Internet, and mobile technologies) that seek to address public audiences for profit or as part of a public service remit, and whose outputs are publicly available. Within this I therefore include major global media corporations such as News Corporation and Time–Warner–AOL, public broadcasters with a primarily national remit such as the BBC in the United Kingdom or PBS in the United States, and niche media producers who are aimed at particular social groups (for example, specific religious audiences) but whose outputs are nevertheless widely available through mainstream or niche distribution outlets. Such media can also be thought of as public in the sense that their outputs implicitly or explicitly construct 'publics', as their imagined audience delineated on grounds of location (for example, a regional or national audience), ideology, or taste.[3] Alongside this definition, the boundaries between public and social media are becoming increasingly blurred. YouTube has become both a site for sharing personal images between friends and a site for being able to engage with a wide range of public media outputs or create one's own set of images for public consumption.[4] Personal images on YouTube can also unintentionally acquire the status of public media phenomena.[5] The practice of sharing links to other Web pages from one's Facebook profile means that that profile may be a means of sharing not simply personal information with one's online social network, but also information and responses to current news events. Similarly, blogs may function as a kind of personalized diary, but are nevertheless generally constructed with a public audience in mind and become another means for the circulation of other public media products. The expanding technological capabilities of new mobile communication devices (such as the i-Phone) enable them to function as social media tools that have become increasingly bound up with the circulation of a wider range of public media. Digital social media are therefore becoming inextricably linked with public media as defined above.

This chapter will initially present a broad argument about the role of public media in relation to the sacred in late modern societies. It will then examine some of the implications of this role for public broadcasters through a more detailed examination of the case of the decision by the BBC not to broadcast a humanitarian appeal relating to Gaza during Israel's military action in the Gaza strip in January 2009. This chapter will demonstrate that, while public media play a vital role in relation to the sacred in contemporary society, this role is not one of acting as an unproblematic structure for ritual re-enactments of the sacred that draw together broad populations (for example, national communities),[6] but of representing the sacred in ways that generate fragmented, overlapping, and often transient forms of collective identification that may perpetuate social conflict as much as integration.

Public media and sacred forms

There is already considerable interest in cultural sociology and media studies about the ways in which public media circulate sacred meanings and make collective sacred experience possible. An important stimulus for this work has been Daniel Dayan and Elihu Katz's widely discussed book *Media Events: The Live Broadcasting of History*, which sought to define a particular media genre that drew audiences into a shared experience in relation to significant cultural meanings.[7] The critical discussion, and subsequent revision, of their ideas have provided an important focus for thinking about the extent to which public media can offer a particular kind of sacred ritual, binding its audience into shared sentiments and responses. Alongside this, there has been a wider literature on media anthropology that has sought to interpret media use in terms of well-established anthropological areas of interest such as symbol, ritual, and myth.[8] Alongside this, Nick Couldry has given a critical account of media rituals that construct public media as offering direct access to the heart of social reality, and in doing so give public media undue symbolic power.[9] The cultural functions of public media have also been discussed by scholars associated with the 'strong programme' of cultural sociology. Here civil society has been defined as a communicative arena in which the symbolic construction of who falls within and beyond the acceptable boundaries of society is continually negotiated and contested. Jeffrey Alexander and Ron Jacobs have explored the ways in which public media are implicated in these processes, including the ways in which niche public media are developed to circulate cultural meanings that are commonly excluded from dominant media outlets.[10] In an early cultural sociological case study of the Watergate crisis, Alexander also discussed the way in which public media could become a 'counter-centre' of the sacred, providing a structure for critique of other key social institutions that had fallen short of their sacred responsibilities.[11]

Drawing on, and extending, this body of work, I wish to make the following claims about the role of public media in relation to sacred forms:

1. In late modern societies, public media are the primary institutional structure through which forms of the sacred are experienced, reproduced and contested.[12] The sacred is reproduced through public media as much by representations of its pollution or breach as by its direct celebration. Public media also act as a primary social

structure through which restitution of the pollution of a particular sacred form is made possible.

2. Through engaging with public media, audiences recursively reproduce sacred forms, bound up with particular ways of thinking, feeling, and acting. Audience members may also regard performances of the sacred through public media with varying degrees of cynicism or disinterest that disrupt the possibility of identification with them.

3. In late modernity, these processes take place in stratified, conflictual societies in which diverse sacred forms are represented and reproduced across an increasingly segmented public media. The representation of particular sacred forms may also be deeply contentious, evoking sympathetic identification or hostility from different audiences,[13] and the media representation of the sacred may therefore evoke conflict and social division, as well as social integration.

4. These processes are shaped by actors who may seek the construction of the sacred through public media for particular social, political, and economic ends,[14] the affordances of historically contingent media industries, technologies, and policies and wider social and political structures.[15] But sacred forms also shape media practice—for example, informing 'news values' of what journalists consider to be newsworthy stories or their criteria for judging the credibility and acceptability of their sources.[16] Journalists' success in constructing narratives that enable widespread identification with sacred forms can also contribute to their status as cultural authorities.[17]

5. While entertainment media (including celebrity culture) offer subject positions for ways of being in the world, and may illustrate particular contemporary value conflicts, the sacred is typically experienced, reproduced, and contested through public media that represent 'actual' events—namely, news media, documentaries, and, in some instances, reality television and chat shows.[18] Entertainment media may evoke the sacred in instances where a narrative presented in an entertainment format 'is based on actual events', or seeks to focus thought and sentiment on historical events that lie behind the narrative.[19]

No great originality can be claimed for many of these observations. As noted above, there has already been substantial exploration of the role of public media in providing moments of focal, sacred experience in the light of Dayan and Katz's theory of 'media events', as well as discussions of ways in which media representation of the sacred is implicated in processes of shaming[20] and restitution.[21] Following Dayan and Katz's earlier assertion of the role of media in integrating broad (for example, national) populations around the performance of shared sacred forms, there has been greater recognition of the disenchantment and cynicism with which audiences may regard attempts to represent the sacred through media,[22] as well as the ways in which the representation of the sacred through media can clarify and perpetuate, rather than overcome, social conflict.[23] Indeed, media events that fix public attention may now less commonly be the ceremonies, contests, and conquests that Dayan and Katz originally imagined drew together broad public audiences (such as the funeral of JFK or the royal wedding of Charles and Diana) than conflicts that dramatize opposing sacred commitments across society (for example, 9/11) or those that evoke disenchantment (for example, Martin Bashir's interview with Princess Diana).[24] This recognition has, in turn, been influenced by wider sociological critiques of the assumption that the representation of the sacred necessarily produces social integration, and that instead point to the role of representations of the sacred in the 'mobilization of bias' in fragmented, stratified, and conflictual societies.[25] Dayan and Katz have, themselves, come to accept much of this critique.

This critique need not lead to a wholesale abandonment of the idea that the audience reception of the sacred through public media can generate 'moral communities' gathered around that sacred form. Johanna Sumiala and Matteo Stocchetti, for example, write of both the formation of 'mediated communities' and a 'post-modern communio sanctorum' in response to the representation of sacred forms through public media.[26] Mervi Pantti and Liesbet van Zoonen have similarly observed the importance of such communities formed around common foci of collective sacred sentiment as a social and political force in late modern societies. Even in Steven Lukes's influential critique of neo-Durkheimian approaches that assume the capacity of sacred ritual to integrate whole societies, Lukes still acknowledged that groups did form around public performances of the sacred, albeit at the level of overlapping and conflicting groups within a wider society.[27] But caution should be taken in assuming that the representation of the sacred through public media *necessarily* leads to widespread, common sentiment.[28] As a series of case studies of public mourning rituals through the media by Johanna Sumiala and Mervi Pantti demonstrate, communities formed around media performances of the sacred are often transient, and it is difficult to determine the extent and boundaries of such collective identification and sentiment. The impression that public media are able to generate widespread communities of shared sacred sentiment is one that is generated by the media itself, reflecting wider conventions that construct the media as giving access to 'reality' and the sacred centre of society.[29]

The claims made above therefore offer a critical understanding of the sacred role of public media. While they largely reflect ideas developed within existing debates on media, ritual, and the sacred, this formulation of them also draws attention to two points that are not always given sufficient emphasis. First, the representation and contestation of the sacred in and through public media takes place primarily in relation to actual, historical events.[30] In the context of the growing literature on media, religion, and culture, much attention has been given to the ways in which religious symbols and discourses are produced and consumed in the context of entertainment media, including film, television, popular music, and video games. The representation, circulation, and reception of the 'religious' and the 'spiritual' through entertainment media are without doubt an important resource of discourses, stories, and images through which people construct their understandings of religion. They may even serve, at times, as a useful guide to changing social attitudes towards religion and the supernatural. Fans can also form significant emotional and imaginative identifications with particular entertainment shows or artists, through which, at times, broader issues of meaning and the nature of the good life may be explored.[31] But the sacred is most commonly experienced in relation to the embodied experiences of real people, whether the death of public figures, forms of suffering that represent a breach of the sacred and that may evoke previous experiences of cultural trauma,[32] or acts that symbolize or celebrate a particular sacred form. Although the mediation of such real sacred dramas may mean that we never get to the experience itself, the postmodern blurring of fiction and fact is not an adequate understanding of how people understand their engagement with the sacred. It is through the representation of concrete experiences of devotion, suffering, love, and sacrifice that sacred forms are made manifest in social life. The construction of particular experiences, for example, as sacrifice, involves the application of particular interpretative frames to particular events. The reference point of those frames, however, remains lived experience. The genocidal killing of six million Jews in the Holocaust, or a million Rwandans, simply matters much more as the destruction of historical lives than the fictionalized representation of genocidal violence in *Star Wars* or *Lord of the Rings*. If we wish to attend to the representation and reproduction of the sacred through public media, it is more useful to focus on media narratives that address 'real' experiences on which sacred realities have a bearing than on fictionalized entertainment.[33]

Second, the sacred role of public media can be understood within a wider debate about the mediatization of society. While the term 'mediatization' has been used with a range of different meanings within media studies,[34] my use is particularly informed by the work of Stig Hjarvard.[35] Hjarvard's theory of mediatization is structured around two key claims. One is that, in late modern society, a growing range of social institutions and practices is performed through the institutional structure of increasingly autonomous, deregulated, and commercialized media. The other is that, as public awareness and engagement with these social forms become more dependent on the media, so the nature of this awareness and engagement is increasingly shaped by particular 'logics' of those media.

It is reasonable to argue that public media have become the primary structure for engaging with the sacred.[36] Media technologies and products saturate everyday life, with considerable amounts of time invested in their use. In 2010, in both the United States and the United Kingdom, around 99 per cent of households had at least one television set,[37] and more than 62 per cent of households in the United States and 71 per cent of households in the United Kingdom had some form of Internet access, with access increasingly available through various public spaces.[38] The amount of media exposure within the wider population is also substantial, with adults in the United Kingdom watching an average of 24–30 hours of television per week in 2009.[39] Much of this media use is for a range of mundane activities and entertainments, but the pervasiveness of public media inevitably gives them a central role in providing representations of social worlds,[40] including those elements taken to be sacred. Although media segmentation means that individual news outlets typically achieve smaller audiences than in previous decades, and circulation figures for national newspapers continue to decline, digital media have become increasingly important as news sources. These include not only websites of broadcasters and newspapers (use of which, by the late 2000s, eclipsed newspaper sales[41]), but the embedding of news content onto a much wider range of websites, including search engines like Yahoo and personal blogs.[42] The range of print, broadcast, and digital media therefore provides a complex, often intersecting network through which society tells stories about itself, and reference to sacred forms is common. Although other social institutions may have important roles in mediating sacred forms for particular social groups (for example, educational institutions for children and young people), this network of public media structures has the greatest reach across society.

Events that acquire sacred significance through public media become a focus for public discussion and action to a greater degree than events given sacred significance through any other contemporary institutional structure. The performance of sacred drama through other institutional structures, such as the criminal justice system, are dependent on media for communicating their sacred symbolism to a wider public audience. Public reaction to celebrations or breaches of the sacred are also fed back for public consumption through the media, continuing the media circulation of sacred forms.

Public media have also acquired a specific cultural role in relation to public engagement with the sacred, as 'counter-centres' through which breaches of the sacred in other institutional contexts can be critiqued and some form of restitution offered. The example of the cultural and political significance of the *States of Fear* documentaries in Ireland in the previous chapter is a good example of this. In this role, public media can be institutionally invisible, purporting to be a neutral means for critiquing the breach of sacred forms. The case of the BBC and the Disasters Emergency Committee (DEC) appeal for Gaza to be discussed later in this chapter represents an occasion in which a public broadcaster becomes implicated in a breach of the sacred, and thus becomes more visible as an institutional actor in the struggle over sacred forms. As media become increasingly important in the construction of public meaning, though, we might reasonably expect such conflicts to become more common.

Public media have also become a primary site for engaging the sacred because of the extent of their reach across public and private spheres. The representation of the sacred through media has transformed domestic spaces into sites for direct encounter with sacred forms (exemplified by watching a news broadcast in one's living room).[43] As domestic life becomes an arena for engaging the sacred through media, it becomes an important resource for stimulating public action. What is happening offline is similarly replicated through new social media, as digital technology ostensibly designed for personal communication becomes an important site for engaging sacred forms through sharing news, giving personal responses to public events, or even participating in social action relating to sacred forms.

The key role of media for public engagement with the sacred reflects Hjarvard's argument about the increasingly influential role of public media in late modern society. However, his claim that aspects of social life become increasingly shaped by media logics is a less convincing basis for thinking about the mediation of the sacred. There is no doubt that, as the media have become the primary site for public engagement with the sacred, so this potentially increases the influence of the practices of media professionals or the effects of particular media institutions, genres, and technologies. As Mervi Pantti and Johanna Sumiala have argued in the context of media representation of public mourning rituals, media professionals have growing power to frame focal, sacred events in particular ways (for example, emphasizing personal expressions of collective grief rather than addressing wider structural questions, or social inclusion rather than conflict).[44] Similarly the dispersal and immediacy of digital media technologies make it possible for influential images of sacred events to be transmitted quickly to a wide audience through a range of media platforms, thus potentially increasing the degree to which they are able quickly to elicit collective responses from their audience, which in turn become the subject of further media coverage.[45] Wider developments within media industries can also be understood as a potentially significant influence. The 'tabloidization' of media,[46] associated with the attempt to hold popular audiences in increasingly competitive media marketplaces through media content that emphasizes human interest stories with a strong emotional content has created a stylistic and economic framework within which narratives of outrage about the breach of the sacred are constructed. Media professionals' decisions about the representation of sacred forms through tabloid (and other competitive) media are therefore made in the context of the need to sell media products, generating suspicion that the construction of outrage at the pollution of the sacred can be a process of creating synthetic emotion for the purposes of commercial profit.[47] Another kind of influence can be found in the regulatory frameworks and technological developments that have made media segmentation possible, as well as attractive in the context of competitive media markets. Such segmentation has, for example, led to the development of broadcasters such as Fox News and MSNBC in the United States, which produce media outputs focused around the sacred commitments of a particular partisan group.

But this pattern of influence is not straightforwardly exerted from media institutions upon their audiences. As Lynn Schofield Clark has argued, it is more accurate to think about media agency as flowing through webs of mutually influencing relationships between media producers, media technologies, audiences, and other social structures.[48] Schofield Clark advocates the concept of 'media affordances' over 'media logics', focusing on what particular media practices, structures, and technologies make possible rather than assuming that media exert a linear influence that shapes social life in predictable ways. Schofield Clark's point is well illustrated by Sumiala and Stocchetti's case study of the way in which public media in Sweden and Finland played a focal role in the construction of a communio sanctorum in the wake of the murder of the Swedish Foreign Minister, Anna Lindh, in 2003. This event drew deeply felt responses among large sections of the Swedish and Finnish public, not only in terms of shared grief at the death of an individual politician and mother but also in terms of identification with the sacred form of a modern, open, egalitarian, and democratic Nordic society symbolically threatened by the murder of a popular figure in a public space. As Sumiala and Stocchetti demonstrate, while public media acted as a primary social structure through which a sense of this shared communio sanctorum was constructed, this was an effect not simply of media agency but of an interplay of actions between the media and members of the public. The decision by members of the public to gather at symbolically important spaces (such as the department store where Lindh was murdered), bringing candles and flowers to lay beside pictures of Lindh, preceded media coverage of these actions. But, by representing these public acts of mourning, the media then played a focal role in the public construction of a mourning community, in which the act of bringing candles and flowers to symbolically significant spaces became authorized as a legitimate expression of identification with this community.[49]

If late modern society is characterized by the mediatization of the sacred, when and how did this happen, and to what extent is it a genuinely contemporary phenomenon? As noted at the start of this chapter, sacred forms have always been mediated, whether through images, sounds, stories, institutional practices and rituals, or embodied sensations. But the more specific sense of the mediatization of the sacred—the way in which public media have become the primary institutional structure for experiencing and reproducing sacred forms—is a modern phenomenon, albeit one that has emerged with the rise of a succession of new media over more than two centuries. Benedict Anderson's influential study of imagined national communities demonstrated how, by the start of the nineteenth century, mass print media provided a structure through which particular kinds of social imaginary could emerge beyond the waning influence of the symbolism offered by the Christian Church. The potential of mass media to present sacred forms was further demonstrated in the twentieth century by the use of print media and the newer electronic media of radio and film by totalitarian regimes, leading to concerns about the role of public media as a propaganda tool for shaping mass psychology. The contemporary phenomenon of encountering sacred forms through public media—whether in the television images of the attacks on the Twin Towers or the newspaper coverage of a convicted paedophile—is not, then, wholly new. Ever since the rise of mass media began to create possibilities for new kinds of social communication, and thus social identification and imagination, public media have always been a means for engaging with sacred forms. The extent of the mediatization of the sacred has, however, arguably increased during the twentieth century. This is due to a number of interrelated factors: the growth of a range of new media technologies (film, television, the Internet, mobile communications); the significant rise in household access to these new media technologies; the speed at which these technologies allow information to flow across the world; and the increasing social role of an expanding, constantly accessible and updated, public media in mediating other social institutions. These factors have meant that the potential for public media to mediate sacred forms has grown as more people spend more time accessing a wide range of media, whose ability to hold their audiences' attention is linked to their increased capacity to present a continually updated flow of images and stories from across the world.

If we are seeing a mediatization of the sacred, this raises further questions about its social and political implications,[50] including the symbolic power that becomes concentrated as much in the *idea* of public media as specific media outputs. But, in addition to these broader theoretical, ethical, and political considerations, it also raises empirical questions about how the role of public media institutions in mediating the sacred is negotiated by media professionals, their audiences, and other interest groups. In the remaining part of this chapter, our attention will turn to a case study in which a public broadcaster's capacity to mediate the sacred was ruptured for a significant part of its audience. Through this case, we will see that there is still nothing inevitable about the mediatization of the sacred, and that the capacity of media institutions to offer engaging mediations of sacred forms is dependent, as Dayan and Katz recognized,[51] on processes of negotiation between media producers, their audiences, and other social groups. It may be that Nick Couldry is right to argue that the mediatization of the sacred involves a concentration of symbolic power in media institutions that does violence to the capacity of late modern societies to engage in genuinely democratic reflection on the meanings of social life. But this symbolic role seems unlikely to be eclipsed by any other social institution for the foreseeable future. By the end of this chapter, I will argue that media professionals need to recognize the presence of the sacred in relation to their work, and that to do so may involve rethinking other principles and policy positions that currently shape their professional practice.

Operation 'Cast Lead': Public media and the Middle East conflict

On 27 December 2008, Israel began a military campaign in Gaza, Operation 'Cast Lead', initially involving air strikes and then subsequently, from 3 January 2009, a major ground offensive. By the time that both Israel and the Hamas-led Gazan administration had independently declared ceasefires on 18 January, NGOs estimated that between 1,387 and 1,417 Palestinians had been killed, and events in this conflict received considerable public attention across the world, not least because the closure of the Gazan borders meant that civilians in this densely populated area were unable to flee the conflict site. During the course of Operation 'Cast Lead', several thousand civilian homes in Gaza were destroyed, more than three hundred factories were severely damaged, and extensive damage was also caused to farms and water and sewerage systems. Thirteen Israelis were also killed during this conflict, of whom three were civilians living in southern Israel.

While any account of events concerning Palestine–Israel invites discussion of the longer historical context of the conflict, the 2008–9 Gazan campaign needs also to be understood in the context of more recent events. These include Israel's withdrawal from Gaza in 2005, the election victory of Hamas in the Palestinian parliamentary elections in 2006, which led to Israel imposing a stringent economic blockade on Gaza, the Lebanon war of 2006, and the conflict between Hamas and Fatah, which led to a breakdown of shared governance between Gaza and the West Bank in 2007. A number of commentators have also situated the decisions made by the Israeli Prime Minister, Ehud Olmert, in the Gaza conflict in the context of forthcoming elections in Israel and the backdrop of sustained criticism of Olmert's handling of the 2006 Lebanon war, the inconclusive outcome of which had been interpreted as weakening the deterrent threat posed by Israel's military capacity. While the Gazan campaign of 2008–9 did represent an intense moment of conflict, with extensive damage caused to Gazan lives and infrastructure, it is also realistic to interpret this, not as a unique moment of conflict but as a continuation of more established patterns. These included Israeli attacks on Gazan infrastructure (such as the bombing of Gaza's main power station in 2006 by Israeli jets following the kidnapping of the Israeli solider Ghalid Shalit), the killing of Gazans by

Israeli military action even after Israel's formal withdrawal from the area, and the sporadic and then increasingly intense rocket fire from Gaza into towns in southern Israel, which also caused injury and death to Israeli civilians.

This case study seeks not to discuss directly the events on the ground in Gaza during that period, but the significance of UK media coverage of these events, focusing particularly on the decision by the BBC not to broadcast a humanitarian appeal in response to the conflict. The intense identifications formed with the Palestinian–Israeli conflict by different religious and political groups across the world are reflected in the importance of a wide range of news media as a source of both information and moral framing of the conflict. In the context of the UK, this has led to intense scrutiny of the BBC's editorial stance in relation to the conflict,[52] in which it has been variously accused of showing bias to Israeli and to Palestinian perspectives. This had previously led to the BBC commissioning the unpublished Balen report of 2004, and the published Thomas report of 2006, which concluded that, while aspects of the BBC's coverage contained implicit bias towards Israel, there was no evidence of any form of systematic bias, and recommended that greater contextualization be given in future news coverage concerning the conflict. Media coverage of events in Gaza in 2008–9 by Western media outlets was made more difficult by Israel's decision not to allow journalists access to Gaza during their assault (most Western journalists having left Gaza in recent years, partly in response to kidnappings of foreign media workers, notably the BBC's Alan Johnston, in 2006). As a consequence, until the end of the fighting in mid-January, Western journalists were unable to report directly on events on the ground in Gaza, relying instead on information and images produced by other local journalists and NGOs. Nevertheless, the prevalence of digital media and news emerging from local sources meant that, despite the restrictions of immediate access for Western journalists, limited information continued to emerge. As a consequence, British media, including the BBC, gave considerable attention to moments of 'spectacular' civilian suffering, such as the killing of 34 Palestinians by Israeli mortar fire in an area near a United Nations school in Jabalya housing more than a thousand civilian refugees,[53] the killing in Zeitoun of 23 members of the Al-Samouni family, who were gathered by Israeli soldiers into a house that was then subsequently shelled,[54] and the images of fragments of phosphorous falling on a UN school at Beit Lahiya, which was serving as another temporary refuge for Palestinian civilians.[55]

My aim here is to consider how a specific incident in the media coverage of the Gazan campaign can be understood in terms of the role of the media as a site for the rehearsal, reproduction, and contestation of the sacred. This case demonstrates the investments that people make in media as sites of collective identification and experience, the significance of collective emotion constructed through media, and the challenges that this sacred role creates for media professionals and audiences in the context of pluralist societies. Through it we will examine how the sacred roles of public media can generate their own internal inconsistencies, producing tensions within media organizations themselves and fragmenting public identification with media organizations as effective sites for engaging sacred forms.

'Today this is not about the rights or wrongs of the conflict': The BBC and the DEC appeal for Gaza

The Disasters Emergency Committee (DEC) is a group of thirteen leading UK charities and aid organizations, which coordinate their activities in cases of sudden major humanitarian need. The DEC has a longstanding agreement with UK television broadcasters that, if it is satisfied that certain conditions are met relating to the urgency of need in a particular case and the viability of a coordinated response, it can request the broadcast of an appeal, which is usually co-produced with those broadcasters and may make use of their news footage. While UK TV broadcasters have usually agreed to these requests, other DEC appeals have previously been refused—for example, appeals for famine victims in East Africa and those suffering from the effects of the Lebanon war, both in 2006.

On 20 January, three weeks into Israel's military campaign in Gaza, the DEC made a formal request to the BBC and other commercial television broadcasters (ITV, Channel 4, Channel 5, and Sky News) to broadcast an appeal for humanitarian relief for suffering caused as a result of the conflict. The following day, following consultation with senior managers, the Director-General of the BBC, Mark Thompson, refused this request. Media coverage of this decision led quickly to growing criticism of the BBC's decision from a wide range of politicians, religious leaders and other public figures, as well as from other media outlets (where left-leaning newspapers critical of Israeli actions found common cause with right-leaning papers happy to find another stick with which to beat the traditionally liberal BBC). The British government minister with responsibility for international development, Douglas Alexander, publicly voiced his concerns about the decision, saying that 'I really struggle to see in the face of the immense human suffering in Gaza . . . that this [concern over impartiality] is in any way a credible argument'. The Archbishop of York, Dr John Sentamu, also released a statement in which he said: 'This is not a row about impartiality, but rather about humanity. . . By declining the [DEC's] request, the BBC has taken sides and forsaken impartiality.'

On 24 January, a demonstration was held outside BBC Broadcasting House, which provided a focal narrative and media images for these ongoing protests (even though this protest had been planned before the announcement of the DEC decision in response to perceived pro-Israeli bias in BBC coverage). The same day, Mark Thompson used an editor's blog on the BBC website to explain his decision, citing the main reasons as being concerns about the ability of DEC charities to deliver aid into Gaza and issues of impartiality in the BBC's coverage of the conflict (although objections based on delivery of aid were subsequently dropped shortly after this).[56] Some news outlets also began to report the anger of some BBC staff about this decision, as well as allegations that staff had been threatened with dismissal if they publicly criticized it. The ambivalence felt towards the decision among BBC staff was perhaps also reflected in an interview with the veteran left-wing politician Tony Benn on BBC News 24, on the morning before the demonstration outside BBC Broadcasting House. Here, Benn was given time to criticize the BBC, publicize the demonstration, and repeatedly read out the postal address for donations for the DEC appeal.[57] More than two years after this interview took place, a clip of it is still available for download from the BBC's own news website, which also includes a link to the DEC website 'for information purposes'.[58]

On 26 January, three other broadcasters (ITV, Channel 4, and Channel 5) broke with the BBC's decision by showing the DEC appeal in their evening schedules, and Mark Thompson appeared on the BBC's flagship radio news programme to defend his decision in the context of a hostile interview with the senior BBC journalist John Humphries.[59] The DEC appeal itself, edited by staff at ITN, focused on the urgent humanitarian need for temporary housing, food, and medical supplies, and explicitly sought to avoid apportioning blame: 'Today, this is not about the rights or wrongs of the conflict; these people simply need your help.'[60] Despite mounting criticism—and threats by some celebrities not to work again with the BBC if the decision was not reversed—Mark Thompson maintained his position over the DEC appeal. By 4 February around 200 appeals had been made to the BBC Trust, which oversees the corporation's work, against the DEC decision, and by 11 February the BBC had received 40,000 complaints against the decision. While this level of complaint is substantial in the context of the BBC complaints system, it should also be understood in the context of other recent, and to some degree coordinated, mass complaints to the BBC, such as the 47,000 complaints over the broadcast of the representation of Christ in *Jerry Springer the Opera*, and 42,000 complaints over offensive comments made by the comedians Russell Brand and Jonathan Ross. The formal process within the BBC was concluded on 19 February, when the BBC Trust ruled in favour of Mark Thompson's decision on the grounds of needing to preserve impartiality in the BBC's coverage of events in the Middle East.[61] The Trust's decision made reference to a substantial report on impartiality produced by the BBC in 2007, which itself had been commissioned against the background of continued allegations of bias in the BBC's Middle East coverage.[62]

Media controversy over the BBC's decision had already begun to abate, even by the time the BBC Trust made its announcement. Events in Gaza swiftly fell down the news agenda after the ceasefires of 18 January, as international attention turned to the presidential inauguration of Barack Obama, even though conditions on the ground for many Gazan civilians remained critical and Israeli economic and humanitarian restrictions remained largely intact. Nevertheless, despite this, the controversy over the BBC's decision has continued to feed wider public debate about the corporation's role, and, in the light of widespread criticism of the BBC's position by British Muslims, contributed to the symbolism surrounding the appointment of the first Muslim to the post of the BBC's Head of Religion later in 2009. This controversy can doubtless be understood in the context of established right-wing criticisms of a publicly funded liberal broadcaster (including criticisms circulated by the BBC's major commercial rival, News International), as well as left-wing criticism of the BBC's editorial stance on Palestine–Israel. However the intensity of the controversy also reflects how media coverage of Operation 'Cast Lead' was inflected with powerful sacred forms, and the perception that the BBC failed to act appropriately in relation to these.

Media images and narratives of the violation of the care of children in Gaza

In the previous chapter, we explored how the care of children has come to have the status of an autonomous sacred form in the modern world. Public media play a central role in reproducing this sacred form. Emotional identification with the sacrality of the care of children is achieved particularly through media images and stories that focus either on the disrupted bond between parents and children (for example, in the case of bereaved parents whose children have been accidentally killed or murdered), or on the breach of the care of children (as in stories of physical and sexual abuse). As Jeffrey Alexander puts it, emotional identification with the sacred is achieved, not simply by 'positive' representations of the sacred, but by stories and images of the evil disruption of that sacred:

Evil is deeply implicated in the symbolic formulation and institutional mainte-nance of the good. Because of this, the institutional and cultural vitality of evil must be continually sustained... Evil is not only symbolized cognitively but experienced in a vivid and emotional way... Through such phenomena as scan-dals, moral panics, public punishments, and wars, societies provide occasions to re-experience and re-crystallize the enemies of the good. Wrenching experiences of horror, revulsion, and fear create opportunities for purification that keep what Plato called 'the memory of justice' alive.[63]

The production and reception of news stories and images of the abuse, suffering, and death of children are therefore loaded with sacred signifi-cance in which emotion and morality are inseparably fused. We see this in both the textual representation of perpetrators of such abuse, who are visually and discursively constructed as profoundly evil, the repetition of images of the child victim, the sense of gravity in the tone of voice of broadcast journalists presenting these stories, and the displaced rage towards anyone thought to be complicit in allowing such suffering (whether families, communities, or statutory agencies). All of these were present, for example, in the extensive media coverage of the case of Baby P, who died in London in 2008,[64] having suffered prolonged abuse and severe injuries at the hands of his carers. This notorious case evoked such a degree of public sympathy and revulsion that there was a significant shift in subsequent social work practice in the UK in remov-ing vulnerable children into care homes.

The suffering and death of children became an important part of Western media coverage of Israel's military action in Gaza. At a conser-vative estimate, between 280 and 313 Palestinian children were killed during the three-week operation. The suffering and death of Palestinian children formed an important part of the 'spectacular' moments of civilian suffering. A notable case was the killing of civilians in the shelled house in Zeitoun. Here, Israeli Defence Force (IDF) soldiers had initially prevented medical aid going to the house after it had been shelled, and, when access was finally granted after three days, Interna-tional Red Cross workers were reported as shocked to have found the surviving children, badly dehydrated and near collapse, and in some cases still holding on to the bodies of their dead mothers.[65] On 4 January, Channel 4 News carried a report on the killing of a 12-year-old boy, Mahmoud Mashharawi, by rocket fire from an unmanned Israeli drone while he was playing on the rooftop of his house;[66] the report was accompanied by live video footage of the assault. After the ceasefires, the BBC journalist Christian Fraser reported for BBC television and radio news on the shooting of 4-year-old Samar Abed Rabbu at close range during an IDF operation in an incident that left her paralysed and her two sisters, aged 7 and 2, dead.[67] Such narratives form powerful instances of the breach of the sacrality of the care of children for those able to form unproblematic identifications with them, and, through such mediated identification, a sense of shared trauma is constructed that potentially binds viewers into a shared moral and emotional ethos.

An important point to note here is that it is not simply the abuse or killing of a child in itself that elicits a sacralized public response. But it is at the point that the abuse or killing of a particular child becomes the focus of public media attention that its socially sacred potentiality is enacted through narrative representation and emotional identification.[68] Through this social process, the suffering and deaths of some children may not be publicly recognized, while those of other children become a focus for intense identification. Thus, while mediated stories of suffering of Gazan children such as Samar Abed Rabbu became potent symbols of the breach of the sacred, little public attention had previously been given to the sixty-eight children killed in Gaza as a result of Israeli military action in 2007–8—or indeed to the thousands of children suffering from malnutrition in Gaza as a result of the economic blockade, effectively endorsed by Western governments.[69] Similarly, who 'counts' as a child is also subject to processes of social and cultural construction (reflected in disputes as to how casualty rates for children should be calculated for the Gaza offensive). Broader historical contingencies also shape the ways in which some forms of human suffering are regarded as worthy of attention through the public space of the media, while other forms of suffering may be neglected. In the context of the Middle East, for example, some have argued that Israeli policies and military actions are subject to an unusually high level of scrutiny and criticism from European audiences, leading to the charge that this scrutiny consciously or unconsciously perpetuates anti-Semitic sentiments that are deeply sedimented in European culture. The persistence of such anti-Semitism is not something to be rejected out of hand, given Europe's tragic history in this regard. But European identification with Palestinian suffering could also be interpreted as bound up with an enduring sense of responsibility of some European societies for the conditions under which the State of Israel was created. Or, perhaps ironically, it is linked more closely to the consistent attempts to represent Israel as a modern, European democracy, which have the effect of leading people in Europe to hold the Israeli government to similar standards as they would their own government or armed forces and to question whether Israeli policies could be easily identified with progressive, Western values. However we interpret the grounds of such identification, however, it is important to note these identifications are historically contingent and partial, rather than natural and inevitable.

The sacred potency of stories of the suffering and death of children should not therefore blind us to the complex relationship between the real lives, suffering, and death of particular human bodies and the ways in which these experiences are taken (or not taken) into the sacred, symbolic realm of the media.[70] I say complex, rather than distinct here, because the reality of children's suffering and the sacralization of this suffering through public media remain intertwined. The social construction and symbolic mediation of this suffering should not make the actual suffering any less morally compelling. As Joe Sacco commented in his recent graphic novel and oral history, *Fragments of Gaza*, although narratives remain vulnerable to the imprecision of memory, behind their inconsistencies are the unchanging raw facts of violent acts that are marked more deeply than narrative in maimed and dead bodies.

The violation of the sacred in stories and images of children's suffering in Gaza clearly evoked different responses in readers and viewers in the UK. For those with little interest in the Middle East conflict, the images formed part of a wider cultural mediation of children's suffering in conflict. For those more familiar with the history of the conflict and critical of Israeli policies, the images reconfirmed a sense of the evils of political policies of constraint and occupation enacted through military force on largely civilian populations. But for those who identified with the State of Israel, and supported the Gazan military offensive as legitimate self-defence, these stories posed a fundamental problem.[71] In the case of the abuse of individual children, it is generally unproblematic to regard the abuser as in some sense fundamentally evil and in some sense separate from the moral community of humanity. But there is an obvious dissonance when the breach of the sacred—the maiming or killing of the child—is perpetuated by someone with whom one identifies as part of a shared moral community. It is a general human trait to find it very difficult to recognize a breach of the sacred in one's own actions, or the actions of someone with whom one strongly identifies. For those, then, who cheered at a rally in Trafalgar Square in support of Israel during the Gaza offensive when the Israeli ambassador to the UK, Ron Prosor, referred to IDF soldiers as 'our sons and daughters', an obvious tension emerges when television coverage reports children's suffering caused by that same military force. Such dissonance cannot be held easily without a profound ability to articulate the tragic, which is rare among politicians, religious leaders, or other public figures, who often require some unambiguous association with the sacred to mobilize support. In the context of Operation 'Cast Lead', this challenge was taken up by the PR work of the IDF, the Israeli government, and other organizations that seek to create a supportive media environment for Israel, such as BICOM.[72]

The Israeli government's decision not to allow foreign journalists access to Gaza during the conflict also reflected an attempt to exercise some control over the flow of information relating to the conflict. IDF and Israeli government spokespeople consistently denied reports of hostile actions by IDF soldiers against Palestinian civilians, suggesting such casualties were caused by Palestinian munitions, or sought to reframe such reports in terms of Israel's right to self-defence. Such PR strategies informed a range of websites and blogs that sought to 'de-construct' evidence of allegations against the IDF or situate these in a narrative of a hostile anti-Semitic campaign against Israel.[73]

A more emotionally nuanced response was demonstrated by the UK's Chief Rabbi, Dr Jonathan Sacks, who at the Trafalgar Square rally sought to downplay the triumphalist atmosphere created by other speakers, and to recognize the human tragedy of events in Gaza. Emphasizing the shared humanity of Palestinians and Jews, Sacks negotiated the tensions of the violation of the sacred posed by the suffering of Gazan children by laying the blame for this at the feet of Hamas, claiming that 'all it took to avoid all the suffering was for Hamas to end firing rockets on innocent Israeli civilians' and that 'the Palestinian future will begin the minute Hamas stops firing rockets on innocent Israelis'.[74] Although the deferral of the Palestinian future since 1948 has doubtless, at different points, been due in part to the political choices of Palestinian leaders, such a simplistic splitting between the evil Hamas and the peace-loving State of Israel bears little relation to the complex facts on the ground. But such splitting and projection of violence into the evil other nevertheless represent an important strategy for maintaining a sense of moral integrity in the face of evidence of violation of the sacred by a community with whom one deeply identifies. As Jeffrey Alexander has observed, the violation of collective forms of the sacred pollutes and taints those associated with it. Through denial, rationalization, splitting, and projection, the threat posed by mediated evidence of the violation of the sacred can thus be managed.

But for those who did not experience such tensions in the face of the violating images and stories of children's suffering in Gaza, the BBC's decision over the DEC appeal often appeared callous, cowardly, and incomprehensible. While the number of complaints to the BBC should be understood partly in terms of the capacity of pro-Palestinian activist networks to mobilize their supporters, the volume of complaints was much higher than the BBC had ever received on any other issue regarding its coverage of Palestine–Israel. The breadth of criticism of the BBC's position, including from government ministers and both the Archbishops of Canterbury and York, also indicated that pressure on the BBC came from a much wider group than the usual pro-Palestinian lobby. The language used in criticism of the BBC's position is also revealing. A common trope used in responses to Mark Thompson's post on the BBC Editors' blog on 24 January is that of shame, in which posters (the vast majority of whom criticize the BBC's decision) either claim to feel ashamed of the BBC's decision or assert that Mark Thompson and other senior BBC managers should feel ashamed. Two examples of such posts are:

You think that

a) people do not see the BBC as biased in its coverage already
b) that by refusing to broadcast it you are making very clear that you ARE partial.

This is an appeal for AID, pure and simple. You either have a very low opinion of your audience or you just ARE biased. Disgraceful, despicable and inhuman, you should be ashamed. Apemantus 2001, 7.42pm, Jan 24th

This is a contemptible decision by the BBC. It is absolutely not impartial—quite the contrary. Most of the hundreds of victims of the recent conflict in Gaza are innocent civilians, including children. The BBCs decision demonstrates contempt for the expertise of the DEC and an appalling disregard for human life. I am ashamed to pay the licence fee. Earthwriter, 7.58pm, Jan 24th

As Stephen Pattison has observed, whereas guilt is typically conceived as an emotional response to a specific action for which a person feels responsible, shame is experienced more as a fundamental tainting or marking of a self or group.[75] The frequent references to shame in these postings might then be understood in terms of a sense of a violation of the sacred that marks those associated with it – either those directly responsible for that violation (BBC management) or even those more loosely associated with it (BBC licence fee-payers).

The violation of something considered sacred within a given social context is typically experienced as a painful wound, for which some kind of restitution is necessary. The fact that the BBC's coverage of the suffering and death of children had offered mediated experiences of the violation of the sacrality of the figure of the child made it all the more difficult, then, for parts of its audience to accept that the BBC was preventing the symbolic restitutive action of supporting a humanitarian appeal to relieve this suffering. The capacity of the BBC in this case, then, to offer both an experience of the violation of the sacred and a necessary form of restitution was fractured, leaving some viewers to experience a fundamental rupture in their identification with the broadcaster symbolized by the threat to withhold their licence fee or to stop supporting the licence fee system. Understanding more about the BBC's decision in this case can further clarify the ways in which public media fail, as much as succeed, in offering effective mediation of sacred forms.

Negotiating between the mediation of the sacred and impartiality

The case of the controversy surrounding the BBC's decision over the DEC appeal demonstrates that the role of public media as a site for engaging the sacred is neither straightforward, nor unproblematic. Indeed, the case demonstrates two elements of the role of public media as sites for rehearsing the sacred that may conflict with each other. The first is the role of the media in providing images and stories informed by sacred forms that are shared by large sections of their audience. News media professionals might not think of this as an explicit part of their role, and might consider such morally inflected reporting to undermine their role as balanced observers and analysts of current events. But, in reality, their ability to create stories that form powerful moments of emotional and moral identification for their audience is dependent on shared cultural forms of the sacred, which shape both the production and the reception of these stories. Indeed, the capacity of journalists to take a moral high ground—in, for example, interviewing politicians about systemic breakdown in child protection systems, which has made child abuse more likely—derives from their use of shared, collective sacred values, symbols, and feelings.

At the same time, however, another important role for broadcasters (particularly those with a public service remit) is to maintain content across its whole range of outputs that is broadly inclusive of its imagined audience. In terms of the sacred, this can be interpreted in terms of a media institution's capacity to function as a focus for collective identification within a wider community. The BBC Trust's 2007 report on impartiality therefore notes the professional obligation for news coverage to maintain a proper distinction between the appropriate reporting of events and expert analysis, and the inappropriate presentation of personal opinions by journalists. It also makes frequent reference to the first public purpose stated in the BBC's new charter, which is to 'sustain citizenship and civil society', and which is taken to mean producing content that does not appear to favour one section of British society to the exclusion of others.

These two roles of public media—to serve as a site for encountering sacred forms and to be a site of shared identification and engagement for a broad public audience—become increasingly problematic and potentially conflictual in pluralist societies in which there are many different sources of sacred identification. This tension becomes more acutely evident when media organizations themselves become the focus of intentional lobbying by ethnic, political, or religious groups on grounds of offence or bias against their particular sacred commitments. The Palestine–Israel conflict has become one of the most enduring examples of this for the BBC and one for which particular organizations (for example, Honest Reporting UK) specialize in sustained criticism of BBC Middle East coverage.

Tensions between these two roles can become particularly acute in the context of decisions over humanitarian appeals. Humanitarian appeals through the media are not, in cultural terms, simply instrumental means of raising charitable donations, but perform important work in marking breaches of the sacred. In cases of natural disasters, such as the Indian Ocean tsunami of 2004, which killed more than 300,000 people, the breach is not the direct cause of human agency. But, even in such cases with no direct human cause, those who have failed to mitigate against the tragedy, for example, through failing to establish early warning systems for underwater earthquakes, may find themselves the focus of a desire to punish in the wake of a violation of the sacred. In other cases, however, breaches of the sacred occur as a direct consequence of the actions of human agents, such as governments, armies, and militia. In such instances, moral identification with the victims performs important work in the construction of evil and thus the reinforcement of the sacred.[76]

In a context of heightened sensitivity to issues of impartiality, humanitarian appeals and campaigns can therefore become particularly contentious. That the humanitarian grounds of a televised appeal typically appear self-evident to their audience is precisely because they are rooted in commonly held sacred forms. As a consequence, political views and campaigns framed within a context of humanitarian concern can have particular moral force. Before the controversy over the Gaza–DEC appeal, there had already been considerable debate within the BBC over issues of impartiality and humanitarian campaigns in relation to the Live 8 concerts, and associated Make Poverty History campaign, in 2005. Although there were no substantial objections to this campaign, BBC senior managers decided that, while the Live 8 concerts could themselves be shown live on BBC television, the Make Poverty History campaign films screened for audiences at those concerts could not be screened directly on the BBC. As a result, whenever the live audiences at the Live 8 concerts were shown a campaign film, BBC editors would cut away either to a BBC-produced film about the issues raised by the campaign or to a celebrity interview—something that the lead singer of Coldplay, Chris Martin, directly criticized from the stage of the Hyde Park concert. Although the BBC's editorial decision reflected a clear attempt to separate news and entertainment coverage from giving a 'free ride' to a particular political campaign, the case of Live 8 also demonstrates the ambiguities of the BBC's position with regard to humanitarian content. The BBC's own Comic Relief annual television fundraiser had been part of the Make Poverty History coalition, and had itself included content on the importance of debt relief for developing countries since 1999, creating a wider public awareness of these issues that formed a context for the subsequent Live 8 events.[77] Indeed, the boundaries between the impartial provision of news coverage and humanitarian action had already been shown to be porous in 1983 when Michael Buerk's emotionally charged news reports of the famine in Ethiopia directly inspired the Band Aid Christmas single and the subsequent Live Aid concerts.

The BBC's editorial approach to humanitarian campaigns, as demonstrated by the Live 8 concerts, thus reflects a fundamental tension between the desire to promote core, sacred values and the desire not to compromise impartiality by offering direct support to a particular political perspective. Given that the Make Poverty History campaign was relatively uncontroversial among the BBC's audience, it is all the more evident why issues of impartiality attracted particular concern in the context of a humanitarian appeal in the highly contested context of Palestine–Israel. In the case of Gaza, then, while the BBC was prepared to show images of the suffering of children as part of its news broadcasts, it was unable to offer symbolic restitution of this by broadcasting a humanitarian appeal to relieve such suffering. To have broadcast such an appeal would, in sacred terms, have entailed drawing the boundaries of a shared moral community around those appalled at the suffering of children, and excluding those who identified with the perpetrators of that suffering. Given that such exclusion would have extended, not only to pro-Israel lobby groups, but to a sizeable number of British Jews and mainstream organizations such as the Board of Deputies of British Jews, such a drawing of moral boundaries became unthinkable in terms of the BBC's policy on impartiality, not to mention the wider cultural resonances of such exclusion in the context of the histories of Western anti-Semitism.

Herein, though, lies the fundamental irony of the case of the DEC–Gaza appeal. In seeking to support and promote 'civil society', the BBC's stance in this case failed to uphold values held sacred by a substantial part of its audience, leading to greater polarization within its wider community of viewers and a breach in identification with the BBC as an effective mediator of the sacred. In failing to offer any restitution to its own representations of the violation of the sacred through the suffering and death of children in Gaza, the BBC became itself tainted with that breach of the sacred, a source of shame and focus for outrage and disgust, and its capacity to function as a focal institution for civil society was fractured. It is not easy to measure the longer-term effects of this perceived failure of the BBC on public life in Britain, or to trace accurately the consequences of such feelings of shame and outrage in sections of the BBC's audience. As noted earlier, it is common for media institutions themselves to act in the role of counter-centres of the sacred in cases where political, cultural, or religious institutions fall short of sacred norms. But, when mainstream media institutions fail as mediators of the sacred, what other counter-centres do people turn to? Perhaps the diversity of media platforms within an organization such as the BBC, in which greater space is given to user-generated content, allows the emergence of such counter-centres within the BBC's own structures—for example, through online message boards. Perhaps the case of the DEC–Gaza appeal also encouraged some sections of the BBC's audience to turn more to alternative media sources that offer less problematic opportunities to rehearse their sacred commitments. Such thoughts are speculative, but demonstrate that public identification with media institutions as mediators of the sacred is fragile and as much subject to failure as powerful moments of collective identification.

Given what the DEC–Gaza case demonstrates about the ambiguous role of public broadcasters as mediators of the sacred, how might we think again about the role of media institutions in the context of societies characterized by a plurality of sacred commitments? It is clear in this case that concerns with impartiality, understood as the inclusion of an imagined public audience, were paramount for the BBC senior management. These concerns also cut across the BBC's ability to offer symbolic restitution for those drawn together in moral outrage through its coverage of children's suffering in Gaza. This case demonstrates that broadcasters' attempts to maintain inclusive structures for their public audience can lose moral force when these work against the mediation of widely held forms of the sacred. For it is sacred forms that have the potential to bind social collectivities together rather than abstract notions of citizenship or civil society. Or, to put it another way, public broadcasters cannot expect to function as powerful sites of collective identification if they do not effectively mediate sacred commitments that are widely held within their audience. A primary emphasis on impartiality (understood as avoiding exclusion of parts of an imagined audience) in public media leads logically to an arid, information-delivery service, which does not seek or achieve any form of powerful, collective fusion of emotion and morality in its audience. Given the importance of public media as primary sites of the mediation of the sacred in contemporary culture, it is not clear that public audiences would necessarily value such emotionally and morally antiseptic media content. There are clearly dangers in public broadcasters uncritically rehearsing sacred values. But, rather than being primarily concerned with impartiality, the DEC–Gaza case suggests that it may be better for public broadcasters to be open and reflexive about their role as mediators of the sacred, provide effective spaces for the rehearsal and reproduction of widely held sacred commitments, and offer structures for public discussion in cases where mediation of particular sacred forms is controversial. It would have been better, in other words, for the BBC to have broadcast the DEC–Gaza appeal, thus providing a symbolic restitution of the violation of the sacrality of care of children, and to have offered public discussion of this decision and the wider context of the Middle East conflict. In the context of societies characterized by plural sacred commitments, what is needed may well not be public media that draw back from any controversy over the mediation of the sacred, but media institutions that recognize the challenges of their sacred role and are open and reflexive about the sacred forms that they mediate.

As a final footnote, the rupture of the mediation of the sacred in the case of the DEC appeal was soon followed by another conflict over the role of the BBC in relation to the mediation of sacred forms. In 2009, Nick Griffin, the leader of the fascist British National Party, was elected as a member of the European Parliament. This led to heated public debate as to whether, as convention would have it, he should then be allowed to participate in mainstream political discussion programmes on the BBC. The BBC subsequently decided to allow Griffin to participate in an edition of *Question Time*, its main weekly political panel discussion held in front of a public audience. This decision gave rise, not only to widespread public debate about the threat of pollution in allowing a racist politician a media platform through the BBC, but physical clashes outside the BBC as protestors attempted to stop the programme being filmed. Despite this, the programme was duly recorded, and, through careful management of the discussion, it was able to present Griffin as ill-informed, engaged in an ill-concealed attempt to present far-right views as in keeping with mainstream British opinion, and almost entirely derided by the studio audience. In the face of the pollution of the sacred centre of the BBC, the programme became a ritual through which panel member contributions and audience reactions demonstrated that Griffin's views fell beyond the acceptable boundaries of the sacred, civil sphere. Some of those who felt alienated by the BBC's decision over the DEC will have identified more closely with the values embedded in its representation of Griffin. Ruptures in the mediation of the sacred, as with moments of identification, are therefore transient and always shifting, as new conflicts and forms of pollution come into the frame.

5

Living with the Light and Shadow of the Sacred

> A man plants a cedar and the rain makes it grow, so that later on he
> will have a tree to cut down ... One half of the wood he burns in the
> fire and on this he roasts his meat ... Then what is left of the wood
> he makes into a god, an image to which he bows down and pros-
> trates himself; he prays to it and says, 'Save me; for you are my god.'
>
> (Isaiah 44: 14–17 (Revised English Bible))

The sacred has a shadow side. While sacred forms symbolize and perpetuate deep moral and existential commitments, they equally have the
capacity to legitimate oppressive social orders, violence, and the breach
of basic human rights of freedom and well-being.[1] Rather than necessarily binding society into a shared order of meanings and values, as
Durkheim suggested, the multiplicity of contemporary forms of the
sacred threatens to fragment society and provides potent symbolic
material for social conflict.

Accepting that the sacred is a cultural structure rather than grounded
in the ontology of the human person or the cosmos itself raises an
important question: do we need the sacred? If sacred forms are as
socially and culturally constructed as the act, mocked by Deutero-Isaiah,
of taking firewood and fashioning it into a god to whom powers of
salvation are attributed, is it possible for us to imagine a society that
moves beyond sacred forms?

To pose this question reflects a more fundamental issue for social
theory about the extent to which social agents are able, through the
exercise of a critical reflexivity, to free themselves from the influence of
particular social or cultural structures. Fundamental questions about the
transformative capacity of critical reflexivity similarly underpin the field
of psychotherapy—for example, between 'optimistic' models such as

solution-focused therapy that emphasize the capacity for individuals to make significant intentional changes to improve their well-being and more 'pessimistic' psychoanalytic approaches that see the battle for self-insight as analogous to the struggle to dam the sea to protect vulnerable, low-lying ground. Jeffrey Alexander's description of cultural sociology as a form of cultural psychoanalysis similarly reflects this sense of tension between what can and what cannot be changed. We may aim, through critical reflection, 'to reveal to men and women the myths that think them so that they can make up new myths in turn',[2] but it is not possible to move social life beyond its predisposition to mythical thinking.

This chapter will explore the limits of our capacity to move beyond the sacred, asking whether such a move is possible or indeed desirable, and what the implications of continuing to live in relation to sacred forms in the modern world might be. Before we turn to this, though, it is important to consider the case for trying to imagine society without the sacred.

Why abandon the sacred?

One of Blaise Pascal's claims, much beloved by the new atheists, was that 'men [*sic*] never do evil so completely and cheerfully as when they do it from religious conviction'. In a similar vein, the Nobel-prize-winning physicist Steven Weinberg has said: 'Religion is an insult to human dignity. With or without it, you'd have good people doing good things and evil people doing evil things. But for good people to do evil things, it takes religion.'[3] But the claim of a direct connection between 'religion' (the meaning of which is self-evident for these writers) and acts of evil is fundamentally mistaken. This association should more accurately be traced back to the sacred, as the phenomenon of collective identification with idealized symbolic forms that can legitimize destructive forms of thinking, feeling, and acting.

This is not a trivial semantic point. If we are appalled by the human capacity for collective evil, it is the sacred—whether in 'religious' or 'secular' guise[4]—of which we should be more wary than religion *per se*. Under the power of the sacred, the normal codes and conventions of mundane life can be suspended. Violence is legitimated and rights can be violated by the symbolic, moral, and emotional demands of sacred forms. The twentieth century provided numerous examples of political orders that unleashed widespread violence against their own, and other, civilian populations: National Socialism in Germany, Stalinist Russia, Maoist China, Imperial reign in Japan, and the Khmer Rouge in

Cambodia. Between them, these political regimes caused the death of more than fifty million civilians through military attack, mass execution, famine, and incarceration. None of these regimes was primarily grounded in religious institutions or symbolism, but all drew their legitimacy from sacred forms—sacred visions of the nation, race, or revolution—that provided moral justification for their violence. René Girard was wrong to claim that societies have an inherent tendency to violence that must necessarily find an outlet through the sacred sacrifice of the scapegoat. On the contrary, in late modern societies, in which the 'civilizing process' has run a long course, there tends to be a strong social aversion to violence, as demonstrated in the substantially lower rates of violent crime in contemporary compared to medieval society. Sometimes social and political actors will make an instrumental decision that violence is the best strategic means to achieve their political ends. To make widespread, collective violence possible, whether state warfare or other acts of systemic violence against civilian populations, it is necessary for people to identify with a symbolic framework that makes such violence seem legitimate.[5] Through cultural narratives of past grievances, Serbs or Hutus were more able to unleash violence upon their former neighbours. As Primo Levi observed, the shocking events of the Holocaust were possible only because of a symbolic narrative in which the Jew became an 'Unter-Mensch', where sights such as Jews crammed into railway carriages for livestock merely confirmed their subhuman status in the eyes of their captors. Violence, in such contexts, may even come to be seen in terms of a ritual expression of sacred commitment.[6]

To understand such collective evil in terms of the sacred is hardly a new insight. As early as the 1920s, religious critics of totalitarian regimes in Europe were likening them to quasi-religious phenomena, emerging out of the anomie of fragmented, secularized societies that promised their adherents a new sacred order towards which their lives should be oriented.[7] This analysis has inspired more sustained academic interest in the sacralization of politics, exemplified by Emilio Gentile's argument that totalitarian regimes can be understood as politicized articulations of sacred forms,[8] which:

(a) define the meaning of life and ultimate ends of human existence; (b) formalize the commandments of a public ethic to which all members of these movements must adhere, and (c) give utter importance to a mythical and symbolic dramatization in their interpretation of history and reality, thus creating their own 'sacred history', embodied in the nation, the state or the party, and tied to the existence of a 'chosen people'...glorified as the regenerating force of all mankind.[9]

Neither was such an analysis alien to these totalitarian movements, which sought, not simply to control the regulative and allocative structures of political power, but to create a new symbolic order for public life. In the Soviet Union, traditional religious rites of passage were marginalized in favour of new ceremonies that recognized the sacrality of the revolution. As one such ceremony, marking the birth of children, put it: 'We cover thee not with a cross, not with water and prayer—the inheritance of slavery and darkness—but with our Red Banner of struggle and labour, pierced by bullets and torn by bayonets...'.[10] Such sacred symbolism was attached not simply to the revolution as a historical event or abstract principle, but to individuals who embodied its sacred essence. Lenin's early death in 1924 led to the establishment of an 'Immortalization Commission', the outcomes of which took material form in both the mummification of Lenin's body and its perpetual display in the mausoleum in Red Square. This cult of personality also took more purely symbolic form through Party declarations such as: 'Lenin lives in the heart of every member of our Party. Every member of our Party is a small part of Lenin. Our whole communist family is a collective embodiment of Lenin.'[11] Following the example of the French Jacobins, in Mussolini's Fascist Italy, a new calendar was introduced in 1926. The 'march to Rome' in October 1922, which led to Mussolini taking power in the Italian state, was designated as the advent of Year I of a new sacred order, and new public holidays were established celebrating the myths and ethos of the Fascist movement.[12] Mussolini himself declared that 'Fascism is a religious conception in which man [sic] in his immanent relationship with a superior law, and with an objective Will that transcends that particular individual, raises him to conscious membership of a spiritual society'.[13] The cult of personality established around Mussolini as an idealized embodiment of this sacred national community even led to the creation of a new School of Fascist Mysticism, led by Mussolini's brother, which devoted itself to the study of Mussolini's thought.[14] In Nazi Germany, the Nuremburg rallies, staged against the backdrop of Albert Speer's 'cathedral of light', provided a spectacular ritual structure for the celebration of the sacred vision of the Nazi movement. The memorialization of the sixteen Nazi activists killed in the failed Munich putsch of 1923 played a central role in the rallies, and in Nazi mythology more generally. The Swastika flag carried in the 1923 revolt, stained with the blood of the fallen, acquired the status of the most sacred relic in the symbolic order of Nazism, with Hitler rubbing this flag against other flags at the culmination of Nuremburg rallies to transfer its mystical power to them. The memory of the Nazi 'heroes' of 1923 was even kept alive, not only by memorials recounting their names and brave deeds, but by rituals in which women would be symbolically married to them as figures of eternal significance. These examples were not simply bizarre cultural manifestations of total-itarian regimes, but represented an intentional effort to colonize the symbolic content of social life in relation to the particular sacred forms to which the Party laid claim. Public identification with the sacred forms around which these totalitarian movements were symboli-cally organized can also partly explain why these movements were able to achieve such widespread public support, beyond explanations based purely on instrumental self-interest or fear of political power.[15]

This is not to suggest that such totalitarian movements functioned on the basis of universal and consistent identification with the sacred symbolism articulated by their primary leaders. As Richard Evans has observed, the notion that Nazism was a unified system directed from a sacred hierarchy focused around Hitler neglects 'the complex competing power centres whose rivalry... drove the regime on to adopt steadily more radical policies'.[16] Identification with sacred forms—in either 'sec-ular' or 'religious' guise—is never uniform within the social collectivities organized in relation to them, nor is their meaning or use simply determined by the official leadership of those movements. Indeed, the officially 'authorized' meanings of sacred forms may be modified 'from below', by those who engage with them from the margins of official structures of authority.[17] Nevertheless, the sacred meanings around which totalitarian regimes have been constructed form part of the social and political frame that, under contingent historical conditions, moti-vates and legitimizes their baleful effects.

Sacred forms are always implicated with power in some sense. At the very least, when sacred forms become an effective focus for collective identification, they exert a symbolic power over their adherents that may also have some effect on the exercise of allocative and regulative power depending on the contingencies of the given social and political context. When social and political elites who possess alloactive and regulative power also strongly identify with particular sacred forms, then the consequences can be highly damaging. The kind of political movement described by Gentile, which both sees itself as having a sacred destiny in effecting radical change and is able to command widespread power, can be motivated to sacrifice human dignity and human life itself to this greater, sacred purpose. It is in such a social and cultural context that the mass extermination of civilians becomes possible. Neither are such effects of the sacred possible only within totalitarian states. As the recent history of the War on Terror demon-strates, democracies provide no inherent protection against the dangers of identification with sacred forms, as practices such as water-boarding and extraordinary rendition, normally unthinkable in mundane society, become justified under the light of America's sacred mission and the shadow of the profane threat of radical Islam. Again, as the case of residential child care in Ireland in Chapter 3 demonstrated, democratic structures provide no bulwark against the dangers of uncritical identification with sacred forms if that identification is so widespread as to form the basis for a wider consensus within which political actors operate. The capacity of sacred forms to command an allegiance in which the ordinary decencies of social life are suspended, whether in totalitarian regimes or democracies, thus gives weight to the suggestion that society may be better without sacred forms.

A second, and related, concern is the potential of sacred forms to become dangerous tools of political and cultural mobilization. This is not to suggest that sacred forms can simply be used as tools to manipulate an unwitting public of cultural dopes, nor that political actors use sacred forms in purely instrumental ways to achieve political ends without any personal identification with them—although this can happen, of course. Used effectively, sacred forms can energize cultural narratives that mobilize groups in accordance with particular political aims. A recent, powerful example of the attempt to stage such a mediatized sacred drama can be seen over the controversy over the proposed construction of the 'Ground Zero Mosque', an Islamic cultural centre to be built two blocks away from the former site of the World Trade Center in New York. The initial media coverage of this building project in December 2009 tended to focus on its multi-faith and progressive ethos, and drew little attention in subsequent months. But the decision of a New York city community board committee to give planning approval for the project in May 2010 was followed by growing media exposure to those opposing the project on the grounds that it gave a symbolic victory to Islamic extremism at the sacred site of the 9/11 attacks.[18] While opposition to the project was particularly voiced, initially, by right-wing activists such as Pamela Geller and Robert Spencer, whose direct access to media was primarily through their blogs and organizational websites or other sympathetic media outlets, it was later adopted by more high-profile public figures such as Sarah Palin, Glenn Beck, and Pat Robertson who had direct access to a wider range of public and social media resources for disseminating their views. Through this process, the proposed community centre became the 'Ground Zero Mosque', a phrase symbolically capturing the pollution of the sacred site ('Ground Zero') with the profane ('Mosque'), leading the Associated Press, among others, to disavow any use of the term in its media outputs because it immediately framed the issue in terms of sacred meanings cast by the project's opponents.[19] While some commentators suggested that attempts by the political right to stoke controversy over the 'Ground Zero Mosque' could be seen as an attempt to mobilize political support ahead of the US mid-term elections in November 2010, the controversy might also be seen as an attempt to control the symbolic meaning of 'Ground Zero' as the anniversary of the 9/11 attacks approached. Indeed, the vast majority of newspaper coverage of the 'Ground Zero Mosque' story peaked in the month immediately preceding 9 September 2010, falling away quickly in the weeks after the anniversary had passed.[20] The apotheosis of the mediatized, symbolic battle over the proper place of Islam within American public life came in the week immediately preceding this anniversary, as pastor Terry Jones's threat to burn copies of the Qur'an achieved a global media audience, allowing the leader of a marginal non-affiliated church to generate intense international reaction.[21] The rival demonstrations held in New York on 9 September 2010, in support of and opposition to the construction of the Islamic community centre—leant further symbolic significance by the presence of Geert Wilders[22]—provided the final climax to this symbolic drama. Although coverage of the 'Ground Zero Mosque' has reduced significantly since then, it remains a latent symbol that actors may choose to reuse at a future time.

The 'Ground Zero Mosque' controversy provides an apposite example of the contestation of sacred meanings through media for public life. The conflict focused on actors' attempts through different media to frame events as breaches of the sacred (by allowing the 'polluting' presence of an Islamic symbol within the heart of the sacred centre of 'Ground Zero') or the protection of the sacred (by safeguarding religious freedom as enshrined in the American constitution). The conflict was not so much between different sacred forms, but over how the sacred form of the American nation might be deployed to construct narratives in support of or opposition to the proposed building project.[23] The shared framework of the sacrality of the American nation meant that some actors were able to justify a shift in their position on the building proposals by presenting new interpretations of the controversy in line with this common sacred reference point. Glenn Beck, for example, initially argued for the right of those behind the project to build a mosque on grounds of the sacrality of religious freedom in America, only later taking the view that the project should be opposed because he had become convinced that those planning it were associated with an 'evil' form of radical Islam that had no place within proper American society.[24]

More specifically, the 'Ground Zero Mosque' controversy demon-strates the power of emotions, elicited in relation to sacred forms, to shape public life. While part of a broader process of political conflict, the controversy provided a symbolic ground for the deepening political polarization of the early years of the Obama presidency. The intensity of the emotion generated by it prompted political actors to define their position in relation to the controversy, even if they had no allocative or regulative authority over the planning process. This provides an exam-ple of the power of mediated emotion in shaping the meanings of citizenship and public life, a phenomenon that has generated both objections to the role of such emotion in undermining the rational basis of the public sphere, and counter-arguments that such emotion inevitably plays a central role in how people interpret, and act in, social life.[25] For those who view the role of emotion in mediated public life with concern, the use of sacred forms as a source of political mobiliza-tion poses a fundamental threat to the capacity of democratic societies to proceed on the basis of balanced, informed, and rational debate, rather than emotionally charged tribal identifications. For those for whom mediated emotion is an inevitable part of contemporary social life, the emotional content of sacred forms may not be a danger *per se*— indeed emotion may serve a powerful communicative role in conveying deep commitments. However, the question then turns to the political ends to which sacred forms are put. If they have the potential to deepen social conflict, to lead people to take to the streets and make violent threats in response to innocuous plans for a community cultural centre, then would society be better without such potent cultural tools at the disposal of political actors? Might public life be better lived in the spirit of banners at Jon Stewart's Rally to Restore Sanity, held on 31 October 2010, which contained slogans such as 'I'm a little annoyed but I'll get over it', 'Somewhat irritated about extreme outrage', and 'Hyperbole is the Anti-Christ'?

Another harmful effect of sacred forms arises out of their construction of emotionally and morally charged in-groups and out-groups. In the previous chapter, the case of the DEC appeal for Gaza demonstrated the ways in which those associated with the pollution of sacred forms can be positioned as inhuman or beyond the boundaries of acceptable moral community. This obviously raises challenges for social institutions— such as public broadcasters—that are intended to have a socially inclu-sive remit, where support for a particular sacred form can be interpreted as unnecessarily alienating a section of the public they are intended to serve. The case of the Gaza–DEC appeal also illustrates the complexities of drawing moral in-groups and out-groups in societies defined by long-sedimented practices of prejudice and exclusion. As previously noted, the moral exclusion of those supporting the actions of the State of Israel can be interpreted by those experiencing that moral exclusion as simply the most recent expression of a longer history of anti-Semitism. Whether such a view is correct or not, this stance demonstrates that the moral exclusion of those associated with the profane does not necessarily lead to restitution but can generate competing moral interpretations that embed conflict more deeply. While allowing powerful symbolic and emotional identification with deep moral commitments, sacred forms are inherently exclusionary. This point has been recognized in Jeffrey Alexander's substantial discussion of civil society as a communicative sphere, in which the sacred boundaries of who can be considered a full member of civic life is always under continual negotiation. Alexander supports the project of an ever-more inclusive civil sphere, in which groups hitherto marginalized from society—for example, on grounds of gender, ethnicity, or sexual orientation—are able to claim the symbolic and practical status of full membership. Yet, at the same time, Alexander recognizes that the symbolic definition of the civil sphere is grounded in the logics of the sacred, in which the sacred centre of civil society is always constituted with reference to the profane that is banished from it. In this sense, then, civil solidarity is ultimately a utopia, albeit one that 'informs every manifestation of the restless and critically demanding spirit that marks democratic life'.[26] It is utopian because attempts to expand the notion of who may participate in the civil sphere always run alongside the constitution of the profane that falls outside the acceptable boundaries of civil life: 'ideal inclusion is always shadowed by pollution and exclusion.'[27] While the promise of civil society continues to offer the possibility of full inclusion for marginalized groups, a truly global civil sphere in which 'civil virtue could not be demonstrated by exterminating the other side'[28] therefore remains perpetually out of reach. As a consequence, 'civil society is, at its very origins, fragmented and distorted in what are often the most heinous ways'.[29]

Sacred forms thus occupy a fundamentally ambiguous position in social life. They symbolize the deepest moral commitments underpinning social life, and as such provide symbolic and emotional resources that mobilize people in the struggle for social justice, equality, and well-being. For those concerned about the imagined anomie of modern life, sacred forms offer a means for the ongoing remoralization of society. Yet, at the same time as promising this, the inherently exclusionary nature of sacred forms can threaten social cohesion. The paradox is that, in deepening our identifications with sacred forms, we may become more morally energized yet less able to live without conflict in pluralist societies.

While each of these arguments suggests the harmful potential of sacred forms for social life, a traditional Durkheimian response might be that, despite such ambiguities, a society without the sacred risks disintegration and a descent into anomie. It can be argued, however, that the sacred is not a necessary condition for social integration. As noted in Chapter 2, Edward Shils argued that sacred identifications are merely one basis for developing social bonds. Indeed, in his view, society is constituted much more on the basis of mundane relationships and interactions:

As I see it, modern society is no lonely crowd, no horde of refugees fleeing from freedom. It is no *Gesellschaft*, soulless, egotistical, loveless, faithless, utterly imper-sonal and lacking any integrative forces other than interest or coercion. It is held together by an infinity of personal attachments, moral obligations in concrete contexts, professional and creative pride, individual ambition, primordial affi-nities, and a civil sense which is low in many, high in some, and moderate in most persons... it is in no danger of internal disintegration. Whatever danger it faces in this respect would be far less from those who are charged with faithful-ness and the inability to rise above their routine concerns, from the philistines, the dwellers in housing estates and new towns, than from those who think that society needs a new faith to invigorate it and give it a new impulse.[30]

In short, 'a large social organization could maintain a high degree of effectiveness— integration—with only a modicum of attachment to its value-system'.[31] This was possible, Shils argued, because strong social bonds in modern society rarely take the form of identification with an ideological cause, but rather with primordial or ecological group struc-tures (for example, kinship, neighbourhoods, professional groups) that need not necessarily have any sacred basis.[32] Indeed, the capacity of large parts of society to function without any reference to a sacred cause is typically a cause for lament among religious or political ideologues. As Shils observed, Lenin regretted that the working classes, if left to their own devices, would be content with making gradual improvements to their lives, and not be inspired with revolutionary fervour.[33]

It is not difficult to see modern social life as constituted around such mundane social bonds—indeed, it is reasonable to claim that this in fact is the most common basis of social life. Moreover, while there may be grounds for anxiety about the potential for identification with sacred forms to generate collective violence, irrationality, and division, there is also reason to doubt that a society grounded purely in the mundane offers any more protection from these. Shils's own research on the commitments and motivations of German and Russian soldiers demonstrated the importance of a core of people committed to the sacred vision of their cause in connecting the mainstream of the armed forces to the symbolic centre of their political movement. However, in practice, Shils argued that most soldiers fought not with a strong sense of commitment to that sacred cause, commenting that

my own examination of the extent to which the ordinary soldier understood and shared in the purposes of war and in the symbols of the state on behalf of which the war was being fought...has shown that acceptance was usually vague, unintense, and although positive, as close to neutrality in concrete situations as it could be without being entirely absent.[34]

Similarly, 'the Soviet army was a very powerful organization which had a great deal of coherence; yet very little of that coherence seemed to come from attachment to ideological or political symbols, or even intense patriotism'.[35] Instead, most smaller fighting units within these armies were constituted on the basis of mundane bonds, such as paternal concern for junior soldiers and a commitment to doing a collective task while keeping each other alive.[36] In other words, the massive damage and loss of life caused by the Second World War were made possible as much, if not more, through the mundane bonds that held armies and communities together as by strong collective identification with sacred forms.

The mundane can provide not only a means for social bonds during times of violent conflict, but also a pattern of life in which collective evil can become invisible or obscured. This point was memorably made by Hannah Arendt's account of Adolf Eichmann's Nazi career as a lesson in the 'banality of evil':

When I speak about the banality of evil, I do so only on the strictly factual level, pointing to a phenomenon that stared one in the face at the trial. Eichmann was not Iago and not Macbeth, and nothing would have been further from his mind than to determine with Richard III to 'prove a villain'. Except for an extraordinary diligence in looking out for his personal advancement, he had no motives at all. And this diligence was in no way criminal; he would certainly never have murdered his superior in order to inherit his post. He *merely*, to put the matter colloquially, *never realized what he was doing*. It was precisely this lack of imagination which enabled him to sit for months on end facing a German Jew who was conducting the police interrogation [of Eichmann], pouring out his heart to the man and explaining again and again how it was that he reached only the rank of lieutenant colonel in the SS and that it had not been his fault he had not been promoted. In principle, he knew quite well what it was all about...He was not stupid. It was sheer thoughtlessness—something by no means identical with stupidity—that predisposed him to become one of the greatest criminals of that period...[One] cannot extract any diabolical or demonic profundity from Eichmann.[37]

As the case of Eichmann demonstrates, the mundane ties that Shils emphasized—friendship, civic pride, a sense of professional responsibility or ambition—can be as complicit in the performance of acts of collective evil as powerful identification with sacred forms. A focus on the mundane bonds and practices of our everyday life can tune us out of systems of structural violence in which we are implicated. In the everyday act of buying a cheap toy for a child, for example, the life-threatening conditions of the workplace in which the toy may have been manufactured remain out of focus. If we wish to avoid the structural or physical violence enacted through the collective structures of social life, we need to maintain as critical a stance towards the mundane as we do towards forms of the sacred.

Sacred forms as communicative structures

A retreat from the sacred to the mundane does not, therefore, offer any certainty of a better society. Even if it did, however, there are good grounds for suggesting that the idea of society without sacred forms is little more than a thought-experiment that proves highly implausible in relation to actual social life.

Chapter 1 noted Durkheim's argument that the experience of the sacred arose out of a particular social ontology, and counter-arguments for rejecting this claim. There is an alternative reading of Durkheim, however, which conceives of the pervasiveness of sacred forms across human societies without referring back to the ontological. This is, as Eric Rothenbuhler has suggested, to read Durkheim's understanding of the sacred as 'positing a theory of the communicative foundations of social life'.[38] In other words, we might think of sacred forms as a common cultural phenomenon because they represent a particular kind of communicative structure around which social life is organized.[39]

The idea of the sacred as a communicative structure is developed initially in Durkheim and Mauss's *Primitive Classification*. In their conclusion to this monograph, Durkheim and Mauss draw out two important points from their earlier discussion of Aboriginal, native American, and Chinese systems of cultural classification. The first is that these systems of classification are not constituted primarily in a rational, systematic comparison; rather, 'it is the emotional value of notions which plays the preponderant part in the manner in which ideas are connected or separated'.[40] Systems of classification are, therefore, grounded primarily in moral sentiment and social sensibility. The value and meaning of objects within that system arise out of the ways in which they are experienced—for example, as nurturing, threatening, welcome, or unwelcome. As a consequence, classificatory systems are not simply made up of abstracted concepts; rather, their elements are 'products of sentiment',[41] objects that are meaningful in relation to the way in which groups have come to experience their worlds emotionally, morally, and aesthetically. This notion that human meaning-making is grounded primarily on sensory–emotional processes, with cognitive representations a second-order consequence of this, has been developed more fully in later phenomenological and pragmatist theories of human knowledge and experience.[42]

A second conclusion drawn by Durkheim and Mauss is that these systems of classification are organized around fundamental concepts, which seek to clarify their relationship to other objects. These fundamental concepts are precisely those that are taken to be sacred within a particular social group. 'The Australian does not divide the universe between the totems of his [sic] tribe with a view to regulating his conduct or even to justify his practice; it is because, the idea of the totem being cardinal for him, he is under a necessity to place everything else that he knows in relation to it.'[43] Sacred forms therefore access absolute realities that are emotionally and morally compelling, in relation to which other aspects of social and cultural experience must be understood.

The sacred can, therefore, be understood as a particular kind of cultural structure that operates in the wider context of human meaning-making, grounded in emotion, moral sensibility, and aesthetics. Given that this cultural structure is made possible through social interaction, it can therefore be thought about more specifically as a particular kind of communicative structure through which people collectively establish the absolute realities around which their lives should be organized. This idea of the sacred as communicative structure has been significantly developed through Eric Rothenbuhler's notion of 'ritual communication'. Rothenbuhler adopts an inclusive, Durkheimian definition of ritual as 'the voluntary performance of appropriately patterned behavior to symbolically affect or participate in the serious life'.[44] Ritual is, therefore, a means of participating in a shared communication about absolute realities that present normative claims on social life. By enacting such shared communication, the absolute realities become more vividly experienced and their claims more acutely felt. Social communication, when it bears upon such absolute realities, can thus be understood in ritual terms, as 'ritual communication'. Such a communicative structure, Rothenbuhler argues, is essential to a viable social life:

Ritual is necessary to social order. It is the symbolic means of crafting the self in social shape, of putting the will in the order of the social. Without it we would have no means of social order between happy cooperation, rational agreement and brute coercion. Real life, so far as we know, cannot always be happy and cooperative—the world we live in is too big for rational agreement among all the interested parties. But neither do we want our world to be brutally coercive . . . We have no evidence that we can live apart and plenty that we can only live together. Ritual is a means for managing that . . . [45]

Social life becomes possible on the basis of symbolic reference points of shared, absolute realities. This communicative structure involves particular kinds of social identification, common meanings, shared sentiments, and frameworks of meaningful social action. Although this communicative structure can be enforced in a coercive way—as totalitarian movements demonstrate—Rothenbuhler makes the point that it need not be, and that it is precisely at its most powerful when people participate in it voluntarily. Contingent, cultural structures are open to change, reform, and critical reflection, and can thus provide a ground on which the struggle for more humane social orders can be pursued.

As we discussed earlier, the communicative structures of sacred forms are not the only basis for the maintenance of social order. Mundane social life provides its own ties, limits, commitments, and sense of obligation, arguably offering the most fundamental basis for the constitution of society. However, social life is never premissed simply on the basis of such mundane ties and interactions. It is always subject to critique with reference to absolute, non-contingent realities, which are regarded as having fundamental normative claims over its conduct. These non-contingent realities are not hard-wired into the consciousness of the pre-social human agent,[46] but are woven into social life through acts of communication. It is through such communicative structures that social agents come to know and to feel the content of a sacred form, and to understand the meaning of their social world in its light. Mundane social interaction may assume certain sacred meanings, but can also take place without any assumed sacred referent, thus allowing mundane exchanges to take place between people whose sacred identifications might otherwise divide them.[47] Although parts of social life may function on the basis of the relative absence of sacred forms, it is impossible to imagine a society in which the communicative structures of the sacred are entirely absent. Social life cannot proceed without the possibility of reference to absolute realities on which it is claimed to be grounded, and it is only with reference to sacred forms that fundamental, normative frameworks for social life are made real. The sacred is inseparable from the very idea of human society because it is with reference to sacred forms that the meaningful, moral foundations and boundaries of human society are made known.[48] Durkheim's basic theory of the origins of the sacred can therefore be reversed. It is not society that generates the idea of the sacred. Rather it is the sacred that generates the idea of human society as a meaningful, moral collective.[49] The sacred remains an ever-present thread in social life, sometimes powerfully shaping social interaction, sometimes not; sometimes explicit, sometimes implicit and existing as a latent force. But society in which the sacred is entirely absent is impossible.

Living with sacred forms

If sacred forms are an inevitable element of social life, then the practical limitations of the thought-experiment of imagining society without the sacred become clear. If we still accept the considerable evidence that sacred forms can have destructive effects, then the question turns from whether we can simply live without the sacred, to how we live with the sacred in ways that mitigate against its shadow side as best as possible.

It is possible that the social and cultural conditions of pluralist, late-modern societies tend to make identification with sacred forms more problematic, and social performances of the sacred more prone to failure.[50] However, while it may be true that reflexivity and cultural pluralism may make it harder for any single form of the sacred to be received uncritically across whole populations in modern societies, there are still enough examples of the power of sacred identifications to suggest that they remain a potent motive force in social life. The murders of Theo van Gogh and Pim Fortuyn, for example, generated widespread identification in Holland with the imagined sacred essence of Dutch society, which was perceived as being under threat from unwelcome outsiders.[51] The continued popularity of Vladimir Putin in Russia testifies to the ongoing power of the sacralization of Russian nationalism. The lack of critical investigation into allegations of war crimes in the prosecution of the Sri Lankan government's war with the Tamil Tigers points to the power of emotionally and morally charged constructions of in-groups and out-groups within Sri Lankan society. Aspects of contemporary social life may weaken or fragment uncritical identifications with the sacred, but the enduring role of this communicative structure means that its social and cultural power persists.

So how can we live with sacred forms in the modern world? A starting point is to nurture practices of critical reflection about the nature and significance both of the sacred as a communicative structure and of specific sacred forms for contemporary social life. The difficulty of this task cannot be underestimated. The sacred is 'naturally refractory to analysis', as Durkheim and Mauss put it, because such analysis requires us to recognize the contingency of sacred forms, which, by their very nature, are regarded by their adherents as non-contingent. To suggest, for example, that the Holocaust became a profound symbol of a unique evil through contingent historical processes can appear offensive, when it is regarded by many simply as a profound breach of the non-contingent sacred. Similarly recognizing the contingent ways in which concepts of human rights have been sacralized can be threatening to the sacred claim of the universality of those rights. To imagine that we can achieve some kind of free-floating attention with regard to sacred forms, in which we suspend any sacred commitments, is neither desirable nor, in reality, achievable. Indeed, to try to place ourselves beyond any sacred claims would be to remove ourselves from the framework of meanings through which social life itself is possible, and, in that sense, to make ourselves less than human. Sacred forms that we experience as exerting a normative claim on our lives are, ultimately, not susceptible to critical analysis, nor can their ontological reality be proven or disproven to their adherents through rational debate. This is not to suggest that identifications with sacred forms are unchangeable. As we know, people who form deep identifications with sacred forms associated with religious and political movements can, over time, disengage from these through sudden or gradual processes of disillusionment. But such cases of 'de-conversion' do not leave a person with no sacred referents for their lives, but simply with a different set of referents. An intellectual or existential stance, beyond all influence of the sacred, is not possible.

What is possible, however, is a nurturing of the capacity for critical reflection on the effects of one's sacred commitments. To achieve this can still be a demanding process. It requires creating a fissure of critical awareness within sacred identifications, which disrupts, however slightly, the assumption that the sacred form is an ontological reality that has specific and unquestionable moral demands and that the pursuit of these is inherently good. Talking about the contingency of sacred forms can help this process to some degree, as this may encourage people not to abandon their sacred identifications but to recognize that these identifications are to some extent an *interpretation* of an underlying absolute reality. Alongside this, historical and contemporary examples of the shadow side of the sacred can also potentially encourage the recognition that the pursuit of one's own sacred commitments might lead to destructive acts. One of the ways in which such reflection is diverted, in the context of debates about the social consequences of religious commitment, is to suggest that those who commit evil in the name of a particular tradition have a distorted or inauthentic grasp of it.[52] This arises particularly in public debate about Islam, in which it is claimed that violent 'extremists' either are holding to a perverted form of Islam or are merely using Islam as a cover for their destructive, political purposes. While the desire to protect the moral rectitude of Islam is understandable against the background of caricatured associations of Islam and terrorism, this particular argument does nothing to help a critical appreciation of the shadow side of the sacred. To claim that evil is done in the name of a sacred form only as a result of a misunderstanding or misuse of that sacred form is a failure to recognize the potential for destructive social action that is embedded within the very structure of the sacred itself. Sacred forms associated with religious traditions that have evolved over many centuries are complex phenomena that give rise to many different forms of identification. To claim that harmful expressions of sacred commitments are simply inauthentic performances of that sacred form neglects aspects of it that allow for such destructive performances. Sacred traditions cannot therefore be assumed to be unambiguously good, but are complex phenomena that require careful cultivation.[53]

If a degree of critical awareness of our sacred commitments is a reasonable aim, the fragmentation of the sacred in late modern societies may prove to be an asset. One of the claims made by some of those who lament the perceived demoralization of contemporary society is that such moral decline is a result of the lack of a clear, shared ethical framework, which is often religious in nature. In reality, the fact that we live in the context of multiple sacred forms and identifications represents a more positive framework for moral reflexivity. In societies where there is a widespread consensus in relation to a single, dominant sacred form, critical reflection on it can be perceived as too threatening to social order to be tolerated. By contrast, as Mary Douglas has put it, 'the more open a community, the less its members are coerced by common beliefs about dangers that defend the community-defined definitions of sin'.[54] The fact that late-modern societies are characterized by multiple sacred forms thus creates the ground for a range of different viewpoints from which the consequences of particular sacred commitments can be critiqued. Projects that attempt to reconstitute society in relation to a single form of the sacred are not only practically doomed to failure, given the irreversibly plural nature of contemporary society, but are morally undesirable. Instead, social life needs to be conducted on the basis of the principle of 'agonistic pluralism', as described by Chantal Mouffe, in which serious difference and moral conflict are an accepted part of the social order. Rather than allowing such difference to become the basis of a polarization between friends (who share our sacred commitments) and enemies (who profane them, and must be destroyed), Mouffe advocates another way of framing such conflict:

While antagonism is a we/they relation in which the two sides are enemies who do not share any common ground, agonism is a we/they relation where the conflicting parties, although acknowledging that there is no rational solution to their conflict, nevertheless recognize the legitimacy of their opponents. They are 'adversaries' not enemies. This means that, while in conflict, they see themselves as belonging to the same political association, as sharing a common symbolic space within which the conflict takes place. We could say that the task of democracy is to transform antagonism into agonism.[55]

Given Jeffrey Alexander's observation about the ways in which the symbolic space of civil society is inevitably constructed in terms of the sacred and profane, the notion of a democratic society in which none is symbolically excluded remains an unrealizable ideal. Mouffe herself argues that, to be accepted as a full participant in such a democratic social order, it is necessary for individuals and groups not to undermine the civic institutions that make that common, democratic life possible.[56] Nevertheless, a commitment to such agonistic pluralism, along with an acceptance that all participants in society are mutually accountable to each other, creates the basis for a common social order in which multiple sacred identifications may be contested without undermining the possibility of peaceful social order itself. The virtues of critical reflection and public exchange required by such agonistic pluralism are at the same time those required to sustain more critical awareness of the light and shadow cast by our particular sacred commitments.[57]

If the multiplicity of sacred forms in modern society can create different vantage points for critical reflection, they can also undermine deeply polarized conflicts that threaten to tear societies apart. This may seem a paradoxical point, as the diversity of sacred commitments is often taken as emblematic of the profound cultural divisions that challenge the cohesiveness of society. Yet, as we have noted at different points through this book, sacred identifications are transient, and the multiplicity of sacred forms can be found not only at the level of society but within the individual subject as well. Debates about multiculturalism can often assume the existence of reified, 'authentic' cultures that have to be negotiated in some sense,[58] and even Mouffe's otherwise helpful analysis assumes we/they divisions in political life that are relatively stable and enduring. But the fragmented nature of the contemporary sacred means that such 'cultures' are not separate, impermeable entities, and that 'we/they' identifications can be similarly unstable. A recent example of this was the shooting of Congresswoman Gabrielle Giffords on 9 January 2011, against the backdrop of increasingly polarized public life in America. The shooting, which left six other people dead, including 10-year-old Christina Taylor Green, generated further performances of this polarized divide over the role of right-wing political discourse in creating conditions for violence. However, the fact that this shooting also threatened sacred forms, such as American democracy (as symbolized in Giffords) or the care of children (as symbolized by Taylor Green), meant other forms of shared identification became possible across the political divide. Two weeks after the shooting, politicians in the houses of Congress, who had been deeply divided before the Christmas break, chose symbolically to sit among each other to hear the President's State of the Union address. This is not to suggest that all social divisions are superficial or that such symbolic reconciliations dissipate all the tensions that threaten to undermine them. Rather, it is important to recognize that the multiplicity of sacred forms creates shifting patterns of identification and conflict that simplistic notions of clashes of cultures or civilizations fail to recognize.

A final, perhaps more parochial, point needs briefly to be made. If critical reflection concerning our sacred identifications is to be encouraged, universities have a central role to play in this. A basic task of academic institutions is to create a space in which non-violent exchange in relation to different sacred commitments can be made possible. The move across different university systems to reframe higher education in primarily neo-liberal terms, as a commodity to be bought by students as an investment for their future career development, is doubtless an expression of some social actors' commitment to neo-liberalism as a sacred form. But this highly reductive view of education is to miss the point of universities as a public good. If we are to live thoughtfully and responsibly under the light and shadow of the sacred, we need spaces, resources, and practices to help us to do this. In pluralist societies, the university is a crucial site for encouraging such work, and subjugating this role to a neo-liberal view of education-as-training risks undermining a vital institutional resource for a viable common life. Perhaps the most important legacy of Durkheim's work will be his example of the pursuit of a humane society through academic reflection on the place of the sacred in social life. Carrying this legacy forward is the challenge ahead of us.

Conclusion: A Theoretical Outline for a Cultural Sociology of the Sacred

A central aim of this book has been to set out a theoretical framework for the sacred that provides a basis for social and cultural analysis. Some core elements of this framework were discussed in the opening two chapters of the book. But the iterative nature of the argument, moving between theoretical generalization, case analysis, and normative reflection, has led to this framework being refined through the book as a whole. In this conclusion, then, a final summary will be given of the theoretical understanding of the sacred reached through the preceding discussion, which remains open to revision, clarification, and extension through future work.

The sacred does not derive directly from the ontological condition of the human person or the cosmos. Rather, the sacred is a communicative structure focused on absolute realities around which the meanings of social life are constituted and that exert normative claims on the conduct of social life. The sacred is not generated by society, as Durkheim suggested, but rather the sacred constructs the idea of human society as a meaningful, moral collective. The nature of the sacred in different contexts remains an empirical question to be pursued through historical, social, and cultural analysis, and caution should be taken in assuming that particular structures of the sacred are universal across all times and places. Nevertheless, it is difficult to imagine a form of human society that does not, at some point, make use of sacred communicative structures about absolute, normative realities.

Sacred forms are specific, contingent instances of the sacred as a communicative structure. Sacred forms consist of specific symbols, as well as patterns of thought, emotions, and actions grounded in the body, which recursively reproduce the sacrality of that particular sacred form, and draw together social collectivities around these shared forms of thinking, feeling, and acting. Sacred forms are historically contingent, in terms of both their content and their structure. The sacrality of a particular sacred form waxes and wanes through time depending on its ability to attract widespread emotional and moral identification, a process influenced by social actors, the spaces and structures through which that sacred form is mediated, and the nature and operation of power in that context. The relative dominance or subjugation of a sacred form in relation to other sacred forms also has a significant bearing on the extent to which its sacrality is widely recognized and it becomes a powerful motive force in social life.

The binary of the sacred and the profane is usefully replaced by the distinction between the categories of the sacred, the profane, and the mundane. The profane is the particular representation of evil constructed in relation to a specific sacred form. The profane threatens to pollute or breach that sacred form, and to taint and shame whatever it comes into contact with. Those who identify with a particular sacred form perceive individuals and groups associated with its profanation as beyond the acceptable boundaries of moral, human community. The profane therefore serves to establish boundaries between moral in-groups and out-groups. It is extremely difficult for an individual or group that identifies with a particular sacred form to acknowledge that they may have been involved in its profanation, unless they have access to some form of cultural mechanism of restitution or are able to draw moral strength from identifying with another sacred form. Instead, it is more common for the threatening sense of one's complicity in the profanation of the sacred to be managed through defences such as projecting the blame for the profanation onto others or providing a rationalization for why an apparently profane act could be deemed acceptable. Beyond such defences lies a sensitivity to the tragic dimension of social life.

The category of the mundane refers to the logics, practices, and aesthetics of everyday life. The mundane can be as great, if not a greater, source of social integration than sacred forms, and much of social life is conducted in the realm of the mundane. The mundane either operates on the implicit assumption of particular sacred forms, or becomes an arena of social life in which the non-explicit nature of sacred forms allows for a common social life to be conducted despite a lack of consensus around sacred forms. While moments of intense identification with sacred forms may be sporadic or transient, sacred forms nevertheless remain a latent force that can erupt into mundane social life.

Such identifications have the capacity to energize, critique, or refashion the conduct of mundane social interaction, as well as remoralize or disrupt mundane social ecologies. In the realm of the mundane, symbols associated with sacred forms can also become routinized, losing their compelling emotional or moral force, and circulate in ways that allow them to be used in banal or instrumental ways.[1] Such banal circulation of sacred symbols can also take place as a result of the relative subjugation of a sacred form in relation to a more dominant form, which constrains the possibilities for widespread or powerful identifications with that subjugated form and generates sentimentalized performances of its sacred symbols, devoid of moral force.

While the nature, content, and significance of sacred forms are always contingent and contextual, some general claims can tentatively be made about the nature of the sacred in late modern societies. In contrast to more homogeneous societies, organized in relation to an overarching sacred form, late modern societies are characterized by the simultaneous presence of multiple sacred forms that exert complementary and conflicting fields of influence. Although some cultural groups attempt to organize their lives with consistent reference to a particular sacred form, in practice this proves very difficult. Even religious groups who believe themselves to be oriented simply around a particular sacred form of their tradition are in reality influenced by other sacred forms such as nationalism, human rights, or the care of children. The fragmentation of the modern sacred does not mean that society is simply organized around different sub-tribes, formed around competing sacred forms, but that social life is negotiated through the complex fields of gravitational pull simultaneously exerted by different sacred forms. The individual human subject in late modernity therefore rarely lives in relation to a single sacred form, but rather in relation to multiple forms in contingent and complex ways.

The social and cultural conditions of late modernity have ambiguous consequences for the possibility of identification with sacred forms. On the one hand, the development of globalized structures such as international law, NGOs, neo-liberal markets, and public media makes it possible for the reach of particular sacred forms (for example, human rights) to be extended over a wide range of societies. At the same time, however, the greater reflexivity and pluralism of modern social life make uncritical identification with sacred forms harder, and sacred performances more likely to be perceived as being instrumental, self-interested, or inauthentic. Arguably the most significant structures through which people reproduce or contest sacred forms in modern society are public media, making it reasonable to make limited claims about the mediatization of the sacred. People have an opportunity for powerful identification with sacred forms, through either their celebration or their pollution, through public media that offer 'real-life' narratives. The sacred role of public media can confer cultural authority on journalists as honest brokers of sacred narratives, but also raises challenges for media professionals and their audiences.

Although the term 'sacred' in its vernacular uses is commonly taken to refer to the 'good', the social effects of the sacred are highly ambiguous. The communicative structure of the sacred draws people into strong identifications with what they experience to be normative realities, but considerable human suffering has been caused throughout history by attempts to sustain or protect sacred forms. On the one hand, sacred forms allow people to communicate about, and collectively experience, realities that provide normative points of reference for social life. They provide a particular source of moralization, in addition to the ethics and norms of polite, professional, or civilized mundane social interactions. Yet, at the same time, identification with sacred forms can legitimate acts of violence, and, when associated with elites who hold substantial allocative and regulative power, form a basis for repressive social orders. Sacred forms can polarize societies and make political life subject more to emotional identifications rather than to critical analysis. Social life entirely divorced from the sacred is impossible, however, because communicative structures of the sacred are inseparable from the concept and practice of human society itself. Furthermore, given the normative significance of sacred forms, it is unrealistic to imagine that those who adhere to them could easily reject them. What is needed, then, is critical reflection upon the effects of sacred commitments, for us to be mutually accountable for these and to support structures that make non-violent and respectful discussion of the nature and consequences of sacred forms possible. Some may view the lack of a single sacred form around which modern society is organized as a dangerous source of godlessness, demoralization, and anomie. In reality, the simultaneous presence of multiple sacred forms creates the potential for more critical spaces and perspectives to emerge that draw attention to the limitations and risks of particular sacred commitments. More harm can be done by those who try to bend society towards a single sacred cause than by those who encourage the democratic, agonistic negotiation of multiple sacred forms.

This, then, is the theoretical framework proposed within this book for identifying and analysing the nature of the sacred in the modern world. There are still a number of questions for further exploration and clarification. How do sacred forms become routinized such that their sacred symbols circulate through society in ways that elicit little emotional or moral power? What specific sacred forms have particular influence over contemporary social life? How do individuals experience and negotiate the pull of multiple sacred forms, and what different kinds of relations exist between sacred forms at the level of society? How might the emotional element of sacred identifications be understood in relation to broader theories of the role of emotion in social life? What role do material objects, aesthetics, time, and space play in the mediation of sacred forms? How can we understand the phenomenon of sacred forms being expressed through a specific person, or think more clearly about the significance of intersubjective relations with persons who are taken to be sacred? Is it possible to make connections between understanding the sacred as a communicative structure and contemporary scientific understanding of brain function, to learn how such cultural structures become ingrained into human perception of the world? All these are important wider questions for a theoretical understanding of the sacred. As we have seen, though, the process of answering these satisfactorily will partly involve more analysis of sacred forms in specific social and historical contexts. Such contextual analysis is also the means through which the critical and therapeutic potential of understanding the significance of the sacred in social life can be realized. In pursuing this project, we have the potential for developing a clearer language for thinking about powerful motive forces that shape society for good and ill. Given the on-going power of the sacred, such insight is essential for understanding what brings us together and divides us, as well as the harm and the good that we do to each other in the wake of our sacred commitments.

Notes

Introduction

1. See, e.g., T. Dant, *Materiality and Society* (Maidenhead: Open University Press, 2005).
2. For a fuller discussion of this, see G. Lynch, *The New Spirituality: An Introduction to Progressive Belief in the Twenty-First Century* (London: I. B. Tauris, 2007).
3. T. Luckmann, *The Invisible Religion* (London: MacMillan, 1967).
4. J. C. Alexander and S. Sherwood, 'Mythic Gestures: Robert N. Bellah and Cultural Sociology', in R. Madsen, W. Sullivan, and A. Swidler (ed), *Meaning and Modernity: Religion Polity, and Self* (Berkeley and Los Angeles: University of California Press, 2002), 1–14, describe Bellah's 1967 article on 'Civil Religion in America' as the first text of the new cultural sociology.
5. See E. Rothenbuhler and M. Coman, *Media Anthropology* (London: Sage, 2005).
6. K. Knott, *The Location of Religion: A Spatial Analysis* (London: Eqiunox, 2005); *Location of* Religion; V. Anttonen, 'Sacred', in R. McCutcheon and W. Braun (eds), *Guide to the Study of Religion* (London: Continuum, 1999), 271–82.
7. See N. Couldry and E. Rothenbuhler, 'Simon Cottle on "Mediatized Rituals": A Response', *Media, Culture, Society*, 29/4 (2007), 691–5.

Chapter 1

1. Although ontological and cultural approaches are based on fundamentally different assumptions, it is also possible to develop a position that brings the two together in some way. Roger Caillois, for example, can be seen as working within a cultural approach to the study of the sacred. In his original introduction to *Man and the Sacred* (1939; Urbana, IL: University of Illinois Press, 2001), Caillois (p. 13) argues that there is no essential content to the category of the sacred other than the fact that it is constructed in opposition to the profane, and his declared interest in studying the 'syntax' of the sacred foreshadows Alexander's semiotic approach. But by the end of the book (pp. 128–38, see also p. 15), Caillois finds it impossible to avoid the conclusion that cultural constructions of the sacred draw on a fundamental, existential awareness of life, mortality, and decay.
2. W. James, *The Varieties of Religious Experience* (London: Longmans, Green & Co., 1902), 31.

3. R. Otto, *The Idea of the Holy* (Oxford: Oxford university Press, 1923), 10 n. 1.
4. Otto, *The Idea of the Holy*, 11.
5. Otto, *The Idea of the Holy*, 112.
6. O. Riis and L. Woodhead, *A Sociology of Religious Emotion* (Oxford: Oxford University Press, 2010), 2.
7. James, *Varieties*, 379–82. Otto also uses terms drawn from longer traditions of mystical writing, such as Meister Eckhart's notion of the ground of the soul (Seelengrund). Other contemporaneous writers focusing on the on-going significance of such mysticism in modernity included Simmel, Troeltsch and Caillois.
8. M. Eliade, *The Sacred and the Profane* (New York: Harcourt, 1959), 10.
9. Eliade, *The Sacred and the Profane*, 16–17. There is a sense, then, for Eliade that the expressions of the sacred may be historically contingent. But, unlike the form of historical contingency I propose below, Eliade still detects a common ontological structure underneath these different cultural expressions, whereas I do not assume any such ontology.
10. This has certain similarities to H. Becker and R. Myers's distinction ('Sacred and Secular Aspects of Human Sociation', *Sociometry*, 5/4 (1942), 355–70) between secular and sacred ways of being, although Becker conceives of the sacred more in terms of traditional, non-rational culture than in terms of any kind of ontological referent.
11. Eliade, *The Sacred and the Profane*, 203.
12. Eliade, *The Sacred and the Profane*, 24, 204–7.
13. Eliade, *The Sacred and the Profane*, 64.
14. Eliade, *The Sacred and the Profane*, 213.
15. We could include Victor Turner's work (e.g. *The Ritual Process: Structure and Anti-Structure* (1969; London: Aldine, 1995)) in this line of scholarship, in some respects. Given Turner's sensitivity to the cultural construction of the sacred through ritual, this might be a surprising move, but his notion of the sacred quality of the liminal, the liminoid, and communitas represents another form of the idea that the sacred is to be found in a particular kind of human experience.
16. It is worth noting that in the extensive literature on Eliade's work there is a debate about whether his notion of the sacred implies an external, intentional agent beyond humanity or simply an integral part of the structure of human experience (R. McCutcheon, *The Discipline of Religion: Structure, Meaning, Rhetoric* (London: Routledge, 2003), 197). As McCutcheon has often pointed out, though, Eliade's concept of the sacred remains somewhat ambiguous through his work. It seems reasonable to read in both Otto and Eliade a reference to an ontological presence that has an existence beyond the structures of human perception, but in both writers the nature of this ontological presence is left largely undefined beyond this fundamental point.
17. See, e.g., R. Orsi, *Between Heaven and Earth: The Religious Worlds People Make and the Scholars who Study Them* (Princeton: Princeton University Press, 2005). The notion that the study of religion, based on such liberal

foundations, could be a source of cultural renewal was explicit in Eliade's work; see R. McCutcheon, *Manufacturing Religion: The Discourse of Sui Generis Religion and the Politics of Nostalgia* (New York: Oxford University Press, 1997), 37–9.

18. McCutcheon, *Discipline of Religion*, 197.

19. See, e.g., McCutcheon, *Discipline of Religion*, 206–7.

20. See, e.g., M. Stausberg, *Contemporary Theories of Religion: A Critical Companion* (London: Routledge, 2009).

21. I am very grateful to Terhi Utriainen for helping me to see this point.

22. Derrida cited in G. Ward, *Theology and Contemporary Critical Theory* (2nd edn; Basingstoke: MacMillan, 2000), 15.

23. Ward, *Theology and Contemporary Critical Theory* 16.

24. See C. Bailey Gill (ed.), *Bataille: Writing the Sacred* (London: Routledge, 1995); S. Kendall, *Georges Bataille* (London: Reaktion Books, 2007).

25. B. Giesen, 'Performing the Sacred: A Durkheimian Perspective on the Performative Turn in the Social Sciences', in J. C. Alexander, B. Giesen, and J. Mast (eds), *Social Performance: Symbolic Action, Cultural Pragmatics and Ritual* (Cambridge: Cambridge University Press, 2006), 325–67.

26. Giesen, 'Performing the Sacred', 332.

27. Giesen, 'Performing the Sacred', 330.

28. For example, in *The Ritual Process*, Victor Turner is primarily interested in the different social and cultural expressions deriving from the foundational, sacral experience of communitas.

29. T. Csordas, 'Asymptote of the Ineffable: Embodiment, Alterity and the Theory of Religion', *Current Anthropology*, 45/2 (2004),164.

30. B. Anderson, *Imagined Communites: Reflections on the Origins and Spread of Nationalism* (London: Verso, 1991), 10–36.

31. See J. C. Alexander, 'Introduction: Durkheimian Sociology and Cultural Studies Today', in J. C. Alexander (ed.), *Durkheimian Sociology: Cultural Studies* (Cambridge: Cambridge University Press, 1988), 3–10, for a broader account of the intellectual reception of Durkheim's work.

32. See Alexander and Sherwood, 'Mythic Gestures', for a fuller account of Bellah's shift from Parsonian theory. Bellah's interest in the ongoing mutual influence of religion, culture, and politics was enabled by Parsons's integrative theory of society, which treated these different elements as inseparable parts of the social system. But Bellah broke from Parsons, not only through the detailed historical treatment of a particular case, grounded in specific social narratives, but in his later rejection of Parsons's evolutionary emphasis, which allowed him to argue the fragility and likely ultimate failure of civil religion in contrast to Parsonian optimism about the evolutionary progress of societies towards ever greater differentiation and renewed integration. Alexander and Sherwood note that Bellah's lament in *The Broken Covenant: American Civil Religion in Time of Trial* (Chicago: University of Chicago Press, 1992) may have been too pessimistic about the prospects for American democracy, but it nevertheless opened the way for developments in cultural sociology

that were sensitive to the ambiguities of history in contrast to the abstract, evolutionary optimism of Parsons.

33. R. Robertson and B. Turner, 'An Introduction to Talcott Parsons: Theory, Politics and Humanity', in R. Robertson and B. Turner (eds), *Talcott Parsons: Theorist of Modernity* (London: Sage, 1991), 1–21, identify four main criticisms of Parsons's structuralist-functionalist theory of society: (1) the inconsistencies in his early and middle accounts of the relationship between agency and structure, in which his early notion that 'human agents select goals through normative choices was incompatible with the idea that human social relations are structured in a systematic fashion as a consequence of the functional imperatives of the social system' (p. 8); (2) that it was too abstract to be of value in the analysis of concrete social systems and its complexity disguised simple and mundane observations about social life; (3) that his work was inherently conservative, not only in terms of Parsons's support for American and capitalist society, but also in terms of his failure adequately to theorize inequality, class, and vested power interests; (4) that his assumption that capitalist societies were inherently capable of progressive improvement represented an unwarranted attempt to overturn Marxist critiques of the capitalist system. Although Parsons's work had fallen from favour among most sociologists by the mid-1970s, there have been subsequent attempts to re-evaluate his work, including Robertson and Turner (eds), *Talcott Parsons*; J. C. Alexander, *Theoretical Logic in Sociology*, iv. *Talcott Parsons* (Berkeley and Los Angeles: University of California Press, 1983), and J. C. Alexander, 'Commentary: Structure, Value, Action', *American Sociological Review*, 55/3 (1990), 339–45.

34. P. Smith and J. C. Alexander, 'Introduction: The New Durkheim', in J. C. Alexander and P. Smith (eds), *The Cambridge Companion to Durkheim* (Cambridge: Cambridge University Press, 2005), 6.

35. Indeed, I would recognize that Giesen's theory is probably much closer to Durkheim's original intent than mine.

36. See P. Smith (ed.), *The New American Cultural Sociology* (Cambridge: Cambridge University Press, 1998), for a broader account of this movement in the USA. Also Riley, '"Renegade Durkheimianism" and the Transgressive Left Sacred', in Alexander and Smith (eds), *The Cambridge Companion to Durkheim*, 274–301.

37. E. Durkheim, *The Elementary Forms of the Religious Life* (Oxford: Oxford University Press, 2001), 3.

38. W. S. Pickering, 'The Eternality of the Sacred: Durkheim's Error?', *Archives de sciences sociales des religion*, 69 (1909), 91–108; S. Meštrović, *Postemotional Society* (London: Sage, 1997).

39. M. Cladis, 'Introduction', in Durkheim, *Elementary Forms*, p. xvi.

40. S. Lukes, *Émile Durkheim: His Life and Work* (London: Penguin, 1975), 478.

41. J. C. Alexander, 'Culture and Political Crisis: "Watergate" and Durkheimian Sociology', in Alexander (ed.), *Durkheimian Sociology*, 190–1.

42. J. C. Alexander and J. Mast, 'Introduction: Symbolic Action in Theory and Practice: The Cultural Pragmatics of Cultural Action', in J. C. Alexander, B. Giesen, and J. Mast (eds), *Social Performance: Symbolic Action, Cultural Pragmatics and Ritual* (Cambridge: Cambridge University Press, 2006), 8–9. But Durkheim himself was much more open than some of his critics acknowledge to the reality of 'confederations' of sacred things that exert complex fields of gravitational pull over individuals and groups (see *Elementary Forms*, 40).

43. Alexander, 'Culture and Political Crisis', 191.

44. N. Couldry, *Media Rituals: A Critical Approach* (London: Routledge, 2003), 8.

45. E. Durkheim and M. Mauss, *Primitive Classification*, trans. R. Needham (1903; London: Cohen & West, 1963), 81–8.

46. Durkheim, *Elementary Forms*, 153, observes that it is the symbolic representation of the totem that conveys sacrality more than the totemic object itself.

47. Durkheim thus had a far more positive view of the socially integrative power of collective emotion than many of his contemporaries, who saw group emotion more in terms of a mass hysteria liable to undermine social order; see M. Richman, 'The The Sacred Group: A Durkheimian Perspective on the College de Sociologie', in C. Bailey Gill (ed.), *Bataille: Writing the Sacred* (London: Routledge, 1995), 58–76.

48. Durkheim, *Elementary Forms*, 155; Cladis, 'Introduction', p. xxvii.

49. P. Mellor and C. Shilling, 'Body Pedagogics and the Religious Habitus: A New Direction for the Sociological Study of Religion', *Religion*, 40 (2010), 27–38; C. Shilling and P. Mellor, 'Retheorizing Emile Durkheim on Society and Religion: Embodiment, Intoxication and Collective Life', *Sociological Review*, 59/1 (2011), 17–41.

50. We could note, for example, that the embodied practice of the Nazi salute ('Heil Hitler') appears to have been far more widespread among supporters of the Nazi movement in the 1920s (indeed compulsory in the movement after 1926) than clearly formulated anti-Semitic beliefs (see R. Evans, *The Coming of the Third Reich* (London: Allen Lane, 2003), 212, 217–25). Robert Orsi (*Between Heaven and Earth*, 108) similarly notes an example of a Catholic woman reporting the experience of reciting a prayer in a dangerous moment in her adult life: 'all of a sudden, when her fear was extreme, she heard one of the old prayers she had memorized as a child sounding in her head. She was not "saying" this prayer, [she] explained to me. The prayer was "echoing in my body".'

51. I am very grateful to Ruth Sheldon for helping me see this, and to think of defining the sacred in terms of normative realities.

52. Durkheim, *Elementary Forms*, 37.

53. Durkheim, *Elementary Forms*, 41.

54. See Smith and Alexander, 'Introduction'.

55. Lukes, *Durkheim*, pp.16–28. Another instance of the limitations of this binary thinking is Durkheim's assumption that the sacred is a collective experience, while profane, everyday existence is simply individualistic and instrumental

(see Cladis, 'Introduction', pp.xxii-xxiii). As a consequence, Durkheim was unable to see the integrative effects of mundane social interaction.

56. Lukes, *Durkheim*, 26–7.

57. See J. C. Alexander, 'Towards a Sociology of Evil: Getting between Modernist Common Sense about the Alternative to the Good', in M. Lara (ed.), *Rethinking Evil: Contemporary Perspectives* (Berkeley and Los Angeles: University of California Press, 2001), 153–72; also R. Stivers, *Evil in Modern Myth and Ritual* (Atlanta, GA: University of Atlanta Press, 1982).

58. Giesen's ontological view of the sacred is, for example, a very reasonable theorizing of the sacred following the ontological thread in Durkheim's own thought.

59. See Durkheim, *Elementary Forms*,154–68.

60. Turner, *The Ritual Process*, 97. This understanding of the sacred significance of the experience of the collective is also central to Maffesoli's understanding of neo-tribes.

61. See, e.g., Riis and Woodhead, *Sociology of Religious Emotion*, 66–7.

62. M. Douglas, *Natural Symbols* (new edn; London: Routledge, 1996), p. xvi.

63. Durkheim, *Elementary Forms*, 154.

64. We can similarly reject Durkheim's assumption that the content and structure of classificatory systems are defined by the structure of social groups, an assumption given elaborate development by Mary Douglas in *Natural Symbols*. An understanding of the contingency of the content and structure of sacred forms is better grounded in the view that classificatory meanings emerge out of the interplay of brain, body, and socio-cultural environment in specific contexts (see M. Johnson, *The Meaning of the Body* (Chicago: University of Chicago Press, 2007), 1–2).

65. Alexander, 'Towards a Sociology of Evil'.

Chapter 2

1. Alexander, 'Introduction', 2–3, notes that Durkheim's application of his concepts of the sacred and symbolic classification to modern society mainly took place in lectures that were published only posthumously, and that he did not develop to the same degree as his major monographs.

2. E. Shils, 'Primordial, Personal, Sacred and Civil Ties', in E. Shils, *Center and Periphery: Essays in Macro-Sociology* (Chicago: University of Chicago Press, 1975),125.

3. Shils, 'Primordial, Personal, Sacred and Civil Ties', 125.

4. The significance of these experiences for Shils's work are described partly in an autobiographical essay in Shils, 'Primordial, Personal, Sacred and Civil Ties'; see also S. Turner, 'The Significance of Shils', *Sociological Theory*, 17/2 (1999), 125–45.

5. E. Shils, 'Center and Periphery', in Shils, *Center and* Periphery, 7. While this represents an ontological claim about human nature, this does not mean that Shils's theory of the sacred is an ontological one. Shils recognizes the

contingent nature of the content and structure of sacred forms rather than seeing these forms as determined by human ontology.

6. Shils, 'Primordial, Personal, Sacred and Civil Ties', 112.
7. E. Shils, 'Charisma', in Shils, *Center and Periphery*, 133–4.
8. Shils, 'Center and Periphery', 3. Note that this interest in the role of the sacred in establishing symbolic centres for society is not original to Shils, but noted by Durkheim and Mauss in *Primitive Classification* (p. 87), as well as being discussed extensively by Eliade in *The Sacred and the Profane*.
9. E. Shils and M. Young, 'The Meaning of the Coronation', in Shils, *Center and Periphery*, 151–2.
10. Shils, 'Center and Periphery', 5.
11. Shils, 'Center and Periphery', 8.
12. Shils, 'Center and Periphery', 6.
13. Shils, 'Charisma', 129, 132–3.
14. Shils and Young, 'The Meaning of the Coronation', 139.
15. See, e.g., R. Jacobs, *Race, Media and the Crisis of Civil Society: From Watts to Rodney King* (Cambridge: Cambridge University Press, 2000).
16. Jacobs, *Race*, 147–8.
17. Shils, 'Center and Periphery', 11.
18. Shils, 'Center and Periphery',11–12.
19. See this work being done explicitly in Shils and Young, 'The Meaning of the Coronation', 139.
20. See, e.g., B. Turner, *Religion and Social Theory* (2nd edn; London: Sage, 1991), 61; A. Giddens, *Durkheim* (London: Fontana, 1997), 103–4.
21. S. Turner, 'The Significance of Shils', 140.
22. Shils and Young, 'The Meaning of the Coronation', 143.
23. R. Bellah, 'Religion and the Legitimation of the American Republic', *Society*, 15/4 (1978), 16–23.
24. Bellah et al., *Habits of the Heart: Individualism and Commitment in American Life* (Berkeley and Los Angeles: University of California Press, 1985).
25. Bellah, *Broken Covenant*.
26. Bellah, 'Civil Religion in America', *Daedalus*, 96/1 (1967), 12.
27. At the preface to the second edition of *The Broken Covenant*, for example, Bellah comments in passing on the 'essence of Christianity', suggesting an essential moral core expressed through, but also standing above, its specific historical instantiations in Christianity. Note this claim does not represent an ontological view of the sacred; it is a normative claim about the ultimate value of a particular sacred form, rather than a claim about an ontological reality that shapes all sacred forms.
28. Bellah, *Broken Covenant*. McCutcheon's dismissal of Bellah as a nationalist propagandist (*Discipline of Religion*, 280–1) seems unfairly to neglect this strong element of social critique in Bellah's work.
29. Bellah, 'Civil Religion', 19 n.1.
30. Durkheim did recognize in the *Elementary Forms*, though, that, within single systems of the sacred (e.g. Catholicism), a plurality of sacred symbols and

allegiances could emerge. But this still tends to locate such diversity in the context of an overarching system of the sacred rather than recognizing the possibility of many different competing sacred systems within the same social space. Where his reference to totemism allowed for the recognition of multiple sacred systems, this was still premissed on the idea that these systems were mutually exclusive in the sense that an individual could be attached to only one totem. Durkheim's framework does not therefore attend to the possibilities of multiple forms of sacred allegiance.

31. Bellah tends to emphasize the distinctiveness of civil religion as a sacred system in his original article on 'Civil Religion in America', but then later emphasized the importance of traditional American religion for encouraging the civic virtues that make civil religion possible (see 'Religion and the Legitimation of the American Republic'. His argument about the co-terminous existence of civil religion and Christianity is a rejoinder to Will Herberg's argument in *Protestant-Catholic-Jew* that mainstream institutional religion in America had degenerated into a celebration of the 'American way of life'.

32. Bellah, 'Civil Religion', 8.

33. Bellah contrasts this positive view of freedom ('freedom to') from the essentially negative view of freedom in the liberal notion of the state as a system of government that offers all but the most necessary constraints upon the individual ('freedom from'); see 'Religion and the Legitimation of the American Republic', 172–3.

34. By identifying civil religion as 'religious' in terms of its focus on particular sacred texts, Bellah actually blurs Durkheim's theory of the sacred with an analogy to a conventional substantive understanding of religion. Sacred texts *per se* do not play an integral role in Durkheim's theory of the sacred.

35. Bellah later saw the Constitution as a more ambivalent document in relation to civil religion; see 'Religion and the Legitimation of the American Republic', 175.

36. Bellah, 'Civil Religion', 1.

37. Bellah, 'Civil Religion', 15.

38. Bellah, 'Civil Religion', 17.

39. Bellah, 'Civil Religion', 12.

40. Bellah, 'Religion and the Legitimation of the American Republic', 184.

41. R. Bellah and P. Hammond, *Varieties of Civil Religion* (New York: Harper Row, 1980).

42. L. Hunt, 'The Sacred and the French Revolution', in J. C. Alexander (ed.), *Durkheimian Sociology: Cultural Studies* (Cambridge: Cambridge University Press, 1988), 25–43.

43. Bellah, 'Religion and the Legitimation of the American Republic', 172.

44. Bellah, 'Religion and the Legitimation of the American Republic', 175.

45. For a broader summary of recent developments within cultural sociology, including the significance of Alexander's contribution to this, see D. Inglis et al., 'Editorial: Sociology, Culture and the Twenty-First Century', *Cultural Sociology*, 1/1 (2007), 5–22.. A useful overview of Alexander's intellectual career and concerns is provided by R. Cordero et al., 'Performing Cultural Sociology:

A Conversation with Jeffrey Alexander', *European Journal of Social Theory*, 11/4 (2008), 523–42.

46. J. C. Alexander, *The Meanings of Social Life: A Cultural Sociology* (New York: Oxford University Press, 2003), 8.

47. Alexander characterizes the later period of Durkheim's work in terms of the development of a 'religious sociology' in which concepts derived from the study of religion might be used in the analysis of society more generally: 'In a series of discussions of education, politics, professional organization, morality and the law, Durkheim demonstrated that these modern spheres must be studied in terms of symbolic classifications. They are structured by tensions between the fields of the sacred and the profane; their central social processes are ritualistic; their most significant structural dynamics concern the construction and destruction of social solidarities' (Alexander, 'Introduction: Durkheimian Sociology', 3). Alexander suggests that Durkheim's death, and the death of many of his students in the First World War, meant that this project was not fully developed. Bellah is less convinced that Durkheim's work can be divided in this way, seeing more continuity of ideas across his work as a whole (R. Bellah (ed.), *Émile Durkheim on Morality and Society* (Chicago: University of Chicago Press, 1973), p. xiii).

48. J. C. Alexander, *Action and its Environments: Towards a new Synthesis* (New York: Columbia University Press, 1988).

49. Alexander, *Meanings of Social Life*, 6.

50. J. C. Alexander, *Fin de siècle Social Theory: Relativism, Reduction and the Problem of Reason* (New York: Verso, 1995).

51. Alexander, *Meanings of Social Life*, 7. See also I. Reed, 'Culture as Object and Approach in Sociology', in I. Reed and J. C. Alexander (eds), *Meaning and Method: The Cultural Approach to Sociology* (Boulder, CO: Paradigm Publishers, 2009), 1–3, on the difference between culture as an object of sociological study and culture as an approach to sociological study.

52. In *Action and its Environments*, 3, Alexander argues that agency is not a universal constant, but that experiences of agency are 'historically variable', and gain their scope and texture in relation to particular codes of symbolic and moral meaning.

53. Alexander, *Meanings of Social Life*, 5; see also Alexander, *Action and its Environments*, 7: 'I would argue that because contingent action is meaningful, a more complex understanding of the nature and dimensions of meaning becomes central to any micro-macro link.'

54. Alexander, *Meanings of Social Life*, 4.

55. The emotional content of classifications organized in relation to the sacred had originally been discussed by Durkheim and Mauss in *Primitive Classification*, pp. 86–7.

56. J. C. Alexander, 'The Computer as Sacred and Profane', in P. Smith (ed.), *The New American Cultural Sociology* (Cambridge: Cambridge University Press, 1998), 4.

57. Alexander, *Meanings of Social Life*, 33. He illustrates this general point through the historical formation in terms of the construction of the Holocaust as a unique evil, serving as a metaphor for the profane.
58. J. C. Alexander, *Remembering the Holocaust: A Debate* (New York: Oxford University Press, 2009).
59. J. C. Alexander et al., *Social Performance: Symbolic Action, Cultural Pragmatics and Ritual* (Cambridge: Cambridge University Press, 2006); see also J. C. Alexander, 'Iconic Consciousness: The Material Feeling of Meaning', *Environment and Planning D: Society and Space*, 26 (2008), 782–94.
60. This point is explored in more detail in relation to the case of Father Edward Flanagan in Ch. 3.
61. J. C. Alexander, 'From the Depths of Despair: Performance, Counter-Performance, and "September 11"', in J. C. Alexander, B. Giesen, and J. Mast (eds), *Social Performance: Symbolic Action, Cultural Pragmatics and Ritual* (Cambridge: Cambridge University Press, 2006), 96.
62. Alexander and Mast, 'Introduction: Symbolic Action', 15.
63. Alexander and Mast, 'Introduction: Symbolic Action', 17.
64. Alexander, *Meanings of Social Life*, 4.
65. See Alexander, *Fin de siècle Social Theory*, 3–4.
66. Alexander, *Meanings of Social Life*, 84.
67. Or as Shils ('Primordial, Personal, Sacred and Civil Ties', 125) put it: 'The growth of [sociological] knowledge is a disorderly movement. It is full of instances of things known and overlooked, unexpected emergencies, and rediscoveries of long-known facts and hypotheses which in the time of their original discovery and no fitting articulation and which found such articulation only after a considerable time.'
68. T. Tweed, *Crossing and Dwelling: A Theory of Religion* (Cambridge, MA: Harvard University Press, 2006), 9–20.
69. In this, I disagree with Caillois's account of the personalization of sacred forms (*Man and the Sacred*, 132–3), which suggests that individuals typically orient their lives around subjectively chosen single forms of the sacred. This neglects both the culturally constructed nature of sacred forms, as well as the fact that people's lives are more commonly conducted in the context of simultaneously present, multiple sacred forms.
70. Alexander, *Meanings of Social Life*, 26; see also Alexander's discussion of Geertz, *Meanings of Social Life*, 23. Alexander's view of whether Geertz's notion of 'thick description' offers an adequate model for this kind of cultural explanation has become more positive over time (compare *Meanings of Social Life* with J. C. Alexander, 'Clifford Geertz and the Strong Program: The Human Sciences and Cultural Sociology', *Cultural Sociology*, 2/2 (2008), 157–68).
71. A. Kane, 'Cultural Analysis in Historical Sociology: The Analytic and Concrete Forms of the Autonomy of Culture', *Sociological Theory*, 9/1 (1991), 56.
72. Alexander, 'Clifford Geertz'.
73. Kane, 'Cultural Analysis', 59.

74. J. C. Alexander and P. Smith, 'The Strong Program in Cultural Sociology: Elements of a Structural Hermeneutics', in Alexander, *Meanings of Social Life*, 26.

75. C. Geertz, *The Interpretation of Cultures* (London: Fontana, 1973), 15.

76. See I. Reed and J. C. Alexander, 'Social Science as Reading and Performance: A Cultural Sociological Understanding of Epistemology', *European Journal of Social Theory*, 12/1 (2009), where this process is characterized as the identification of 'truth signs [which] participate in a *double* system of reference, in the world of meaning that is social scientific theory, on the one hand, and the world of meaning that "surrounds" social action, on the other... Empirical objects do "speak to us", and we strive mightily to "know" them, and what explains them in an honest way. But all we can really do is to "know" them in the way we know aesthetic objects, through our hopes, sensibilities, mental maps and expectations... Instead of a logic of scientific discovery, social scientists are continually involved in a sort of epistemological deep play, putting our inner meanings at risk in attempting to grasp the inner meanings of other people and things whose reality is outside ourselves' (pp. 30–1).

77. Alexander, 'Clifford Geertz', 158.

78. D. Spence, *Narrative Truth and Historical Truth* (New York: W. W. Norton, 1982).

79. See Cordero et al., 'Performing Cultural Sociology', 528.

Chapter 3

1. See *Irish Times*, Saturday, 24 Apr. 1954.

2. D. Ferriter, 'Report', in *Report of Ryan Commission to Inquire into Child Abuse* (2006), vol. V, ch. 5, 26–7. All material from the final report of the Ryan Commission to Inquire into Child Abuse was downloaded from the report website, www.childabusecommission.ie/rpt/pdfs (accessed 10 Mar. 2010).

3. B. Arnold, *The Irish Gulag* (Dublin: Gill and MacMillan, 2009), 57.

4. This followed a broader pattern of complaints by parents and former residents, as well as some government officials, to the Department of Education failing to generate any substantial inquiries or reforms.

5. While it is not surprising that the Ryan Commission has proven controversial among some of the religious orders responsible for the running of the industrial and reformatory schools, it has also been subject to criticism from people supporting former residents. For example, it has been argued that, given that more girls were committed to industrial schools than boys (M. Raftery and E. O'Sullivan, *Suffer the Little Children: The Inside Story of Ireland's Industrial Schools* (Dublin: New Island, 1999), 14), the Ryan Commission gave insufficient attention to institutions for girls (and indeed excluded a number of these from its investigation); see Arnold, *Irish Gulag*, 311–12.

6. Ryan Commission, *Report of Ryan Commission to Inquire into Child Abuse* (2009), vol. I, ch. 5, 5.32, www.childabusecommission.ie/rpt/pdfs (accessed 10 Mar. 2010); see also Arnold, *Irish Gulag*, 8; Ferriter, 'Report', 1.

7. See Arnold, *Irish Gulag*, 80–6.
8. Arnold, *Irish Gulag*, 87–97.
9. By the end of the nineteenth century, there were 61 industrial schools across the 26 counties of Ireland (56 of which were Catholic and 5 Protestant), compared to only 7 reformatory schools (Ryan Commission, vol. I, ch. 2, 2.08–2.09.
10. Ryan Commission, vol. I, ch. 2, 2.15.
11. See, e.g., Arnold, *Irish Gulag*, 5. Raferty and O'Sullivan, *Suffer the Little Children*, 23, state that between 1870 and 1944, 19% of girls and 10% of boys committed to industrial schools were aged under 6 at the time of their admission.
12. Ferriter, 'Report', 12, 15.
13. Ferriter, 'Report', 29.
14. Ryan Commission, vol. I, ch.3, 3.01–3.02. Raferty and O'Sullivan, *Suffer the Little Children*, 20, give a lower total figure for 1868–1969 of 105,000 residents.
15. Raferty and O'Sullivan, *Suffer the Little Children*, 20.
16. O'Sullivan, 'Residential Child Welfare in Ireland 1965–2008: An Outline of Policy, Legislation and Practice', in *Report of Ryan Commission to Inquire into Child Abuse* (2009), vol. 4, ch. 4, 4.44.
17. O'Sullivan, 'Residential Child Welfare', 4.490.
18. The Anglo-Irish Treaty of 1921 had allowed for the establishment of an Irish State under the dominion of the British Empire, whose subjects were to swear an oath of loyalty to the King. This treaty, designed to end the Irish nationalist uprising against British rule, proved deeply divisive, with some nationalists regarding it as the most realistic opportunity for Irish independence and Republicans objecting to it as a vestige of British colonialism. Following tight votes for its ratification in the Dáil, the Irish Free State was established in December 1922, leading both to the six counties of Northern Ireland exercising their legal right to opt out of the Irish Free State within a month of its formation and to the Irish civil war of 1922–3 in which the Republicans were defeated. Following a national referendum, the Irish Free State was replaced by the Republic of Ireland in 1937 and adopted a new constitution.
19. Ferriter, 'Report', 6; Rollinson, 'Residential Child Care in England 1948–1975: A History and Report', in *Report of Ryan Commission to Inquire into Child Abuse* (2009), vol. V, ch. 6, 6.2, 6.3.
20. Orsi, *Between Heaven and Earth*, 77. See also C. Jenks (ed.), *The Sociology of Childhood: Essential Readings* (London: Batsford, 1982), 9–25; C. Castenada, *Figurations: Child, Bodies, Worlds* (Durham, NC: Duke University Press, 2002).
21. Arnold, *The Irish Gulag*, 53–5.
22. Although poor records make it difficult to assess the extent of their involvement, local officers of the National Society for the Prevention of Cruelty to Children did play an active role in the committal of children to industrial schools. For a short period after 1949, the NSPCC's annual report criticized the excessive use of the option of sending children to industrial schools,

although, when the Archbishop of Dublin, Dr John McQuaid, became a patron of the society in 1956, this critical perspective was dropped.

23. Ryan Commission, *Executive Summary, Conclusions*, 5.
24. Ryan Commission, vol. IV, ch. 2, 2.89.
25. Arnold, *Irish Gulag*, 29.
26. Ryan Commission, *Executive Summary, Conclusions*, 33.
27. Arnold, *Irish Gulag*, 29.
28. Ryan Commission, vol. I, ch. 4, 4.02.
29. Ryan Commission, *Executive Summary, Conclusions*, 32.
30. Arnold, *Irish Gulag*, 82.
31. A. Staines et al., 'An Assessment of the Health Records of Children Detained at Irish Industrial Schools 1940–1983', in *Report of Ryan Commission to Inquire into Child Abuse* (2009), vol. V, ch. 4, noted that the standard of children's health records in the schools was 'very limited, very variable and generally of very poor quality' (pp. 1–2).
32. Arnold, *Irish Gulag*, 340.
33. Ryan Commission, *Executive Summary, Conclusions*, 38.
34. See Ryan Commission, vol. IV, ch. 2; Arnold, *Irish Gulag*, 76, argues that the religious orders consistently refused to provide independent, audited accounts to the Department of Education.
35. See, e.g., Ryan Commission, vol. IV, ch. 2, 2.20. The schools typically resisted attempts to establish more transparent and independently verified accounting systems, as in 1951, where an attempt by the Department of Education to set up an inquiry into the financial management of the schools involving the Departments of Finance and Social Welfare was successfully faced down by the schools' resident managers association (Ryan Commission, vol. IV, ch. 2, 2.37 ff.).
36. The Ryan Commission, for example, reviewed the case of Carriglea industrial school, run by the Christian Brothers, which was closed in 1954 in the light of falling numbers of children being admitted into the industrial school system. By 1953, the school had accumulated a surplus of £11,000, which the Christian Brothers' own auditor suggested should be transferred into the institution's building fund in such a way as not to draw government attention to the scale of the surplus. Such a transfer of funds did take place, and, on the closure of the Carriglea school, this was used to finance the setting-up of a new juniorate for the order at the same site rather than to support their industrial school work (Ryan Commission, vol. I, ch. 10, 10.17–10.24). During this same period, the school at Carriglea had become increasingly dysfunctional because of understaffing and the lack of recreational facilities for its residents. The fabric of the buildings was in poor repair, and, despite the fact that the school ran a large, commercial farm, former residents of the school have complained of never receiving milk and being given egg only once a year at Easter (Ryan Commission, vol. I, ch. 10, 10.122 ff.). The Mazar's report concludes that, although some smaller schools without additional sources of income or working farms did struggle financially, schools that

were more financially successful did not provide any better standards of care or nutrition (see Ryan Commission, vol. IV, ch. 2, 2.221).

37. Arnold, *Irish Gulag*, 317.

38. See, e.g., Ryan Commission, vol. III, ch.19, 19.06.

39. Ryan Commission, vol. III, ch. 7, 7.15. It is also indicative of the normalization of this level of violence that the Redress Board established to compensate former residents of the school did not make payments for those who experienced only physical abuse.

40. Ryan Commission, *Executive Summary, Conclusions*, 7.

41. See, e.g., Ryan Commission, vol. III, ch. 7, 7.07; also vol. III, ch. 19, 19.07. Also Arnold, *Irish Gulag*, 46.

42. Ryan Commission, *Executive Summary, Conclusions*, 9–17. These conclusions were contested by religious orders, who claimed that such violence was not widespread, and, where evident, reflected wider cultural practices of disciplining children current at that time. The hierarchy of punishment in the regulations for corporal punishment suggests that this was not the case, however.

43. Ryan Commission, vol. I, ch.10, 10.75.

44. Ryan Commission, *Executive Summary, Conclusions*, 9.

45. This figure was significantly higher in a study conducted by the Commission on 'The Psychological Adjustment of Adult Survivors of Institutional Abuse' (Ryan Commission, vol. V, ch. 3), which interviewed 247 people who had testified to the Commission and who had experienced abuse in the context of industrial and reformatory schools. Within this sample, around 80% were found to have had significant psychological difficulties, with a similar proportion forming insecure attachments in adult life. Among those who had memories of living with their families prior to admission to the residential school system, around a third reported some form of abuse or neglect in their family environment.

46. The Irish case is not entirely unique in this regard. In Australia and Canada, for example, church-run residential schools were established in the context of broader projects of nation-building and, in these cases, with the specific aim of removing indigenous Aboriginal and Indian children from their family contexts in order to Christianize and 'civilize' them. The conditions and longer-term effects of this residential care system have similarly generated a sense of public scandal. As in Ireland, this has led to formal government apologies, and inquiry processes have been established through the Canadian Indian Residential Schools Truth and Reconciliation Commission and the Australian *Bringing Them Home* report.

47. Raftery and O'Sullivan, *Suffer the Little Children*, 15–16.

48. V. Zelizer, *Pricing the Priceless Child: The Changing Social Value of Children* (New York: Basic Books, 1985), is part of a longer intellectual project she has pursued in exploring the framework of meanings and values that shape the operation of markets.

49. See, e.g., Arnold, *Irish Gulag*, 94–5.

50. Ryan Commission, vol. I, ch. 1, 1.99; see also a more outright rejection of claims not proven by court convictions at 1.141.

51. The Commission received verbal evidence of abuse and neglect in 216 different contexts of institutional child care, mainly (though extending beyond) the industrial and reformatory school system; Ryan Commission, vol. III, ch. 19, 19.04.

52. See Ryan Commission, vol. III, ch. 19, 19.14. Religious orders claimed that 'sexual abuse' was not properly understood in the earlier decades of the twentieth century, and that they had responded to it as a moral than a criminal offence. But it is clear, for example, in the evidence of Garda Commissioner Eoin O'Duffy to the Carrigan Committee in 1932, that sexual offences against children were known about, and actively prosecuted by the Irish police. Religious orders decided not to report members suspected of sexual abuse to the police, but to subject them to internal disciplinary reviews in which offenders were usually moved to another institution, often in roles that gave them continued access to children. This often represented a sustained attempt to manage scandal by preventing knowledge of such abuse coming more widely into the public domain through the media or court system.

53. Alexander, *Meanings of Social Life*, 33.

54. See, for example, the importance of Ireland as a Christian nation in the political rhetoric of de Valera (T. Brown, *Ireland: A Social and Cultural History, 1922–2001* (London: Harper Perennial, 2010), 26–7).

55. P. Murray, *Oracles of God: The Roman Catholic Church and Irish Politics, 1922–37* (Dublin: UCD Press, 2000), 6–7.

56. Brown, *Ireland*, 56.

57. Murray, *Oracles*, 414 ff.

58. Murray, *Oracles*, 410.

59. Murray, *Oracles*, 415.

60. Murray, *Oracles*, 411.

61. Murray, *Oracles*, 8.

62. It is possible to see how a culture of 'economic prudence...puritanical, repressive sexual mores and nationalistic conservatism' was recursively reproduced in a society characterized by small farms, the importance of family structures, and ecclesiastical and political elites that had been formed through such conservative contexts (Brown, *Ireland*, 16).

63. Brown, *Ireland*, 18–19.

64. K. Whelan, 'The Cultural Effects of the Famine', in J. Cleary and C. Connolly (eds), *The Cambridge Companion to Modern Irish Culture* (Cambridge: Cambridge University Press, 2005), 137 ff.

65. Whelan, 'Cultural Effects', 138.

66. Brown, *Ireland*, 35–67. Part of the failure of traditional Irish folk culture post-1852 can also be attributed to the growing strength of the Catholic 'devotional revolution' in the latter part of the nineteenth century in which

traditional practices such as keening became regarded as morally and spiritually suspect (Whelan, 'Cultural Effects', 141–2).

67. See, e.g., Murray, *Oracles*, 1, 4.
68. Brown, *Ireland*, 17.
69. Brown, *Ireland*, 77. See also Whelan, 'Cultural Effects', 138–40.
70. Brown, *Ireland*, 28–9.
71. T. Inglis, 'Religion, Identity, State and Society', in J. Cleary and C. Connolly (eds), *The Cambridge Companion to Modern Irish Culture* (Cambridge: Cambridge University Press, 2005), 64–5.
72. Brown, *Ireland*, 10.
73. Whelan, 'Cultural Effects', 140.
74. Inglis, 'Religion, Identity, State and Society', 65.
75. Brown, *Ireland*, 11–14.
76. This included a ban of books by Marie Stopes (Brown, *Ireland*, 58, 65). Censorship also reflected the projection of immorality into surrounding nations, with British publications particularly liable to censorship on moral grounds (Brown, *Ireland*, 59).
77. Ferriter, 'Report', 13 ff.
78. Brown, *Ireland*, 18. See also Ferriter, 'Report', 15. This mobilization led to various forms of legal prohibition, including the 1929 Censorship Act and the 1935 Dance Hall Act, which sought much tighter controls over the management of public dances, and sought largely to close down informal dances held within the home; see Whelan, 'Cultural Effects', 145.
79. Brown, *Ireland*, 29–30.
80. H. Ferguson, 'Abused and Looked after Children as "Moral Dirt": Child Abuse and Institutional Care in Historical Perspective', *Journal of Social Policy*, 36 (2007), 132, 134.
81. Ryan Commission, *Executive Summary, Conclusions*, 23.
82. See Ferguson, 'Abused', esp. 130 ff.
83. 'Re-moralising children meant returning them to "innocence" by knocking the devil out of them' (Ferguson, 'Abused', 134).
84. Ryan Commission, *Executive Summary, Conclusions*, 3.
85. See, e.g., Brown, *Ireland*, 22–2, on the uncritical culture within Catholic theological education in Ireland in the early part of the twentieth century.
86. Accounts of twentieth-century practices in Irish industrial schools bear close resemblance, for example, to Mintz's account of residential school life in the 1840s and 1850s (S. Mintz, *Huck's Raft: A History of American Childhood* (Cambridge, MA: Belknapp, 2006), 160). The first White House conference on childcare in 1909 made it an explicit goal to reduce the dependence on institutional forms of care (Mintz, *Huck's Raft*, 179).
87. P. Aries, *Centuries of Childhood: A Social History of Family Life* (New York: Vintage Books, 1962), 128.
88. As Aries, *Centuries of Childhood*, 411, points out, for example, the classical Greek concept of paedia designated a transitional stage between early infancy and adulthood, largely unrecognized in the medieval period.

Notes

89. Aries, *Centuries of Childhood*, 329.
90. Comparing Aries's account with Mintz's (see, e.g., Mintz, *Huck's Raft*, 3) suggests that this process took somewhat longer to take hold in the United States, with the American emphasis on the long childhood emerging from the mid-eighteenth century.
91. Aries, *Centuries of Childhood*, 412–13f.
92. Aries, *Centuries of Childhood*, 331–3.
93. Mintz, *Huck's Raft*, 155. Children were also vulnerable given the high mortality rates for parents; in the nineteenth century, nearly half of all children had lost a parent before they reached 20, and, by 1900, 20–30% of children had lost a parent before they reached 15. Migration also played a significant role in disrupting family structures. Death of fathers was particularly likely to cause significant economic hardship and lead to further family dispersal (Mintz, *Huck's Raft*, 157). In the United States, the rate of expansion of these institutions began to grow significantly only towards the turn of the twentieth century: between 1870 and 1915, the numbers of children in school almost tripled from seven million to twenty million. But the massification of these institutions really took place only in the first half of the twentieth century: by 1915, still only 20% of American children attended high school, but by 1928 this figure had risen to around 50% (Mintz, *Huck's Raft*, 172–4). It was also from the end of the eighteenth century that children became a more visible and sustained focus in literature; see Jenks (ed.), *The Sociology of Childhood*, 42–7.
94. A. Turmel, *A Historical Sociology of Childhood: Developmental Thinking, Categorization and Graphic Visualization* (Cambridge: Cambridge University Press, 2008).
95. Mintz, *Huck's Raft*, 134. Child labour also remained important for agricultural production (p. 135). The nature of this employment also remained largely gendered with boys more likely to work in factory settings, and girls in domestic service (pp.138–42).
96. Mintz, *Huck's Raft*, 2.
97. I am grateful to Erika Wallander for drawing my attention to Key's work.
98. Zelizer, *Pricing the Priceless Child*, 3.
99. By the turn of the twentieth century, not only was child labour being opposed simply on moral grounds, but newly emergent trade unions campaigned against child labour on the grounds that these depressed adult wages (Mintz, *Huck's Raft*, 182).
100. At all points in this narrative, it is important to avoid the impression of sudden or distinct phases of sacred or moral discourse in relation to childhood. The notion of children's rights had been discussed in the American press in the 1850s, and the rise of new societies to protect against cruelty to children from the 1870s also implied a wider sense of moral concern for child protection (although the standards of what constituted cruelty to children for some of these early organizations would have been much less exacting than standards by the post-war period; Mintz, *Huck's Raft*, 168).

101. The sacrality of the care of children is, therefore, better understood as the universalizing and autonomous definition of a sacred form whose origins lay in Christian cultural practices, rather than as a purely 'secular' form of the sacred.
102. See, e.g., M. Woodhead, 'Psychology and the Construction of Children's Needs', in A. James and J. Prout (eds), *Constructing and Reconstructing Childhood* (New York: Falmer, 1990), 60–77.
103. A pseudonym.
104. Ryan Commission, vol. I, ch. 10, 10.57.
105. Ryan Commission, vol. I, ch. 10, 10.52.
106. *Irish Times*, Monday, 10 June 1946, p. 6.
107. *Irish Times*, Thursday, 20 June 1946, p. 3.
108. *Irish Times*, Monday, 24 June 1946, p. 7.
109. *Irish Times*, Monday, 8 July 1946, p. 6.
110. *Irish Times*, Monday, 8 July 1946, p. 6.
111. *Irish Times*, Wednesday, 24 July 1946, p. 7.
112. *Irish Times*, Friday, 28 Mar. 1947, p. 4.
113. *Irish Times*, Friday, 28 Mar. 1947, p. 4.
114. *Irish Times*, Thursday, 25 July 1946, p. 5.
115. See, e.g., *Irish Times*, Saturday, 31 Aug. 1946, p. 4; Saturday, 7 Sept. 1946, p. 4; Saturday, 21 Sept. 1946, p. 4; Saturday, 12 Oct. 1946, p. 4. The focus on prisons also had a political context, given that Republican prisoners were still being held in jail, and voluntary organizations were campaigning in relation to their conditions and release; see Saturday, 14 Sept. 1946.
116. See Raftery and O'Sullivan, *Suffer the Little Children*, 195–7, for further discussion of MacCarthy's relatively isolated position within the judicial system on the treatment of children brought before the courts.
117. *Irish Times*, Saturday, 31 Aug. 1946, p. 4.
118. *Irish Times*, Saturday, 7 Sept. 1946, p. 4.
119. *Irish Times*, Saturday, 14 Sept. 1946, p. 4.
120. *Irish Times*, Saturday, 21 Sept. 1946, p. 4.
121. Raftery and O'Sullivan, *Suffer the Little Children*, 192.
122. *Irish Times*, 19 Oct. 1946, p. 4.
123. Raftery and O'Sullivan, *Suffer the Little Children*, 195.
124. Raftery and O'Sullivan, *Suffer the Little Children*, 192, 195.
125. Raftery and O'Sullivan, *Suffer the Little Children*, 216.
126. www.paddydoyle.com/whistleblower-paddy-doyle-i-walked-in-i-didnt-walk-out (accessed 13 Mar. 2010).
127. D. Ferriter, *Occasions of Sin: Sex and Society in Modern Ireland* (London: Profile Books, 2009), 335–8.
128. Ferriter, *Occasions of Sin*, 343–8.
129. In the revision to this Act made in 1967, any proscribed publication automatically had its ban lifted after twelve years, which meant that this change in legislation led to publications banned earlier in the century becoming

immediately available (C. Morash, *A History of the Media in Ireland* (Cambridge: Cambridge University Press, 2010), 180).

130. Ferriter, *Occasions of Sin*, 349.
131. Ferriter, *Occasions of Sin*, 362–3.
132. Ferriter, *Occasions of Sin*, 365.
133. Ferriter, *Occasions of Sin*, 364.
134. Ferriter, *Occasions of Sin*, 528–31.
135. Brown, *Ireland*, 232, points out that it had been possible for people on the eastern side of Ireland to pick up British television some years before this. Indeed, the *Irish Times* regularly began publishing TV listings for BBC programmes from 1954 (Morash, *History of the Media in Ireland*, 168).
136. Morash, *History of Media in Ireland*, 171.
137. J. Hogan, *Irish Media: A Critical History since 1922* (London: Routledge, 2001), 84–91.
138. Morash, *History of Media in Ireland*, 177–8.
139. Morash, *History of Media in Ireland*, 173–4.
140. Morash, *History of Media in Ireland*, 179–80.
141. Ferriter, *Occasions of Sin*, 376–9.
142. The increasing length of newspapers in the 1960s and 1970s allowed the relatively new phenomenon of longer investigative pieces by Irish journalists (Morash, *History of Media in Ireland*, 180–1).
143. Ferriter, *Occasions of Sin*, 443–4.
144. Arnold, *Irish Gulag*, 63–9.
145. Raftery and O'Sullivan, *Suffer the Little Children*, 378–80; see also Arnold, *Irish Gulag*, 69–78.
146. www.iro.ie/EU-structural-funds.html (accessed 14 Mar. 2010).
147. See, e.g., C. Kuhling and K. Keohane, *Cosmopolitan Ireland: Globalization and Quality of Life* (London: Pluto Press, 2007).
148. Report by the Commission of Investigation into the Archdiocese of Dublin (2009), 1.113, www.justice.ie/en/JELR/Pages/PB09000504 (accessed 14 Mar. 2010).

Chapter 4

1. See B. Meyer, 'Religious Sensations: Why Media, Aesthetics and Power Matter in the Study of Contemporary Religion', in H. de Vries (ed.), *Religion: Beyond a Concept* (New York: Fordham University Press, 2008), 704–23; D. Morgan, *The Sacred Gaze: Religious Visual Culture in Theory and Practice* (Berkeley and Los Angeles: University of California Press, 2005); Orsi, *Between Heaven and Earth*, 73–109.
2. Alexander's 'Iconic Consciousness' has been one of the initial attempts to do this within the 'strong programme'.
3. On the role of media in the construction of publics, see, for example, J. Tiitsman ('The Occasion is not a Local One: Making a Public for the Atlantic Telegraph', paper presented at the Media, Religion and Culture

group of the Annual Meeting of the American Academy of Religion, Chicago, 2008), who extends this notion beyond public media to communication technologies more generally to demonstrate how advocates of the new media technology of telegraphy in the mid-nineteenth century described this in terms of the construction of a new global social order. Guadeloupe (*Chanting down the New Jerusalem: Calypso, Christianity and Capitalism in the Caribbean* (Berkeley and Los Angeles: University of California Press, 2008), also demonstrates how the encoding of particular media content may establish an implied contract between broadcaster and audience focused around a common identity, attitudes, or values.

4. L Van Zoonen et al., 'Performing Citizenship on YouTube: Activism, Satire and Online Debate around the Anti-Islam Video Fitna', *Critical Discourse Studies*, 7/4 (2010), 249–62.

5. L. Schofield Clark, 'Considering Religion and Mediatisation through a Case Study of *J+K's Big Day* (The J K Wedding Entrance Dance): A Response to Stig Hjarvard', *Culture and Religion*, 12/2 (2011), 167–84.

6. An important issue that I will not address directly in this chapter is whether engagement with the sacred through public media can usefully be understood in terms of 'ritual'. The notion of ritual has been applied to public media in a wide range of ways, from Dayan and Katz's original notion (*Media Events: The Live Broadcasting of History* (Cambridge, MA: Harvard University Press, 1992)) of 'media events' as public rituals (an idea extended by S. Cottle, 'Mediatized Rituals: Beyond Manufacturing Consent', *Media, Culture and Society*, 28/3 (2006), 411–32). Pantti and Sumiala's ('Til Death Us Do Join: Media, Mourning Rituals and the Sacred Centre of the Society', *Media, Culture, Society*, 31/1 (2009), 119–35) use the concept of mediated mourning rituals to refer both to the coverage of specific mourning rituals (e.g. funerals, memorial events) and to a wider sense of a ritual process of public mourning in which public media are deeply implicated. E. Rothenbuhler (*Ritual Communication: From Everyday Conversation to Mediated Ceremony* (London: Sage, 1998)) provides more general notions of the ritual nature of communicative and symbolic acts (see also S. Lukes, 'Political Ritual and Social Integration', *Sociology*, 9/2 (1975), 289–308). Couldry (*Media Rituals*) understands 'media rituals' as everyday acts that perpetuate the symbolic status of the media as giving access to reality and the sacred centres of society. The value of applying notions of ritual to public media has itself been contested (see Couldry and Rothenbuhler, 'Simon Cottle'), reflecting critiques within anthropology of the value of broad concepts of 'ritual' and 'belief' as a basis for cross-cultural analysis. Couldry and Rothenbuhler's work is useful in demonstrating the socially constructed status of public media, and the symbolic significance of communicative acts more generally, and this provides a helpful conceptual framework for thinking about the engagement with the sacred through public media. But the case for thinking about the experiencing, reproduction, and contestation of the sacred through public media primarily

in terms of ritual (e.g. as suggested by Cottle) has still to be convincingly made, and I have elected not to use the concept of ritual in this sense. I do, however, return to Rothenbuhler's concept of ritual communication in the following chapter.

7. See also N. Couldry et al. (eds), *Media Events in a Global Age* (London: Routledge, 2010).

8. See, e.g., Rothenbuhler and Coman, *Media Anthropology*; J. Sumiala, *Median rituaalit: Johdatus media-antropologiaan* (Tampere: Vastapaino, 2010). My interests here, for example, touch on discussions of the role of news media in the construction and circulation of cultural myth; see e.g., Lule, 'News as Myth: Daily News and Eternal Stories', in E. Rothenbuhler and M. Coman (eds), *Media Anthropology* (London: Sage, 2005), 101–10, and M. Coman, 'News Stories and Myth: The Impossible Reunion?' , in E. Rothenbuhler and M. Coman (eds), *Media Anthropology* (London: Sage 2005), 111–20, although these debates tend to turn more on technical discussions of the defining feature of 'myth' and arguably add less value to this analysis than other work on media ritual or on media within the 'strong programme'.

9. Couldry, *Media Rituals*.

10. J. C. Alexander and R. Jacobs, 'Mass Communication, Ritual and Civil Society', in T. Liebes and J. Curran (eds), *Media, Ritual and Identity* (London: Routledge, 1998), 23–41; J. C. Alexander, *The Civil Sphere* (New York: Oxford University Press, 2006), 75–84; Jacobs, *Race*.

11. Alexander, 'Culture and Political Crisis'.

12. When using the term 'institution' in the context of this claim, I have in mind the definition used by Anthony Giddens (*The Constitution of Society* (Cambridge: Polity, 1984), 17) in his theory of structuration: 'The most deeply embedded structural properties, implicated in the reproduction of societal totalities, I call *structural principles*. Those practices which have the greatest time-space extension within such totalities can be referred to as *institutions*.'

13. See J. Sumiala-Seppänen and M. Stocchetti, 'Father of the Nation of Arch-Terrorist? Media Rituals and Images of the Death of Yasser Arafat', *Media, Culture, Society*, 29/2 (2007), 336–43, on the ways in which the media coverage of the death of Yasser Arafat evoked very different symbolic interpretations among Arab and Israeli audiences.

14. Pantti and Wieten's discussion ('Mourning Becomes the Nation: Television Coverage of the Murder of Pim Fortuyn', *Journalism Studies*, 6/3 (2005), 301–13) of Dutch media coverage in the wake of the murder of Pym Fortuyn demonstrates that mediated public ceremony may consciously be used as a tool for social integration by key social actors (in that case, Dutch politicians) attempting to shore up their societies through periods of social disintegration and conflict. See also Pantti and Sumiala, 'Til death', 133.

15. See, e.g., J. Thompson, *Political Scandal: Power and Visibility in the Media Age* (Cambridge: Polity, 2000).

16. See, e.g., S. Allan, *News Culture* (3rd edn; Maidenhead: Open University Press, 2010), 72–4, 82–3. Sacred forms can structure journalistic perceptions of what constitutes significant stories of conflict, personalization, or cultural specificity, as well as their sense of who is an obvious, controversial, or unacceptable source.

17. Drawing on Durkheim, Giddens, and Halbwachs, Barbie Zelizer, *Covering the Body: The Kennedy Assassination, the Media and the Shaping of Collective Memory* (Chicago: University of Chicago Press, 1992), has argued that the journalistic process crafting narratives that draw upon and constitute collective memory constructs the cultural authority of journalists as well as helping to establish models of what it means to undertake appropriate journalistic practice. Journalists are positioned as trusted witnesses whose presence at crucial events is inseparable from the media's ability to construct sacred meanings in relation to them (see A. Richards and J. Mitchell, 'Journalists as Witnesses to Violence and Suffering', in R. Fortner and M. Fackler (eds), *The Handbook of Global Communication Ethics* (Wiley: Blackwell, 2010).

18. The case of the public conflict over the racist bullying of Shilpa Shetty by Jade Goody and other members of the Celebrity Big Brother show in 2007 demonstrates how reality TV can, occasionally, represent events that have sacred significance (see also K. Lofton, *Oprah: The Gospel of an Icon* (Berkeley and Los Angeles: University of California Press, 2011). Alexander, *Civil Sphere*, 75–80, argues that fictional media should also be given serious regard as mediators of the semiotics of the sacred. While he makes a strong case for the ways in which fictional narratives represent cultural codes of inclusion and exclusion, the examples of sacred identification that he gives (e.g. Harriet Beacher Stowe's *Uncle Tom's Cabin*) are at their strongest when they clearly map onto 'real' experiences of society or articulate breaches of the sacred in a focused narrative that are perceived as present in a more diffuse way throughout society.

19. Examples of this would include the dramatization of 'The Diary of Anne Frank' (cf. Alexander, *Meanings of Social Life*, 57–9), or Stephen Spielberg's film version of *Schindler's List*.

20. J. Carey, 'Political Ritual on Television: Episodes in the History of Shame, Degradation and Excommunication', in T. Liebes and J. Curran (eds), *Media, Ritual and Identity* (London: Routledge, 1998), 42–70.

21. Alexander, 'Culture and Political Crisis'; Alexander and Jacobs, 'Mass Communication'.

22. Alexander and Mast, 'Introduction: Symbolic Action'; J. C. Alexander, 'Cultural Pragmatics: Social Performance between Ritual and Strategy', in J. C. Alexander et al. (eds), *Social Performance: Symbolic Action, Cultural Pragmatics and Ritual* (Cambridge: Cambridge University Press, 2006), 29–90; D. Dayan, 'Beyond Media Events: Disenchantment, Derailment, Disruption', in N. Couldry et al. (eds), *Media Events in a Global Age* (London: Routledge, 2010), 23–3.

23. Rothenbuhler, *Ritual Communication*, 42; Alexander, 'From the Depths of Despair'.
24. E. Katz and T. Liebes, '"No more peace!" How Disaster, War and Terror Have Upstaged Media Events', in N. Couldry et al. (eds), *Media Events in a Global Age* (London: Routledge, 2010), 32–42.
25. Lukes, 'Political Ritual'.
26. J. Sumiala-Seppänen and M. Stocchetti, 'Mediated Sacralization and the Construction of Postmodern *communion sanctorum*: The Case of the Swedish Foreign Minister Anna Lindh', *Material Religion*, 1/2 (2005), 229–34.
27. See Lukes, 'Political Ritual', 300.
28. See, e.g., R. Turnock, *Interpreting Diana: Television Audiences and the Death of a Princess* (London: BFI, 2000), on Princess Diana.
29. Pantti and Sumiala, 'Til death', 133; Couldry, *Media Rituals*.
30. In this sense, then, I agree with Dayan and Katz's contention that the study of media and the sacred should focus on the 'broadcasting of history', though I would include a much wider range of media representations of historical experience than their notion of 'media events' includes.
31. See, e.g., G. Turner, *Understanding Celebrity* (London: Sage, 2004).
32. Sumiala-Seppänen and Stocchetti, 'Mediated Sacralization', 244; Pantti and Sumiala,'Til death'; R. Eyerman, *The Assassination of Theo van Gogh: From Social Drama to Cultural Trauma* (Durham, NC: Duke University Press, 2008).
33. It can be argued that fiction provides a way of reflecting on sacred commitments, away from the immediacy of specific historical referents. Artists would typically be cautious about the idea of producing objects or performances that elicit common sentiments, seeing this more as propaganda than authentic art, which allows different experiences and interpretations within its audience. But art and fiction have the potential for creating an imaginative space through which the nature and consequences of particular sacred forms can be critically thought about. My point here, then, is not that art and fiction have no significance in relation to the sacred, but that it is through the mediation of 'real-world' experiences that the sacred becomes most acutely expressed, experienced, and contested in social life. While art and fiction create opportunities for critical engagement with the sacred, they do not in themselves have the capacity to inspire the kind of sacred sentiments for which people will die or kill, or allow their political representatives to undertake actions normally regarded as morally abhorrent. Representations of the sacred in relation to actual events can motivate political action, for example; representations of the sacred in fiction (unless tied to a specific 'real-world' referent), in general, do not.
34. K. Lundby (ed.), *Mediatization: Concepts, Changes, Consequences* (New York: Peter Lang, 2009).
35. S. Hjarvard, The Mediatization of Society: A Theory of the Media as Agents of Social and Cultural Change', *Nordicom Review*, 2 (2008), 105–34, and 'The Mediatization of Religion: A Theory of the Media as Agents of Religious Change', *Northern Lights*, 6 (2008), 9–26.

36. It is clear that this claim cannot be held as universally true for all people living in late modern societies. For some, for example, the sacred may still primarily be mediated through embodied religious rituals in local places of worship. But, even in such cases, public media often represent an important supplement to their localized practices of the sacred, either through religious media, which extend or amplify their particular religious construction of the sacred, or through wider public media, which act as a way of negotiating the meaning of their sacred commitments in wider society. While individual exceptions can doubtless be identified, the claim that public media are the primary site for engaging the sacred in late modern societies appears robust.

37. www.census.gov/Press-Release/www/releases/archives/facts_for_features_ special_editions/012025.html; www.statistics.gov.uk/CCI/nugget.asp?ID= 823&Pos=2&ColRank=2&Rank=640 (accessed 17 Jan. 2010).

38. www.census.gov/Press-Release/www/releases/archives/communication_ industries/013849.html; note this figure is for 2007, so is likely to be considerably lower than rates of access in 2011; www.statistics.gov.uk/cci/nugget.asp? ID=8 (accessed 17 Jan. 2010).

39. www.barb.co.uk/graph/weeklyViewing?data_series%5B%5D=2009&submit= View+Graph (accessed 17 Jan. 2010).

40. Couldry, *Media Rituals*, 37 ff. See also Alexander, *Civil Sphere*, 80.

41. In November 2009, the number of original users of the *Guardian* website reached thirty-six million, globally, nearly double the entire number (nineteen million) of all daily national newspapers sold in the UK in the same month: www.guardian.co.uk/media/table/2009/dec/11/abcs-national-news-papers; www.guardian.co.uk/media/table/2009/dec/11/abcs-national-news-papers1; www.guardian.co.uk/media/2009/dec/22/abces-guardian-35m-user-barrier (accessed 18 Jan. 2010).

42. On 4 Jan. 2010, yahoo.co.uk's third highest search was for Wootton Bassett, a town in the UK that had become a ceremonial centre for receiving the bodies of British soldiers killed in Afghanistan, in response to a news story that an Islamist group planned a counter-march against the war in the same village. This story, which clearly illustrated competing sacred commitments, led the PM Gordon Brown to declare the proposed Islamist march 'abhorrent'.

43. Dayan and Katz, *Media Events*, 77.

44. Pantti and Sumiala, 'Til death', 133.

45. See Sumiala and Stocchetti, 'Mediated Sacralization', 234, 241, on the role of images as 'determining structures' in forming the postmodern communio sanctorum.

46. M. Conboy, *Tabloid Britain: Constructing a Community through Language* (London: Routledge, 2005); C. Kitch, 'Tears and Trauma in the News', in B. Zelizer (ed.), *The Changing Faces of Journalism: Tabloidization, Technology and Truthiness* (London: Routledge, 2009), 29–39. For a critique of the analytical usefulness of the concept of tabloidization, see S. E. Bird, 'Tabloidization: What Is It, and Does It Really Matter?', in B. Zelizer (ed.), *The Changing Faces of*

Journalism: Tabloidization, Technology and Truthiness (London: Routledge, 2009), 40–50.

47. See, e.g., Meštrović, *Postemotional Society.*
48. L. Schofield Clark, 'Mediatization and Media Ecology', in K. Lundby (ed.), *Mediatization: Concepts, Changes, Consequences* (New York: Peter Lang, 2009), 85–100.
49. Sumiala-Seppänen and Stocchetti, 'Mediated Sacralization', 237. See also Sumiala-Seppänen and Stocchetti, 'Father of the Nation', for another example of this cycle in which images of the Palestinian leader printed in the press were then used in public forms of mourning across the Middle East.
50. See, e.g., R. Silverstone, *Media and Morality: On the Rise of the Mediapolis* (Cambridge: Polity, 2007).
51. Dayan and Katz, *Media Events*, 54–77.
52. BBC Trust, 'From Seesaw to Wagon Wheel: Safeguarding Impartiality in the 21st Century', report (2007), p. 43, www.bbc.co.uk/bbctrust/our_work/other/century21.shtml (accessed 2 June 2009): 'every judgment made in the Israeli-Palestinian situation, for instance, is fraught with difficulty, and is parsed in minute detail by specialists and apologists in the audience.'
53. http://news.bbc.co.uk/1/hi/world/middle_east/7814054.stm (accessed 28 May 2009).
54. http://news.bbc.co.uk/1/hi/world/middle_east/7819937.stm (accessed 28 May 2009).
55. http://news.bbc.co.uk/1/hi/world/middle_east/7841406.stm (accessed 28 May 2009).
56. www.bbc.co.uk/blogs/theeditors/2009/01/bbc_and_the_gaza_appeal.html (accessed 28 May 2009).
57. www.youtube.com/watch?v=ix5CkWWeSmI.
58. http://news.bbc.co.uk/1/hi/7848673.stm (accessed 28 May 2009).
59. http://news.bbc.co.uk/today/hi/today/newsid_7850000/7850617.stm (accessed 28 May 2009).
60. www.youtube.com/watch?v=smBSqO90k4c (accessed 28 May 2009).
61. www.bbc.co.uk/bbctrust/our_work/complaints_appeals/dec_gaza/appeal_findings.shtml (accessed 28 May 2009).
62. www.bbc.co.uk/bbctrust/assets/files/pdf/review_report_research/impartiality_21century/report.pdf (accessed 28 May 2009).
63. Alexander, *Meanings of Social Life*, 115.
64. http://news.bbc.co.uk/1/hi/uk/7708398.stm (accessed 30 May 2009).
65. www.guardian.co.uk/world/2009/jan/20/gaza-israel-samouni-family; www.guardian.co.uk/world/2009/jan/10/gaza-zeitoun-attack-deaths (accessed 30 May 2009).
66. www.channel4.com/news/articles/politics/international_politics/tale+of+a+young+palestinians+death/2897187 (accessed 30 May 2009).
67. http://news.bbc.co.uk/1/hi/programmes/from_our_own_correspondent/7843307.stm (accessed 30 May 2009).

68. For example, see J. Mitchell, *Media Violence and Christian Ethics* (Cambridge: Cambridge University Press, 2007), on the effects of differential media coverage of events that elicit powerful sacred identifications.
69. www.pchrgaza.org/files/Reports/English/pdf_spec/Blood%20on%20their%20hands.pdf (accessed 30 May 2009).
70. Butler, *Frames of War*.
71. On the complexities of Jewish and Zionist identification with Israel, see J. Rose, *The Question of Zion* (Princeton: Princeton University Press 2005).
72. BICOM: Britain Israel Communications and Research Centre, www.bicom. org.uk (accessed 27 June 2011).
73. See, e.g., www.goldstonereport.org (accessed 30 May 2009).
74. www.chiefrabbi.org/ReadArtical1446.aspx (accessed 30 May 2009).
75. S. Pattison, *Shame: Theory, Therapy, Theology* (Cambridge: Cambridge University Press, 2000).
76. See, in relation to this, Alexander's discussion (*Remembering the Holocaust*) of the significance of the publication and dramatization of Anne Frank's diaries for expanding sympathy with victims of the Holocaust.
77. www.comicrelief.com/what_we_do/campaigns/past_campaigns (accessed 2 June 2009).

Chapter 5

1. When talking about human rights in this context, I recognize that the sacralization of human rights has a particular Western history (L. Hunt, *Inventing Human Rights: A History* (New York: W. W. Norton, 2007), and that what is taken to be a human right is inseparable from contingent, cultural constructions of what it means to be a person (C. Mouffe, *On the Political* (London: Routledge, 2005), 119–26; C. Taylor, 'The Politics of Recognition', in A. Gutman and C. Taylor, *Multiculturalism and 'The Politics of Recognition'* (Princeton: Princeton University Press, 1992), 25–75). At the same time, the normative argument developed in this chapter proceeds on the, culturally grounded, assumption of the importance of basic human rights to life, freedom of expression, and fairness in legal and political process.
2. Alexander, *Meanings of Social Life*, 4
3. R. Dawkins, *The God Delusion* (London: Bantam, 2006), 283.
4. This is a rhetorical point to emphasize the dangers of equating the threat of the sacred with religion. As the discussion through the book as a whole suggests, distinguishing between religious and secular forms of the sacred is not straightforward or even useful. Autonomous sacred forms, such as the care of children or human rights, can be conceived of as forms of a 'secular sacred', but, historically, have strong religious origins that are still reflected in their content. Similarly, to think of the sacred worlds of religious groups as somehow distinct from the 'secular sacred' fails to recognize the ways in which religious subjectivities are constructed in relation to a range of sacred

forms that are not simply encapsulated by their explicit religious tradition or affiliation.

5. P. Smith, *Why War? The Cultural Logic of Iraq, the Gulf War and Suez* (Chicago: University of Chicago Press, 2005).

6. M. Burleigh, *Sacred Causes: Religion and Politics from the European Dictators to Al Qaeda* (London: Harper Perennial, 2006). 57. 'Even the violence with which society reacts against attempts at dissidence, whether by blame or physical repression, helps to reinforce its hold by forcefully demonstrating the heat of common conviction' (Durkheim, *Elementary Forms*, 156).

7. E. Gentile, 'Political Religion: A Concept and its Critics—a Critical Survey', *Totalitarian Movements and Political Religions*, 6/1 (2005), 26; Cattaruzza, 'Introduction to the Special Issue of *Totalitarian Movements and Political Religions*: Political Religions as a Characteristic of the 20th Century', *Totalitarian Movements and Political Religion*, 6/1 (2005), 4–6. See also Burleigh, *Sacred Causes*, 38–9.

8. See also K.-G. Riegel, 'Marxism-Leninism as a Political Religion', *Totalitarian Movements and Political Religion*, 6/1 (2005), 97–126, and K. Vondung, 'National Socialism as a Political Religion: Potentials and Limits of an Analytical Concept', *Totalitarian Movements and Political Religions*, 6/1 (2005), 87–95, although these articles also demonstrate the analytical confusion by unreflectively importing elements of substantive definitions of religion into theories of the sacralization of political movements. While the concept of the sacralization of politics can be valuable in drawing attention to the role of cultural meanings in authoritarian political regimes, there is a risk that generalized concepts can also fail to give adequate account of historical specificity. As Richard Evans (*Coming of the Third Reich*, p. xxvii) puts it: 'Whatever the similarities between these various regimes, the differences between the forces that lay behind the origins, rise and eventual triumph of Nazism and Stalinism are too strikingly different for the concept of totalitarianism to explain very much in this area. In the end, it is more useful as a description than an explanation, and it is probably better at helping us understand how twentieth-century dictatorships behaved once they had achieved power than in accounting for how they got there.'

9. Gentile, 'Political Religion', 29.

10. Burleigh, *Sacred Causes*, 51.

11. Burleigh, *Sacred Causes*, 53–4.

12. Burleigh, *Sacred Causes*, 59.

13. Burleigh, *Sacred Causes*, 62.

14. Burleigh, *Sacred Causes*, 64.

15. Gentile, 'Political Religion'; H. Maier, 'Political Religion: A Concept and its Limitations', *Totalitarian Movements and Political Religion*, 8/1 (2007), 5–16. But again these are complex contingent phenomena. As Hugh McLeod (private communication) commented to me, identification with the sacred forms of the Party could explain identification with Nazism among its most enthusiastic supporters, but popular support for Germany in the Second

World War also drew on a wider sacred identification with the Fatherland, which drew on a longer tradition of German nationalism, not identical to the racialized understanding of the German nation sacralized by the Nazis.

16. Evans, *Coming of the Third Reich*, p. xxix.

17. See, e.g., R. Orsi, *The Madonna of 115th St* (New Haven: Yale University Press, 1986); H. Luckey, 'Believers Writing for Believers: Traces of Political Religion in National Socialist Pulp Fiction', *Totalitarian Movements and Political Religion*, 8/1 (2007), 77–92.

18. For a summary of this process, see www.salon.com/news/politics/war_room/2010/08/16/ground_zero_mosque_origins (accessed 13 Nov. 2010).

19. www.npr.org/blogs/thetwo-way/2010/08/20/129319644/ap-memo-to-reporters-editors-don-t-use-ground-zero-mosque-construction (accessed 13 Nov. 2010).

20. In a Nexis UK search of US newspaper headlines containing the phrase 'Ground Zero Mosque', three stories were published in May 2010, 2 in June 2010, 7 in July 2010, 58 in August 2010, 10 in September 2010, and 2 in October 2010.

21. Jones subsequently carried out this symbolic act in March 2011, leading to further violent responses in reaction to his profane act.

22. The Dutch MP responsible for the production of the controversial film *Fitna*, which made direct links between Qur'anic teaching and violence.

23. See I. Reed, 'Social Dramas, Shipwrecks, and Cockfights: Conflict and Complicity in Social Performance', in J. Alexander, B. Giesen, and J. Mast (eds), *Social Performance: Symbolic Action Cultural Pragmatics, and Ritual* (Cambridge: Cambridge University Press, 2006), 146–68.

24. www.foxnews.com/story/0,2933,599162,00.html (accessed 15 Nov. 2010).

25. M. Pantti and L. van Zoonen, 'Do Crying Citizens make good citizens?', *Social Semiotics*, 16/2 (2006), 205–24, provides a useful summary of recent literature on emotion and public life.

26. Alexander, *Civil Sphere*, 550.

27. Alexander, *Civil Sphere*, 551. He also writes: 'Even in this more differentiated and civil situation, however, dichotomous evaluations of persons and events continue to be made, for pollution and purification are structural features of civil society as such' (Alexander, *Civil Sphere*, 84).

28. Alexander, *Civil Sphere*, 552.

29. Alexander, *Civil Sphere*, 202.

30. Shils, 'Primordial, Personal, Sacred and Civil Ties', 112.

31. Shils, 'Primordial, Personal, Sacred and Civil Ties', 122.

32. Referring to his analysis of data from the 1948 US presidential election, Shils observed that 'those with intense and continuous responses to symbols referring to the central value system were in a very small minority' ('Primordial, Personal, Sacred and Civil Ties', 124).

33. Shils, 'Primordial, Personal, Sacred and Civil Ties', 115.

34. Shils, 'Primordial, Personal, Sacred and Civil Ties', 123.

35. Shils, 'Primordial, Personal, Sacred and Civil Ties', 121.

36. Shils, 'Primordial, Personal, Sacred and Civil Ties', 116.

37. H. Arendt, *Eichmann in Jerusalem: A Report on the Banality of Evil* (London: Penguin, 1977), 288.

38. Rothenbuhler, *Ritual Communication*, p. xi.

39. In using the term 'structure', I have in mind Giddens' definition (*Constitution of Society*, 377) of structure as 'rules and resources, recursively implicated in the reproduction of social systems. Structure exists only as memory traces, the organic basis of human knowledgeability, and as instantiated in action.'

40. Durkheim and Mauss, *Primitive Classification*, 86.

41. Durkheim and Mauss, *Primitive Classification*, 85.

42. See Riis and Woodhead, *Sociology of Religious Emotion*, 26–7; M. Johnson, *The Body in the Mind: The Bodily Basis of Meaning, Imagination and Reason* (Chicago: University of Chicago Press, 1987).

43. Durkheim and Mauss, *Primitive Classification*, 81–2.

44. Rothenbuhler, *Ritual Communication*, p. ix.

45. Rothenbuhler, *Ritual Communication*, 130.

46. This is an epistemological, rather than an ontological, point. I am not claiming that there is no ontological basis for normative commitments to human rights or the care of children. But I am arguing that we come to these powerful normative commitments only through the social phenomena of sacred, communicative structures. In other words, we do not have any direct knowledge of the Good, but can come to an understanding of the good only through processes of cultural communication and formation. This is not to embrace a moral relativism in which all sacred commitments are equally valid, but to suggest that our knowledge and practices of the Good are only ever possible through contingent cultural structures.

47. John Gray ('Modus vivendi', in J. Gray, *Gray's Anatomy* (London: Penguin, 2010), 36–7), for example, argues that, under the correct structural conditions, the market can function as a framework for such mundane interaction between people who might, in other contexts, have competing goals or values.

48. On the importance of symbolic and moral boundaries for the constitution of society, see M. Douglas, *Purity and Danger* (London: Routledge, 1996), e.g. 141–59.

49. To be symbolically excluded from human society as moral community is, therefore, to lay oneself open to the charge of being an 'animal' (i.e. not properly human).

50. This argument has been noted in Ch. 2 in relation to Alexander's work, and in Ch. 4, in relation to the critical discussion around Dayan and Katz's concept of media events.

51. Eyerman, *Assassination*.

52. For a critique of such constructions of religious authenticity, see R. McCutcheon, *Religion and the Domestication of Dissent: Or How to Live in a Less than Perfect Nation* (London: Equinox, 2005), 47–63.

53. E. Shils, *Tradition* (Chicago: University of Chicago Press, 1981).

54. Douglas, *Natural Symbols*, p. xviii.
55. Mouffe, *On the Political*, 20. I am grateful to Anna Strhan for suggesting that I look at Mouffe's work in this context.
56. Mouffe, *On the Political*, 120: 'A democratic society cannot treat those who put its basic institutions into question as legitimate adversaries.'
57. For a rich account of these virtues, see W. Connolly, *Pluralism* (Durham, NC: Duke University Press, 2005).
58. For example, in John Gray's thoughtful discussion ('Modus vivendi') of different forms of liberalism, there is nevertheless an emphasis on 'ways of life' that suggests relatively stable cultural ways of being (even though he does recognize that these interpenetrate and that a person may participate in more than one way of life ('Modus vivendi', 30)).

Conclusion

1. M. Billig, *Banal Nationalism* (London: Sage, 1995), is a useful resource for further discussion of these processes.

Bibliography

Alexander, J. C., *Theoretical Logic in Sociology*, iv. *Talcott Parsons* (Berkeley and Los Angeles: University of California Press, 1983).

Alexander, J. C., *Action and its Environments: Towards a New Synthesis* (New York: Columbia University Press, 1988).

Alexander, J. C., 'Introduction: Durkheimian Sociology and Cultural Studies Today', in J. C. Alexander (ed.), *Durkheimian Sociology: Cultural Studies* (Cambridge: Cambridge University Press, 1988), 1–22.

Alexander, J. C., 'Culture and Political Crisis: "Watergate" and Durkheimian Sociology', in J. C. Alexander (ed.), *Durkheimian Sociology: Cultural Studies* (Cambridge: Cambridge University Press, 1988), 187–224.

Alexander, J. C. (ed.), *Durkheimian Sociology: Cultural Studies* (Cambridge: Cambridge University Press, 1988).

Alexander, J. C., 'Commentary: Structure, Value, Action', *American Sociological Review*, 55/3 (1990), 339–45.

Alexander, J. C., *Fin de siècle Social Theory: Relativism, Reduction and the Problem of Reason* (New York: Verso, 1995).

Alexander, J. C., 'The Computer as Sacred and Profane', in P. Smith (ed.), *The New American Cultural Sociology* (Cambridge: Cambridge University Press, 1998), 29–46.

Alexander, J. C., 'Towards a Sociology of Evil: Getting between Modernist Common Sense about the Alternative to the Good', in M. Lara (ed.), *Rethinking Evil: Contemporary Perspectives* (Berkeley and Los Angeles: University of California Press, 2001), 153–72.

Alexander, J. C., *The Meanings of Social Life: A Cultural Sociology* (New York: Oxford University Press, 2003).

Alexander, J. C., 'Cultural Pragmatics: Social Performance between Ritual and Strategy', in J. C. Alexander, B. Giesen, and J. Mast (eds), *Social Performance: Symbolic Action, Cultural Pragmatics and Ritual* (Cambridge: Cambridge University Press, 2006), 29–90.

Alexander, J. C., 'From the Depths of Despair: Performance, Counter-Performance, and "September 11"', in J. C. Alexander, B. Giesen, and J. Mast (eds), *Social Performance: Symbolic Action, Cultural Pragmatics and Ritual* (Cambridge: Cambridge University Press, 2006), 91–114.

Alexander, J. C., *The Civil Sphere* (New York: Oxford University Press, 2006).

Alexander, J. C., 'Clifford Geertz and the Strong Program: The Human Sciences and Cultural Sociology', *Cultural Sociology*, 2/2 (2008), 157–68.

Alexander, J. C., 'Iconic Consciousness: The Material Feeling of Meaning', *Environment and Planning D: Society and Space*, 26 (2008), 782–94.

Alexander, J. C., *Remembering the Holocaust: A Debate* (New York: Oxford University Press, 2009).

Alexander, J. C., and Jacobs, R., 'Mass Communication, Ritual and Civil Society', in T. Liebes and J. Curran (eds), *Media, Ritual and Identity* (London: Routledge, 1998), 23–41.

Alexander, J. C., and Mast, J., 'Introduction: Symbolic Action in Theory and Practice: The Cultural Pragmatics of Cultural Action', in J. C. Alexander, B. Giesen, and J. Mast (eds), *Social Performance: Symbolic Action, Cultural Pragmatics and Ritual* (Cambridge: Cambridge University Press, 2006), 1–28.

Alexander, J. C., and Sherwood, S., 'Mythic Gestures: Robert N. Bellah and Cultural Sociology', in R. Madsen, W. Sullivan, and A. Swidler (eds), *Meaning and Modernity: Religion, Polity, and Self* (Berkeley and Los Angeles: University of California Press, 2002), 1–14.

Alexander, J. C., and Smith, P., 'The Strong Program in Cultural Sociology: Elements of a Structural Hermeneutics', in J. Alexander, *The Meanings of Social Life* (New York: Oxford University Press, 2003), 11–26.

Alexander, J. C., Giesen, B., and Mast, J. (eds), *Social Performance: Symbolic Action, Cultural Pragmatics and Ritual* (Cambridge: Cambridge University Press, 2006).

Allan, S., *News Culture* (3rd edn; Maidenhead: Open University Press, 2010).

Anderson, B., *Imagined Communities: Reflections on the Origins and Spread of Nationalism* (London: Verso, 1991).

Anttonen, V., 'Sacred', in R. McCutcheon and W. Braun (eds), *Guide to the Study of Religion* (London: Continuum, 1999), 271–82.

Arendt, H., *Eichmann in Jerusalem: A Report on the Banality of Evil* (London: Penguin, 1977).

Aries, P., *Centuries of Childhood: A Social History of Family Life* (New York: Vintage Books, 1962).

Arnold, B., *The Irish Gulag* (Dublin: Gill and MacMillan, 2009).

Bailey Gill, C. (ed.), *Bataille: Writing the Sacred* (London: Routledge, 1995).

BBC Trust, 'From Seesaw to Wagon Wheel: Safeguarding Impartiality in the 21st Century', report (2007), www.bbc.co.uk/bbctrust/our_work/other/century21.shtml (accessed 2 June 2009).

Beckford, J., *Religion and Social Theory* (Cambridge: Cambridge University Press, 2003).

Becker, H., and Myers, R., 'Sacred and Secular Aspects of Human Sociation', *Sociometry*, 5/4 (1942), 355–70.

Bellah, R., 'Civil Religion in America', *Daedalus*, 96/1 (1967), 1–21.

Bellah, R. (ed.), *Émile Durkheim on Morality and Society* (Chicago: University of Chicago Press, 1973).

Bellah, R., 'Religion and the Legitimation of the American Republic', *Society*, 15/4 (1978), 16–23.

Bellah, R., *The Broken Covenant: American Civil Religion in Time of Trial* (Chicago: University of Chicago Press, 1992).

Bellah, R., and Hammond, P., *Varieties of Civil Religion* (New York: Harper Row, 1980).

Bellah, R., Madsen, R., Sullivan, W., Swidler, A., and Tipton, S., *Habits of the Heart: Individualism and Commitment in American Life* (Berkeley and Los Angeles: University of California Press, 1985).

Billig, M., *Banal Nationalism* (London: Sage, 1995).

Bird, S. E., 'Tabloidization: What Is It, and Does It Really Matter?', in B. Zelizer (ed.), *The Changing Faces of Journalism: Tabloidization, Technology and Truthiness* (London: Routledge, 2009), 40–50.

Brown, T., *Ireland: A Social and Cultural History, 1922–2001* (London: Harper Perennial, 2010).

Burleigh, M., *Sacred Causes: Religion and Politics from the European Dictators to Al Qaeda* (London: Harper Perennial, 2006).

Butler, J., *Frames of War: When is Life Grievable?* (London: Verso, 2009).

Caillois, R., *Man and the Sacred* (1939; Urbana, IL: University of Illinois Press, 2001).

Carey, J., 'Political Ritual on Television: Episodes in the History of Shame, Degradation and Excommunication', in T. Liebes and J. Curran (eds), *Media, Ritual and Identity* (London: Routledge, 1998), 42–70.

Castenada, C., *Figurations: Child, Bodies, Worlds* (Durham, NC: Duke University Press, 2002).

Cattaruzza, M., 'Introduction to the Special Issue of *Totalitarian Movements and Political Religions*: Political Religions as a Characteristic of the 20th Century', *Totalitarian Movements and Political Religion*, 6/1 (2005), 1–18.

Cladis, M., 'Introduction', in E. Durkheim, *The Elementary Forms of the Religious Life* (Oxford: Oxford University Press, 2001), pp. vii–xxxv.

Coman, M., 'News Stories and Myth: The Impossible Reunion?', in E. Rothenbuhler and M. Coman (eds), *Media Anthropology* (London: Sage 2005), 111–20.

Conboy, M., *Tabloid Britain: Constructing a Community through Language* (London: Routledge, 2005).

Connolly, W., *Pluralism* (Durham, NC: Duke University Press, 2005).

Cordero, R., Carballo, F., and Ossandon, J., 'Performing Cultural Sociology: A Conversation with Jeffrey Alexander', *European Journal of Social Theory*, 11/4 (2008), 523–42.

Cottle, S., 'Mediatized Rituals: Beyond Manufacturing Consent', *Media, Culture and Society*, 28/3 (2006), 411–32.

Couldry, N., *Media Rituals: A Critical Approach* (London: Routledge, 2003).

Couldry, N., and Rothenbuhler, E., 'Simon Cottle on "Mediatized Rituals": A Response', *Media, Culture, Society*, 29/4 (2007), 691–5.

Couldry, N., Hepp, A., and Krotz, F.(eds), *Media Events in a Global Age* (London: Routledge, 2010).

Csordas, T., 'Asymptote of the Ineffable: Embodiment, Alterity and the Theory of Religion', *Current Anthropology*, 45/2 (2004), 163–85.

Dant, T., *Materiality and Society* (Maidenhead: Open University Press, 2005).

Dawkins, R., *The God Delusion* (London: Bantam, 2006).

Dayan, D., 'Beyond Media Events: Disenchantment, Derailment, Disruption', in N. Couldry, A. Hepp, and F. Krotz (eds), *Media Events in a Global Age* (London: Routledge, 2010), 23–31.

Dayan, D., and Katz, E., *Media Events: The Live Broadcasting of History* (Cambridge, MA: Harvard University Press, 1992).

Douglas, M., *Purity and Danger* (London: Routledge, 1996).

Douglas, M., *Natural Symbols* (new edn; London: Routledge, 1996).

Durkheim, E., *Sociology and Philosophy* (New York: MacMillan, 1974).

Durkheim, E., *The Elementary Forms of the Religious Life* (Oxford: Oxford University Press, 2001).

Durkheim, E., and Mauss, M., *Primitive Classification*, trans. R. Needham (1903; London: Cohen & West, 1963).

Effler, E. Summers, *Laughing Saints and Righteous Heroes: Emotional Rhythms in Social Movement Groups* (Chicago: University of Chicago Press, 2010).

Eliade, M., *The Sacred and the Profane* (New York: Harcourt, 1959).

Evans, R., *The Coming of the Third Reich* (London: Allen Lane, 2003).

Eyerman, R., *The Assassination of Theo van Gogh: From Social Drama to Cultural Trauma* (Durham, NC: Duke University Press, 2008).

Ferguson, H., 'Abused and Looked after Children as "Moral Dirt": Child Abuse and Institutional Care in Historical Perspective', *Journal of Social Policy*, 36 (2007), 123–39.

Ferriter, D. 'Report', in *Report of Ryan Commission to Inquire into Child Abuse* (2006), vol. V, ch. 5, www.childabusecommission.ie/rpt/pdfs/CICA-VOL5-07A.pdf (accessed 8 Feb. 2010).

Ferriter, D., *Occasions of Sin: Sex and Society in Modern Ireland* (London: Profile Books, 2009).

Festinger, L., Riecken, H., and Schachter, S., *When Prophecy Fails* (London: Pinter & Martin, 1956/2008).

Geertz, C., *The Interpretation of Cultures* (London: Fontana, 1973).

Gentile, E., 'Political Religion: A Concept and its Critics—a Critical Survey,' *Totalitarian Movements and Political Religions*, 6/1 (2005), 19–32.

Giddens, A., *The Constitution of Society* (Cambridge: Polity, 1984).

Giddens, A., *Durkheim* (London: Fontana, 1997).

Giesen, B., 'Performing the Sacred: A Durkheimian Perspective on the Performative Turn in the Social Sciences', in J. C. Alexander, B. Giesen, and J. Mast (eds), *Social Performance: Symbolic Action, Cultural Pragmatics and Ritual* (Cambridge: Cambridge University Press, 2006), 325–67.

Gray, J., *Black Mass: Apocalyptic Religion and the Death of Religion* (London: Penguin, 2008).

Gray, J., 'Modus vivendi', in J. Gray, *Gray's Anatomy* (London: Penguin, 2010), 21–51.

Guadeloupe, F., *Chanting down the New Jerusalem: Calypso, Christianity and Capitalism in the Caribbean* (Berkeley and Los Angeles: University of California Press, 2008).

Herberg, W., *Protestant–Catholic–Jew: An Essay in American Religious Sociology* (Chicago: University of Chicago Press, 1960).

Hjarvard, S., 'The Mediatization of Religion: A Theory of the Media as Agents of Religious Change', *Northern Lights*, 6 (2008), 9–26.

Hjarvard, S., 'The Mediatization of Society: A Theory of the Media as Agents of Social and Cultural Change', *Nordicom Review*, 2 (2008), 105–34.

Hogan, J., *Irish Media: A Critical History since 1922* (London: Routledge, 2001).

Hunt, L., 'The Sacred and the French Revolution', in J. C. Alexander (ed.), *Durkheimian Sociology: Cultural Studies* (Cambridge: Cambridge University Press, 1988), 25–43.

Hunt, L., *Inventing Human Rights: A History* (New York: W. W. Norton, 2007).

Inglis, D., Blaikie, A., and Wagner-Pacifici, R., 'Editorial: Sociology, Culture and the Twenty-First Century', *Cultural Sociology*, 1/1 (2007), 5–22.

Inglis, T., *Moral Monopoly: The Rise and Fall of the Catholic Church in Modern Ireland* (2nd edn; Dublin: University College Dublin Press, 1998).

Inglis, T., 'Religion, Identity, State and Society', in J. Cleary and C. Connolly (eds), *The Cambridge Companion to Modern Irish Culture* (Cambridge: Cambridge University Press, 2005), 59–77.

Jacobs, R., *Race, Media and the Crisis of Civil Society: From Watts to Rodney King* (Cambridge: Cambridge University Press, 2000).

James, W., *The Varieties of Religious Experience* (London: Longmans, Green & Co., 1902).

Jenks, C. (ed.), *The Sociology of Childhood: Essential Readings* (London: Batsford, 1982).

Johnson, M., *The Body in the Mind: The Bodily Basis of Meaning, Imagination and Reason* (Chicago: University of Chicago Press, 1987).

Johnson, M., *The Meaning of the Body* (Chicago: University of Chicago Press, 2007).

Kane, A., 'Cultural Analysis in Historical Sociology: The Analytic and Concrete Forms of the Autonomy of Culture', *Sociological Theory*, 9/1 (1991), 53–69.

Katz, E., and Liebes, T., '"No more peace!" How Disaster, War and Terror Have Upstaged Media Events', in N. Couldry, A. Hepp, and F. Krotz (eds), *Media Events in a Global Age* (London: Routledge, 2010), 32–42.

Kendall, S., *Georges Bataille* (London: Reaktion Books, 2007).

Key, E., *The Century of the Child* (New York: Bantam, 1909).

Kitch, C., 'Tears and Trauma in the News', in B. Zelizer (ed.), *The Changing Faces of Journalism: Tabloidization, Technology and Truthiness* (London: Routledge, 2009), 29–39.

Knott, K., *The Location of Religion: A Spatial Analysis* (London: Eqiunox, 2005).

Kuhling, C., and Keohane, K., *Cosmopolitan Ireland: Globalization and Quality of Life* (London: Pluto Press, 2007).

Lofton, K., *Oprah: The Gospel of an Icon* (Berkeley and Los Angeles: University of California Press, 2011).

Luckey, H., 'Believers Writing for Believers: Traces of Political Religion in National Socialist Pulp Fiction', *Totalitarian Movements and Political Religion*, 8/1 (2007), 77–92.

Luckmann, T., *The Invisible Religion* (London: MacMillan, 1967).

Lukes, S., *Émile Durkheim: His Life and Work* (London: Penguin, 1975).

Lukes, S., 'Political Ritual and Social Integration', *Sociology*, 9/2 (1975), 289–308.

Lule, J., 'News as Myth: Daily News and Eternal Stories', in E. Rothenbuhler and M. Coman (eds), *Media Anthropology* (London: Sage, 2005), 101–10.

Lundby, K. (ed.), *Mediatization: Concepts, Changes, Consequences* (New York: Peter Lang, 2009).

Lynch, G., *The New Spirituality: An Introduction to Progressive Belief in the Twenty-First Century* (London: I. B. Tauris, 2007).

Lynch, G., 'Living with Two Cultural Turns: The Case of the Study of Religion', in S. Frosh and S. Roseneil (eds), *Social Research after the Cultural Turn* (Basingstoke: Palgrave-MacMillan, 2011), in press.

McCutcheon, R., *Manufacturing Religion: The Discourse of Sui Generis Religion and the Politics of Nostalgia* (New York: Oxford University Press, 1997).

McCutcheon, R., *The Discipline of Religion: Structure, Meaning, Rhetoric* (London: Routledge, 2003).

McCutcheon, R., *Religion and the Domestication of Dissent: Or How to Live in a Less than Perfect Nation* (London: Equinox, 2005).

Maier, H., 'Political Religion: A Concept and its Limitations', *Totalitarian Movements and Political Religion*, 8/1 (2007), 5–16.

Mellor, P., and Shilling, C., 'Body Pedagogics and the Religious Habitus: A New Direction for the Sociological Study of Religion', *Religion*, 40 (2010), 27–38.

Meštrović, S., *Postemotional Society* (London: Sage, 1997).

Meyer, B., 'Religious Sensations: Why Media, Aesthetics and Power Matter in the Study of Contemporary Religion', in H. de Vries (ed.), *Religion: Beyond a Concept* (New York: Fordham University Press, 2008), 704–23.

Mintz, S., *Huck's Raft: A History of American Childhood* (Cambridge, MA: Belknapp, 2006).

Mitchell, J., *Media Violence and Christian Ethics* (Cambridge: Cambridge University Press, 2007).

Morash, C., *A History of the Media in Ireland* (Cambridge: Cambridge University Press, 2010).

Morgan, David, *The Sacred Gaze: Religious Visual Culture in Theory and Practice* (Berkeley and Los Angeles: University of California Press, 2005).

Mouffe, C., *On the Political* (London: Routledge, 2005).

Murray, P., *Oracles of God: The Roman Catholic Church and Irish Politics, 1922–37* (Dublin: UCD Press, 2000).

Orsi, R., *The Madonna of 115th St* (New Haven: Yale University Press, 1986).

Orsi, R., *Between Heaven and Earth: The Religious Worlds People Make and the Scholars who Study Them* (Princeton: Princeton University Press, 2005).

O'Sullivan, E., 'Residential Child Welfare in Ireland 1965–2008: An Outline of Policy, Legislation and Practice', in *Report of Ryan Commission to Inquire into Child Abuse* (2009), vol. 4, ch. 4, www.childabusecommission.ie/rpt/pdfs/CICA-VOL4-10.pdf (accessed 23 Feb. 2010).

Otto, R., *The Idea of the Holy* (Oxford: Oxford University Press, 1923).

Pantti, M., and Sumiala, J., 'Til Death Us Do Join: Media, Mourning Rituals and the Sacred Centre of the Society', *Media, Culture, Society*, 31/1 (2009), 119–35.

Pantti, M., and Wieten, J., 'Mourning Becomes the Nation: Television Coverage of the Murder of Pim Fortuyn', *Journalism Studies*, 6/3 (2005), 301–13.

Pantti, M., and Zoonen, L. van, 'Do Crying Citizens Make Good Citizens?', *Social Semiotics*, 16/2 (2006), 205–24.

Parsons, T., and Shils, E., *Toward a General Theory of Action: Theoretical Foundations for the Social Sciences* (Cambridge, MA: Harvard University Press, 1951).

Pattison, S., *Shame: Theory, Therapy, Theology* (Cambridge: Cambridge University Press, 2000).

Pickering, W. S., 'The Eternality of the Sacred: Durkheim's Error?', *Archives de sciences sociales des religions*, 69 (1990), 91–108.

Raftery, M., and O'Sullivan, E., *Suffer the Little Children: The Inside Story of Ireland's Industrial Schools* (Dublin: New Island, 1999).

Reed, I., 'Social Dramas, Shipwrecks, and Cockfights: Conflict and Complicity in Social Performance', in J. C. Alexander, B. Giesen, and J. Mast (eds), *Social Performance: Symbolic Action, Cultural Pragmatics and Ritual* (Cambridge: Cambridge University Press, 2006), 146–68.

Reed, I., 'Culture as Object and Approach in Sociology', in I. Reed and J. C. Alexander (eds), *Meaning and Method: The Cultural Approach to Sociology* (Boulder, CO: Paradigm Publishers, 2009).

Reed, I., and Alexander, J. C., 'Social Science as Reading and Performance: A Cultural Sociological Understanding of Epistemology', *European Journal of Social Theory*, 12/1 (2009), 21–41.

Report by Commission of Investigation into Catholic Archdiocese of Dublin (2009), www.justice.ie/en/JELR/Pages/PB09000504 (accessed 20 Feb. 2010).

Richards, A., and Mitchell, J., 'Journalists as Witnesses to Violence and Suffering', in R. Fortner and M. Fackler (eds), *The Handbook of Global Communication Ethics* (Wiley: Blackwell, 2010).

Richman, M., 'The Sacred Group: A Durkheimian Perspective on the College de Sociologie', in C. Bailey Gill (ed.), *Bataille: Writing the Sacred* (London: Routledge, 1995), 58–76.

Riegel, K.-G., 'Marxism-Leninism as a Political Religion', *Totalitarian Movements and Political Religion*, 6/1 (2005), 97–126.

Riis, O., and Woodhead, L., *A Sociology of Religious Emotion* (Oxford: Oxford University Press, 2010).

Riley, A., '"Renegade Durkheimianism" and the Transgressive Left Sacred', in J. C. Alexander and P. Smith (eds), *The Cambridge Companion to Durkheim* (Cambridge: Cambridge University Press, 2005), 274–301.

Robertson, R., and Turner, B., 'An Introduction to Talcott Parsons: Theory, Politics and Humanity', in R. Robertson and B. Turner (eds), *Talcott Parsons: Theorist of Modernity* (London: Sage, 1991), 1–21.

Robertson, R., and Turner, B. (eds), *Talcott Parsons: Theorist of Modernity* (London: Sage, 1991).

Rollinson, R., 'Residential Child Care in England 1948–1975: A History and Report', in *Report of Ryan Commission to Inquire into Child Abuse* (2009), vol. V, ch. 6, www.childabusecommission.ie/rpt/pdfs/CICA-VOL5-08A.pdf (accessed 10 Feb. 2010).

Rose, J., *The Question of Zion* (Princeton: Princeton University Press 2005).

Rothenbuhler, E., *Ritual Communication: From Everyday Conversation to Mediated Ceremony* (London: Sage, 1998).

Rothenbuhler, E., and Coman, M., *Media Anthropology* (London: Sage, 2005).

Ryan Commission, *Report of Ryan Commission to Inquire into Child Abuse* (2009), www.childabusecommission.ie/rpt/pdfs (accessed 2 Feb. 2010).

Sacco, J., *Fragments of Gaza: A Graphic Novel* (New York: Metropolitan Books, 2009).

Schofield Clark, L., 'Mediatization and Media Ecology', in K. Lundby (ed.), *Mediatization: Concepts, Changes, Consequences* (New York: Peter Lang, 2009), 85–100.

Schofield Clark, L., 'Considering Religion and Mediatisation through a Case Study of *J+K's Big Day* (The J K Wedding Entrance Dance): A Response to Stig Hjarvard', *Culture and Religion*, 12/2 (2011), 167–84.

Shilling, C., and Mellor, P., 'Retheorizing Emile Durkheim on Society and Religion: Embodiment, Intoxication and Collective Life', *Sociological Review*, 59/1 (2011), 17–41.

Shils, E., 'Center and Periphery', in E. Shils, *Center and Periphery: Essays in Macro-Sociology* (Chicago: University of Chicago Press, 1975), 3–16.

Shils, E., 'Charisma', in E. Shils, *Center and Periphery: Essays in Macro-Sociology* (Chicago: University of Chicago Press, 1975), 127–34.

Shils, E., 'Primordial, Personal, Sacred and Civil Ties', in E. Shils, *Center and Periphery: Essays in Macro-Sociology* (Chicago: University of Chicago Press, 1975), 111–26.

Shils, E., *Tradition* (Chicago: University of Chicago Press, 1981).

Shils, E., and Young, M., 'The Meaning of the Coronation', in E. Shils, *Center and Periphery: Essays in Macro-Sociology* (Chicago: University of Chicago Press, 1975), 135–52.

Silverstone, R., *Media and Morality: On the Rise of the Mediapolis* (Cambridge: Polity, 2007).

Smith, P., 'The New American Cultural Sociology: An Introduction', in P. Smith (ed.), *The New American Cultural Sociology* (Cambridge: Cambridge University Press, 1998), 1–14.

Smith, P. (ed.), *The New American Cultural Sociology* (Cambridge: Cambridge University Press, 1998).

Smith, P., *Why War? The Cultural Logic of Iraq, the Gulf War and Suez* (Chicago: University of Chicago Press, 2005).

Smith, P., and Alexander, J. C., 'Introduction: The New Durkheim', in J. C. Alexander and P. Smith (eds), *The Cambridge Companion to Durkheim* (Cambridge: Cambridge University Press, 2005), 1–37.

Spence, D., *Narrative Truth and Historical Truth* (New York: W. W. Norton, 1982).

Staines, A., Boilson, A., Craven, F., and Wyse, E., 'An Assessment of the Health Records of Children Detained at Irish Industrial Schools 1940–1983', in *Report of Ryan Commission to Inquire into Child Abuse* (2009), vol. V, ch. 4, www.childabusecommission.ie/rpt/pdfs/CICA-VOL5-06A.pdf (accessed 24 Feb. 2010).

Stausberg, M., *Contemporary Theories of Religion: A Critical Companion* (London: Routledge, 2009).

Stivers, R., *Evil in Modern Myth and Ritual* (Atlanta, GA: University of Atlanta Press, 1982).

Sumiala, J., *Median rituaalit: Johdatus media-antropologiaan* (Tampere: Vastapaino, 2010).

Sumiala-Seppänen, J., and Stocchetti, M., 'Mediated Sacralization and the Construction of Postmodern *communion sanctorum*: The Case of the Swedish Foreign Minister Anna Lindh', *Material Religion*, 1/2 (2005), 228–49.

Sumiala-Seppänen, J., and Stochetti, M., 'Father of the Nation of Arch-Terrorist? Media Rituals and Images of the Death of Yasser Arafat', *Media, Culture, Society*, 29/2 (2007), 336–43.

Taylor, C., 'The Politics of Recognition', in A. Gutman and C. Taylor, *Multiculturalism and 'The Politics of Recognition'* (Princeton: Princeton University Press, 1992), 25–75.

Thompson, J., *Political Scandal: Power and Visibility in the Media Age* (Cambridge: Polity, 2000).

Tiitsman, J., 'The Occasion is not a Local One: Making a Public for the Atlantic Telegraph', paper presented at the Media, Religion and Culture group of the Annual Meeting of the American Academy of Religion, Chicago, 2008.

Turmel, A., *A Historical Sociology of Childhood: Developmental Thinking, Categorization and Graphic Visualization* (Cambridge: Cambridge University Press, 2008).

Turner, B., *Religion and Social Theory* (2nd edn; London: Sage, 1991).

Turner, G., *Understanding Celebrity* (London: Sage, 2004).

Turner, S., 'The Significance of Shils', *Sociological Theory*, 17/2 (1999), 125–45.

Turner, V., *The Ritual Process: Structure and Anti-Structure* (1969; London: Aldine, 1995).

Turnock, R., *Interpreting Diana: Television Audiences and the Death of a Princess* (London: BFI, 2000).

Tweed, T., *Crossing and Dwelling: A Theory of Religion* (Cambridge, MA: Harvard University Press, 2006).

Vondung, K., 'National Socialism as a Political Religion: Potentials and Limits of an Analytical Concept', *Totalitarian Movements and Political Religions*, 6/1 (2005), 87–95.

Ward, G., *Theology and Contemporary Critical Theory* (2nd edn; Basingstoke: MacMillan, 2000).

Whelan, K., 'The Cultural Effects of the Famine', in J. Cleary and C. Connolly (eds), *The Cambridge Companion to Modern Irish Culture* (Cambridge: Cambridge University Press, 2005), 137–55.

Woodhead, M., 'Psychology and the Construction of Children's Needs', in A. James and J. Prout (eds), *Constructing and Reconstructing Childhood* (New York: Falmer, 1990), 60–77.

Zelizer, B., *Covering the Body: The Kennedy Assassination, the Media and the Shaping of Collective Memory* (Chicago: University of Chicago Press, 1992).

Zelizer, V., *Pricing the Priceless Child: The Changing Social Value of Children* (New York: Basic Books, 1985).

Zoonen, L. van, Vis, F., and Mihelj, S., 'Performing Citizenship on YouTube: Activism, Satire and Online Debate around the Anti-Islam Video Fitna', *Critical Discourse Studies*, 7/4 (2010), 249–62.

Index

Index

taboo 19, 81
Thompson, Mark 87,
   100–2, 107
Turner, V. 19–20, 26

utopian potentiality 33, 37

violence 2, 38, 45, 48, 55–6, 61–3, 66–7, 69,
   83, 92, 97, 105–6, 114–6, 123–5, 130,
   132, 136
   against children 55–6, 61–3, 66–7, 69, 105

Zelizer, V. 64, 72

Printed in the USA/Agawam, MA
February 27, 2014

585690.116